In Love and War

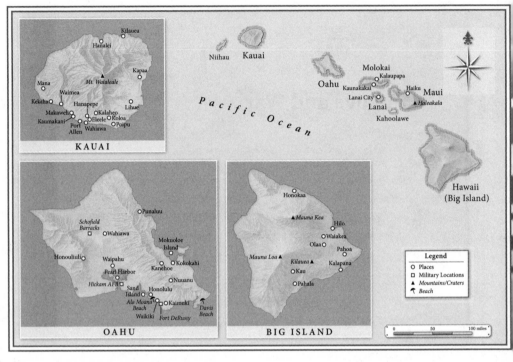

Map of the Hawaiian Islands.
Map by Gerry Krieg. Copyright © 2015, University of Oklahoma Press.

In Love and War

THE WORLD WAR II COURTSHIP LETTERS OF A NISEI COUPLE

Melody M. Miyamoto Walters

University of Oklahoma Press : Norman

Publication of this book is made possible through the generosity
of Edith Kinney Gaylord.

Library of Congress Cataloging-in-Publication Data
Ogata, Yoshiharu, 1919–2007.
  In love and war : the World War II courtship letters of a Nisei couple
/ [edited by] Melody M. Miyamoto Walters.
      pages cm
    Includes bibliographical references and index.
    ISBN 978-0-8061-4820-5 (paperback : alkaline paper) 1. Ogata,
Yoshiharu, 1919–2007—Correspondence. 2. Tsukiyama, Naoko, 1917—
Correspondence. 3. Japanese Americans—Hawaii—Correspondence.
4. Couples—Hawaii—Correspondence. 5. Courtship—Hawaii—
History—20th century—Sources. 6. Love-letters—Hawaii.
7. Hawaii—Biography. 8. World War, 1939–1945—Hawaii. 9. Martial
law—Social aspects—Hawaii—History—20th century. 10. Patriotism—
Hawaii—History—20th century. I. Tsukiyama, Naoko, 1917–
II. Walters, Melody M. Miyamoto, 1975– III. Title.
    DU624.7.J3O35 2015
    305.8956'09690922—dc23
                                                      2014047966

The paper in this book meets the guidelines for permanence and
durability of the Committee on Production Guidelines for Book
Longevity of the Council on Library Resources, Inc. ∞

In honor of my grandparents,
Naoko and Yoshiharu Ogata,
and Chieko and Tadao Miyamoto.
And for Jeff and Amelia Walters.

Okage sama de.

When you have two mothers, one who brought you into this world and one who brought you up, you owe much more obligation and respect toward the mother who brought you up.

—H. S. KAWAKAMI

CONTENTS

ILLUSTRATIONS

PREFACE

THE urgency of completing a project dependent on oral sources from World War II becomes increasingly clear each day. Famed news anchor Tom Brokaw dubbed American young adults of that era as "the Greatest Generation," and their heroic efforts have served as the plots for countless books, movies, and family stories. Many lived inconspicuous lives and faded into the background of the American tapestry. Yet it is their stories, their individual experiences toward a national effort, that make up the history of World War II.

This project began in 2007 when my mother and I were cleaning out my grandparents' closet in their home in Waimea, Kauai, Hawaii. My grandfather Yoshiharu Ogata had just died that June. Both he and my grandmother, formerly Naoko Tsukiyama, had occasionally spoken of their experiences during the war (such as watching the bombs drop onto Pearl Harbor or teaching in basements when the U.S. Army took over school classrooms). But neither had mentioned that they had saved the courtship letters they wrote to each other during the war. Upon finding and reading through the letters, we realized that theirs was a touching love story, but their correspondence was also a lesson in history as it documented the war and the varying concepts of race and ethnicity in Hawaii. Their letters are excerpted and edited here to provide a framework for study.

The letters, dating from July 1941 to June 1943, provide rich source material from which to draw conclusions about life in Hawaii during

World War II. In addition to providing its own primary and epistolary source material, this narrative tells a personal story contextualized in the history of World War II and the history of race in Hawaii, drawn from both primary and ample secondary sources. The statistical information comes from several books that served generations as classics in Hawaiian history classes. Scholarship on Japanese Americans in World War II and the war's impact on American mainland and island society also continues to grow in popularity. More recent works on race and generational changes in Hawaii highlight the need to step beyond a dichotomy of White versus Other in order to study "local" identity in Hawaii. This book seeks to address the complex question of what it meant to be a Japanese American living in Hawaii during World War II.

Both written and oral sources provide the personal information about the Tsukiyama and Ogata families. Naoko Tsukiyama's parents wrote memoirs that chronicle their upbringing, their migration from Japan to Hawaii, their own acculturation and the "Americanization" process, and their experiences of living in Hawaii as Japanese Americans. The Ogata family has no such written records but does have a written family tree that provides names and birthdates. Specific information not recorded in books about Hawaii or held in the University of Hawaii archives came from family members. Some of the stories were passed down from generation to generation, while others were the recollections of the Tsukiyama and Ogata families. Yoshiharu Ogata died before this book went into its research stage. Naoko Ogata, in her nineties when this project began, was "too busy" to sit for a formal interview. Instead, she provided information through a number of conversations and reminiscences as she reread the letters and flashed back to her past. Interestingly, she never wanted to write her memoirs, regardless of the numerous requests for her to do so. She believed that if she wrote her story, she would be part of history and, thus, old.

Other family members contributed to this work as well. Ted Tsukiyama, my great-uncle and a prolific writer and recorder of his own memoirs, provided identifications for many of the names mentioned in the letters; these identifications are in the notes. My mother, Joy Miyamoto (née Ogata), and her brother, Jon Ogata—Yoshiharu and Naoko's two children—provided information on family members and cultural references. Joy Miyamoto stayed with her father in the last days of his life as he reflected on his past. Some of the information presented here came from what she recorded while sitting with him, while other pieces were fit together from discussions that she remembers. My sister, Misty Tsukayama (née Miyamoto), is the Ogatas' eldest grandchild and provided a family tree of both the Ogata and Tsukiyama families. Overall, this is a personal story. It is a family story. The information gleaned came not through the rigorous standards of academe or through the impersonal tallies of human subject forms. Scholars wishing to verify the details will find general information that corresponds, but as with so many family stories, specifics reside with the family members themselves.

As the editor and author of this book, I had to make the hard decisions of what to include, emend, and edit. I chose to retain phrases that may be unfamiliar to some readers. Some of them were colloquial to the era and the location of the letter writers. I have given definitions for some, while others simply have no accurate English translation. Some terms that were not used by the letter writers, such as "Issei" and "Nisei," appear throughout the text, because they have gained in popularity with the increased scholarship and interest on the history of Japanese Americans. I have incorporated popular terms still used in Hawaii today, including "local," "haole," and "the mainland," along with explanations of their usage to help the reader navigate the differences in mentality between residents of Hawaii and residents of the continental United States. After much deliberation, I chose not to use glottal stops (*okina*) or macrons (*kahako*) in my narrative. The two letter writers did not, and I wanted to remain consistent in transcribing their correspondence. Additionally, my goal was to appeal not only to scholarly readers familiar with Hawaii but also to a general audience who may not be familiar with the Hawaiian language. By omitting those markings, I recognize that I have spelled words incorrectly. Although I mean no disrespect to Hawaiian-language speakers and writers, I hoped not to complicate the narrative with markings foreign to many readers.

The bulk of the research for this project came from primary sources housed at the University of Hawaii archives. The Romanzo Adams Social Research Laboratory holds letters, newspaper clippings, and other materials from Hawaii during World War II. The collection began as a sociology study of Hawaii in 1922. It primarily focuses on race relations and includes information on cultural conflict during World War II, as students wrote about themselves, their families, and their communities. Throughout the war years, the research laboratory worked with the military government on issues such as race relations, morale, and labor. The collection also contains interviews and surveys conducted by University of Hawaii sociologists with people of various ethnicities throughout the Hawaiian Islands. Students also contributed to the collection through their class papers, journals and diaries, and interviews regarding race and ethnicity, as well as intergenerational conflict. Their papers are filed by ethnic background, demonstrating race as a category for organization and distinction. The Confidential Research Files at the University of Hawaii Archives provided information about living in the islands during the war and in the postwar era.[1] The archives also contain the Hawaii War Records Depository, with files from various military committees and subcommittees, along with other information about life during wartime.

My goal for editing and annotating the courtship letters of Yoshiharu Ogata and Naoko Tsukiyama was to remain true to the integrity of the original documents. Paragraphs and parts of paragraphs that are not crucial to the story have been omitted, even though they arguably add to our understanding of the tedium of living under martial law in remote places. I attempted to preserve Ogata's and Tsukiyama's styles of writing to reveal their levels of education, their cultural backgrounds, and even their personalities. Each of the writers seems to have proofread many of their letters after writing a first draft. I did not change their spelling, punctuation, or grammar in their letters, because the mistakes show the education, emotion, and enthusiasm of the writers; a minor punctuation correction in the epigraph at the beginning of chapter 1 is the single exception. However, I did delete words that the letter writers had crossed out. I avoided using "[*sic*]," so as not to take away from the narrative, and I added bracketed insertions only when the text needed clarification. Long dashes indicate a line or flourish drawn by the letter writer, and long dashes enclosed in square brackets indicate a blank space or blank line within the letter. I have taken editorial liberties with the formatting of the letters. The line breaks are not preserved. Also, I placed the date and location of the letter writer (town and island) at the top right of each letter and added the year when the writer did not. When "Hawaii" is used as a location marker, it references the Big Island of Hawaii, not the chain of Hawaiian Islands. I placed the closing of each letter at the bottom left, though they were usually placed on the right.

Explanatory notes identify people, places, cultural references, and popular culture of the time. When "Tsukiyama" appears as the name of an individual in the text or notes, it refers to Naoko Tsukiyama. She is also called "Naoko," "Naoko Tsukiyama," and rarely, when appropriate, "Naoko Ogata." Yoshiharu Ogata is referred to as "Yoshiharu" and "Ogata," as well as by his first and last name. Tsukiyama's family nicknamed him "Ogie," but he is never called "Yoshi," as that was the prefix for all of his brothers' names too. The Tsukiyamas are referred to by first name or by first and last names. Similarly, the Ogata family members are referred to by first name, or by first name and married name. In the letters, both Yoshiharu Ogata and Naoko Tsukiyama called each other by their full first names, then used terms of endearment as their relationship intensified. Because theirs is such a personal story, I generally used "Naoko" and "Yoshiharu" when referring to them.

As the editor, I have photocopies and digital scans of the letters and photos, as well as access to the originals. The letters still sit in their original "Air Mail" envelopes and, until early in the twenty-first century, remained in brown paper grocery bags in the Ogatas' bedroom closet. The couple also kept collections of letters to and from the Tsukiyama family members on Oahu that Naoko wrote and received as a young wife. One day, all of these will be donated to the University of Hawaii Archives and join the other war records, including letters from her family, that are already there.

ACKNOWLEDGMENTS

First and foremost, my appreciation goes to the residents of Hawaii, both in the World War II era and in the present day. I have had the privilege to live and learn among a community that has truly created the Aloha State.

Although this project officially began in 2007, its technical beginning came before I even found the letters. A project in an English class at Waimea High School led my friends and me to interview senior citizens of Waimea, Kauai, about their experiences of living there during World War II. My "frenz-4-eva"—Ann Abeshima, Jill Uyeda, and Elizen Vallo—worked with me on that, and Ashley Newton supported me through the countless positives and negatives. My thanks to Grace-leanor Baird, who promoted that project, and to Gloria Matsuba, who told me to write with passion. Training to become a historian at Arizona State University ingrained me with skills for this project, and my thanks go to Robert A. Trennert, Jr., who knew I was an Asian American historian even before I did, and to Susan E. Gray and Beth Luey for introducing me to the wonderful world of documentary editing. The Association for Documentary Editing, the Summer Institute for the Editing of Historical Documents, and the National Historical Publications and Records Commission trained me in the skill of documentary editing. The Asian Pacific American Studies Program, currently under the direction of Karen Leong, provided me a formal entry into that field. Azusa Ono lent her knowledge of the Japanese language and of Japanese culture. Laurie Arnold, Peter Blodgett, Brian Collier, Mary Dillman, and Sara Martin contributed to my graduate school experiences and my training as a historian.

Generous support from Coe College and Collin College allowed me to complete this project, and the Perrine Foundation at Coe College provided me with funding to pursue the project. My thanks to James Phifer, Marie Baehr, Derek Buckaloo, Ed Burke, David Nordmann, Glenn Janus, and Monica Fuertes-Arboix for their company and support during the Iowa years. Vaclav Shatillo and Megan Johnson provided immeasurable help with the initial phase of the project, transcribing and copying the original letters. My thanks also to the administration at Collin College, to my colleagues Steven Short, David Cullen, and Keith Volanto for reading drafts, and to Lisa Kirby for her unwavering support.

I have called this foray into Asian American history "my giving-back project," and my appreciation goes to those who have paved the way for me. As with all undertakings such as this, I am grateful for the help of others and recognize that any mistakes or shortcomings are my own. Franklin Odo's study provided an example of scholarly work and respect for a generation of Hawaii's residents that I have tried to emulate. David Farber, whose work with Beth Bailey established my background for World War II Hawaiian society, generously read a chapter draft. John Rosa, expert in local identity and all-around good guy, also provided expert knowledge and generous encouragement. My thanks as well go to Sherman Seki at the University of Hawaii at Manoa Archives, who went above and beyond the call of duty in responding to my search for answers.

Publishing my first book has been a great experience, and to do so, I have stood on the shoulders of giants in the field. Gerry Krieg, of Krieg Mapping, provided the map of the Hawaiian Islands. Sherrye Young compiled the index. Bob Clark, whose eyes lit up with interest from the first time I mentioned this project, has been a great mentor and friend.

Jay Dew listened and listened and listened, and gave wise advice. The University of Oklahoma Press has been a joy to work with. The unsung marketing department promoted my project across land and sea, reaching to the middle of the Pacific Ocean. Chuck Rankin supported this project from its inception. Anthony Roberts produced a cover that captured the spirit of my grandparents' relationship. Rosemary Wetherold provided a careful eye, generous encouragement, and expert knowledge in the copyediting process. Emily Jerman Schuster, my manuscript editor, has been referred to as "the best to work with" and I wholeheartedly agree. And of course, my editor, Kathleen Kelly, whose patience is exceeded only by her brilliance, took me through every step of the publication process. It has been both an honor and a pleasure to work with all of them.

My family has provided unending support and information for this project. Jon Ogata and Ted Tsukiyama supplied photographs and information on family members and friends. My mother, Joy Miyamoto, who still wanted to know how the story ended, has the heart of a historian and now the training of one as well. My father, Lynn Miyamoto, supported all of our crazy adventures. My siblings, Misty Tsukayama and Matt Miyamoto, and their families, as well as the rest of the extended Miyamoto, Urata, Tsukiyama, and Ogata families, embrace local identity and the aloha spirit. Of course, my thanks go to my grandmother Naoko Ogata, whose remarkable life spanned the historic events that only the Greatest Generation has known, and who always emphasized the importance of speaking proper English. I would also like to extend a heartfelt *mahalo* to the Walters family, who welcomed me and know the true meaning of *ohana*. And a big aloha to Jeff and Amelia Walters, who will straddle the line between Texan and local, creating the identity of the next generation.

In Love and War

Dec. 7

This is the most incredible thing that has ever happened to us. All day long we have hoped that the reports were false. It can't happen here; it's impossible — we have been telling ourselves. It is 4:30 now and I believe now that the incredible has happened. Martial law has been declared in this Territory by the Governor and it is true that Pearl Harbor and other areas have been attacked by planes. Japanese planes they say and I hear over a mainland broadcast that Japan has declared war on U.S. I can hardly believe such a thing has happened, after these 'peace talks' by special envoys in which I had hoped so much for success. To think that Japan can do this to us is unbelievable — that a nation whose people have some of the finest qualities I have known, should resort to such tactics. I am ashamed, even humiliated to think I can trace my ancestors back to that country. Maybe it isn't the country, but the leaders that have planned so hateful a thing. We cannot hate Germany as much as its leader. Nevertheless we are Japanese and a feeling of contempt for such low-handed methods is fully justifiable I think. We are Americans here and think and feel the same as any other peoples but we also have to suffer the humiliation

First page of the reflection written by Naoko Tsukiyama on December 7, 1941. Photo in author's collection.

1 We Should Be Made to Suffer

This is the most incredible thing that has ever happened to us. All day long we have hoped that the reports were false. 'It can't happen here,' it's impossible—we have been telling ourselves. It is 4:30 now and I believe now that the incredible has happened. Martial law has been declared in this Territory by the Governor and it is true that Pearl Harbor and other areas have been attacked by planes. Japanese planes they say and I hear over a mainland broadcast that Japan has declared war on U.S. I can hardly believe that such a thing has happened, after these 'peace talks' by special envoys in which I had hoped so much for success. To think that Japan can do this to us is unbelievable—that a nation whose people have some of the finest qualities I have known, should resort to such tactics. I am ashamed, even humiliated to think I can trace my ancestors back to that country. Maybe it isn't the country, but the leaders that have planned so hateful a thing. We cannot hate Germany as much as its leader. Nevertheless, we are Japanese and a feeling of contempt for such low-handed methods is fully justifiable I think. We are Americans here and think and feel the same as any other peoples, but we also have to suffer the humiliation of such truths as this. If it will make us even more strongly Americans in every way, I don't mind that we should be made to suffer for it. I hope this will give us a chance to show we are as American as we can possibly be. If so, I am thankful for the chance. Teddy went so eagerly this morning when the call came for the University ROTC. He has been gone all day but I hope he will be back and is safe in whatever he is doing. He said he would be the first to volunteer in case of such an emergency, so I know he is serving gladly as are many of his friends. 104 were killed and 300 injured are the news reports from the mainland. Radio stations here are cut off except for important reports that are official. We are going into blackout at dusk and we must boil water that we drink. Emergency units, construction workers, defense and everybody like that has been called to help. I'm sure most men folk are gone. This is war, but it is so incredible. The sun continues to set over Waikiki, it is quiet except for the wind in the trees. There is no panic, neighbors talk together, we prepare buckets of water, and we are told to be calm. I'm sure our military forces are strong enough to ward off any attack. Whatever happened, they were caught off guard this morning. I heard the dull roar of shooting this morning. The telephone was disconnected, so that's how we found out about all this first. I hope and pray it won't be worse than this. It is the beginning of something terrible in political and economic relations between East and West there is no doubt. Japan is committing suicide, but let her do so if this is her method. Jimmy is there but this is no time to hope for official protection because he is my brother. We chose our ways to go and this is so, it can't be helped at a time like this.

—*Naoko Tsukiyama's reflection, written December 7, 1941*

THE events of December 7, 1941, changed the lives of many Americans and people around the world. But the bombing of Pearl Harbor hit much closer to home for those living in Hawaii. Two of those people were my grandparents, Naoko Tsukiyama and Yoshiharu Ogata, second-generation immigrants (or Nisei) who were living in Honolulu. These two Japanese Americans spoke English, participated in Christian church activities and the YMCA, and trained to teach in Hawaii's public schools. They considered themselves Americans, although their ethnic heritage was Japanese and Hawaii was a territory of the United States. A young woman at the time of the attack on Pearl Harbor, Naoko had grown up in Honolulu, with well-off merchant parents who participated in Americanizing activities, including being members of the Christian church, going to the YMCA, speaking English, and even reading American magazines. Yoshiharu had grown up on a sugar plantation camp on the rural island of Kauai, in a large family that had little money. They both saw their friends and family members enlist in the U.S. military while other Japanese Americans faced threats of internment.

To the outsider, Naoko and Yoshiharu were both considered "Japs," despite their differences in class and cultural upbringing. Still, they both dealt with the war at home, participating in USO events, adjusting to martial law, and working as public servants. As circumstances of the time demanded, the two taught on different islands, she on the Big Island of Hawaii, he on Oahu and then on Kauai. For nearly two years, they wrote to each other, and thus they shared and joined their lives as two ordinary people living during an extraordinary time. Yet, they did not see the time as extraordinary. They went about their daily activities, and through their letters, they courted and formed a bond that led them to marriage. All the while, they shared their experiences and struggles of dealing with the hardships of the time. They were in love, and in war.

※※※

Yoshiharu Ogata and Naoko Tsukiyama met in the summer of 1941. World War II had already begun, and for American citizens, the threat of a war at home loomed large. But for twenty-three-year-old Naoko, a new phase in her life also beckoned. As a recent college graduate, she was about to start her first full-time job. She prepared to leave her parents' home and live independently, on a different island from the rest of her family. She made her move to Hilo (on the Big Island of Hawaii), traveling from Oahu by boat. But as she began to settle into her new job as an elementary school teacher at a small, rural school, she contracted bronchitis and had to return to her family's home in Honolulu in September of 1941. Less than three months after she returned to Oahu, the infamous day occurred, and it shaped the rest of her life.

Naoko Tsukiyama wrote of her beliefs like "it can't be helped" and "we should be made to suffer" in her reflection on Pearl Harbor Day, ideas that became constant themes for Japanese Americans, as did her statements such as "we are Americans" and "serving gladly." Indeed, many of her fears and predictions became realities over the next four years. In their courtship correspondence, she and Yoshiharu Ogata chronicled the impact of war, the ideas of gender roles, and the notions of race and ethnicity in World War II Hawaii, islands that stood apart culturally, ethnically, and geographically, from the mainland United States.

The complex story of race for the Japanese in Hawaii combines traditional Japanese values, American ideals, and Hawaiian influences. It began with the first sugar mill, which opened on Kauai in 1835. From as early as 1868, immigrants left Japan, primarily from Hiroshima, Yamaguchi, Fukuoka, and Kumamoto.[1] Contract laborers received a paid passage in exchange for three years of labor, for which they received a payment of nine dollars a month (six times what they would have earned in Japan), plus food, lodging, and medical care. By the 1890s, sugar plantations, then Hawaii's main industry, called for laborers from across Asia, and the Japanese responded in the largest numbers. With Japan suffering economically, many small farmers saw immigrating to Hawaii as an opportunity to fulfill their dreams of making money (despite restrictions on property rights), a much more appealing option than moving to the cities of Japan to work in the factories.[2] Between 1885 and 1924, about 200,000 Japanese moved to Hawaii, and 180,000 went to the mainland.[3] Hawaii benefited from the influx of labor, but mainlanders neither recruited nor welcomed as warmly the growing Japanese population.[4] Nativism, racialized laws, and hostility increased on the mainland, and the Japanese saw Hawaii as the place with an "eternal summer" and sincere, kind, and gentle people.[5] After the primary male immigration, women went to Hawaii as "picture brides." Hawaii had no law prohibiting interracial marriage,[6] but as the willingness of Japanese women to move to Hawaii created a more even sex ratio among the immigrants, little interracial marriage occurred.[7]

Once in Hawaii, the first-generation immigrants, or Issei, worked on the sugar plantations and kept many traditions of their home country. Plantation owners gave Buddhist missions their monetary and moral support, and allocated lands for temples on the plantations. The owners considered Buddhism a "stabilizing influence," a way to manage laborers, because Buddhism preached nonviolence, peace, and tolerance. At the same time, some people believed that the "heathen" religion made Japanese immigrants seem more foreign and tied them more closely to Japan.[8] Many plantation workers spoke Japanese and even sent their children to Japanese-language schools. Together, they formed a community based on a local Japanese identity that allowed them to share memories of Japan as well as stories of their new experiences in Hawaii.[9]

Prior to World War I, the Japanese in Hawaii generally identified with Japan and raised their children according to traditional Japanese practices so that they could be "good subjects of the Emperor." However, after World War I, they experienced a shift to focus on life as American citizens.[10] Japanese-language schools had once taught Japanese culture and worship of the emperor, but by 1922, Hawaii's Department of Public Instruction required the schools to obtain a permit and to teach nothing that would contradict American ideals or institutions. In acculturation practices, it required its teachers to have a grasp of the English language, American history, and ideals of democracy. Japanese schools also emphasized moral codes, including respecting elders, having harmonious relationships with others, being tidy and punctual, and helping needy people, with teachers serving as models of morality, religion, and social obligation.[11] The island-born plantation workers formed a distinctive Japanese-Hawaiian-American culture and oftentimes were simply referred to as "local Japanese." This was the typical experience of Japanese immigrants as they made Hawaii their home.

"We didn't come to Hawaii to work on the plantations—we were merchants," Naoko Ogata often told her grandchildren. The usual image of Japanese immigration to Hawaii was that of the plantation worker, an immigrant from Japan hoping to earn money and make a better life for himself. After a few years of work, the lonely bachelor then sought out the company of a wife, through matchmaking services that provided a photograph of a suggested match (a picture bride). The couples paired based on the pictures and family recommendations, and the woman in Japan would then move to Hawaii, where she sought out her husband (who sometimes did not look like the picture he had used). The couple lived together in plantation housing and raised their children to participate in the activities of the Buddhist temple in the plantation camp. Such was not the case for Naoko's family, the Tsukiyamas. Instead, Naoko's father and mother, Seinosuke and Yoshiko, raised their children in the city, "under Christian influence," and because of their American education, they were able to read parenting magazines like *Ladies' Home Journal* and learned how to care for babies and raise them "properly."[12] Furthermore, as active Christians, the Tsukiyamas shared a religion with "haoles," giving them a commonality with the elite in Hawaii and with the majority of Americans at the time. (The term "haole," often translated as "without breath," is the Hawaiian word for "foreigner" and refers to whites, except for Portuguese and Puerto Rican plantation workers).[13] That also meant, though, that they did not share the same religious beliefs as most of the local Japanese families.

Naoko Tsukiyama had two brothers and two sisters. Her older brother, James (Jimmy) Kagawa, was born on May 15, 1915. (Although he was also a Tsukiyama, his family name was Kagawa. Because Yoshiko Tsukiyama was an only child, she and Seinosuke had agreed that their first-born son would keep her maiden name and thus carry it on.) The next child was Naoko, the eldest daughter, born on November 28, 1917. Daughter Kazu followed, on January 13, 1919. The fourth child and second son, Ted, was born on December 20, 1920. The youngest Tsukiyama daughter was Martha, born on October 6, 1923.

The Tsukiyama family exemplified many of the stereotypes associated with the townsfolk of Honolulu. When comparing the Japanese in the city of Honolulu with those in rural areas, one Kauai boy explained that the city Japanese dressed better, knew better English, and were worldlier.[14] Additionally, because Seinosuke Tsukiyama was a merchant and the family lived in a working-class community, they seldom socialized

The Tsukiyama family's Easter photo, ca. 1926. *Left to right, bottom row:* James and Ted. *Middle row:* Kazu and Naoko. *Top row:* Yoshiko, Martha, and Seinosuke. Photo in author's collection.

with their neighbors. Instead, their peers included Seinosuke's business associates and those with whom the children attended school. The family also had little contact with Buddhist families. They were not part of the bourgeoisie (their race prevented the automatic admission that their economic status should have allowed), nor were they part of the local plantation community (their economic status prevented the automatic admission that their race should have allowed.)[15] Being Christian was unusual for Issei before World War II, but both Seinosuke and Yoshiko had been Christians prior to leaving Japan.[16] Once in Hawaii, they saw that the Christian church not only intended to save souls but also created organizations that gave immigrants a sense of friendship, intimacy, and social support; provided food, clothing, and shelter; and Americanized them by teaching them English. The Christian church (as well as the local YWCA) also taught women sewing, American customs, and cooking and provided child day-care centers.[17] The Tsukiyamas spoke standard U.S. English, which was a determinant of social class and status in Hawaii.[18] The family were steeped in the American culture, and they had no doubt that they were Americans.

Naoko Tsukiyama and her siblings received an education typical of American children in her generation, but unusual for Japanese Americans in Hawaii. She went to Queen Liliuokalani Elementary School in Kaimuki for first and second grades, and from the third grade on, she attended Aliiolani Elementary School in Kaimuki, on the island of Oahu. Aliiolani was the second of the "English Standard Schools" established in Honolulu, which required students to show proficiency in standard English in order to be admitted. When she was twelve, Naoko traveled to Japan to care for her maternal grandmother. Her year away from Hawaii delayed her formal education, and when she returned, she was placed in the same grade as her younger sister Kazu. She next attended Honolulu's Roosevelt High School, which had begun in 1929 as an English Standard School, and most of its students were white. In fact, it stood as "a powerful metaphor for the race and class divide"

The Tsukiyama children with their peers, ca. 1924. *Left to right, back row:* Barton Eveleth (the Tsukiyamas' neighbor); Leslie Hegenberger (their neighbor and son of Lt. Albert F. Hegenberger, who in 1927 was the navigator for the army's first flight from California to Hawaii); James Kagawa; Kenji Ikeda (whose father was first cousin to Seinosuke Tsukiyama and also immigrated to Hawaii to work for the Isoshimas); Joseph Silva (identified as Portuguese, not haole); Koji Ikeda (brother of Kenji); and Donald Napier (their neighbor). Hidden behind Joseph Silva is the infant Martha Tsukiyama, carried by an unidentified person. *Front row:* Helen Eveleth (sister of Barton), Ted Tsukiyama, Toshi Sasano (another neighbor), Kazu Tsukiyama, Albert Hegenberger (brother of Leslie), and Naoko Tsukiyama. Photo in author's collection.

between haole and non-haole.[19] That she was a Japanese American attending this school made her and her family very different from most Hawaiians of Japanese ancestry—it made them more similar to whites than to the local Japanese who worked on the plantations. After graduating high school in 1936, Naoko attended the University of Hawaii. She graduated from the university's Teachers' College in 1940 with a bachelor's degree in education and then continued for a fifth year to earn her teaching certificate, a requirement for all teachers. Throughout her career, Naoko worked as an elementary school teacher and librarian.

Yoshiharu Ogata's early life is much more typical of the Japanese who settled in Hawaii. His father, Zenzo Ogata, and his mother, Jyo Ogata, had their roots in the Fukuoka Prefecture of Japan. They immigrated to Hawaii, in 1899 as part of the large influx of plantation workers in the late 1800s and early 1900s. They resided on the island of Kauai, the most geographically separated of the four main islands, and the island most socially and politically dominated by plantations.[20] Zenzo Ogata worked as a plantation *luna*, a supervisor who rode around the sugarcane fields on horseback, and Jyo contributed as a housewife. Yoshiharu was born in Wahiawa, Kauai, on February 3, 1919. He had four older sisters—Sakae (born 1903), Hiruyo (born 1905), Tomoe (born 1908), and Momoe (born 1910)—and one younger sister, Sueko (born 1922). Yoshiharu was the youngest of the four sons, all of whose names began with "Yoshi," meaning "good." His brothers were Yoshio (born 1911), Yoshitaka (born 1914), and Yoshiyuki (born 1917). Plantation life allowed for a tight-knit Japanese community in the camps, and Yoshiharu's family, like many others there, grew and shared vegetables, attended public and Japanese-language schools, and went to Buddhist temples on plantation land.

The Ogatas stand in stark contrast to the Tsukiyamas. Little written record of them exists, for they did not write memoirs as the Tsukiyamas did. They also spoke little English, so their stories are lesser known to the current living family members. It is unknown if Sakae, Hiruyo, or Tomoe graduated from high school. As an adult, Sakae did domestic work, then toiled as a housewife, and her husband, Chu Iimura, was a butcher. Hiruyo worked with her husband, Sueji Haraguchi, on his taro farm. Tomoe worked in a pineapple cannery, and her husband, Tomoiichi Yamamoto, was a police officer. Momoe graduated from McKinley High School in Honolulu and, after receiving clerical training at Honolulu Business College, did office work. Her husband, Yoshio Inouye, taught at a Japanese-language school on Kauai, even into the 1980s. After graduating from Waimea High School, the youngest Ogata daughter, Sueko, trained in Honolulu to become a cafeteria manager and then worked at Eleele Elementary School. Family members believe that all of the Ogata sons except Yoshiharu graduated from Kauai High School in Lihue. The eldest, Yoshio, married Kimiko Nishimura and became an electrician. Yoshitaka worked as a repairman at the Dole Cannery and married Akiko Nagata. The third son, Yoshiyuki, enlisted in the army and never married. Yoshiharu's family were members of the Kauai Soto Zen Temple Zenshuji, the Buddhist temple that originated in the Wahiawa plantation camps.[21] His parents and a number of his siblings are interred at the columbarium there. Yoshiharu was not a regular temple-goer and in his adulthood spent more Sundays golfing than attending religious services. The second generation of Ogatas moved off the sugar plantations, epitomizing the upward mobility of the Nisei, and Yoshiharu's life became a prime example of this.

Yoshiharu Ogata's traditional Japanese upbringing, combined with his American aspirations of upward mobility and moving away from the plantation, led him to develop his own set of standards and values, which eventually shaped his decisions during the war. Yoshiharu attended Eleele Elementary School and finished Waimea High School in 1937 as part of its first graduating class to attend the ninth through twelfth grades. He told stories of having to ride a horse to school, since the family did not have a car that he could use. He next attended the Stout Institute in Menomonie, Wisconsin (today the University of Wisconsin–Stout), completing the requirements for a degree to teach industrial arts. His family sacrificed their money, as well as his contributions to the family economy, in order to send him to college. Like many Japanese families, the Ogatas believed that schooling would increase their children's prestige, self-respect, and standard of living.[22] His Japanese training ingrained in Yoshiharu the ideas of unquestionable obedience to his father, obligation to his parents, and a sense of duty. Furthermore, Japanese children's loyalty fell first to their father, then to their eldest

Yoshiharu Ogata in 1941, on his way back to Hawaii after graduating from the Stout Institute. Photo in author's collection.

brother. Thus, when Yoshiharu returned to the islands, he felt obligated to pay back his educational debt, and by the time he returned to his family after graduating from college, he was the only son still living at home. The responsibility of caring for the family fell to him, as did the respect that would have been due to the oldest son. Yoshiharu put his college education to use and worked as a teacher of industrial arts for his entire career.

The Tsukiyamas differed from the Ogatas in other ways as well. Although all of the Tsukiyama children attended a Japanese-language school, most of the Tsukiyamas' family friends were haoles. The Tsukiyama boys were Boy Scouts and YMCA members so that they could participate in the camps and other organized activities, and Naoko took piano lessons from the nuns at Sacred Hearts Academy. The family joined the Harris United Methodist Church, which began in 1888 after the Reverend Kenichi Miyama arrived on Oahu with the intent of converting Japanese immigrants and eliminating drinking and gambling. Miyama also helped found the Japanese YMCA, the precursor to the Nuuanu YMCA.[23] At the time when Naoko attended Harris United

Methodist Church, its members included English-speaking young people and students from the University of Hawaii.[24]

By 1941, when Yoshiharu and Naoko began corresponding, Yoshiharu had just graduated (in December 1940) from the Stout Institute. He earned his degree in only three and a half years, rather than four—he had taken classes throughout the year because he could not afford to return home to Hawaii during the summer. Yoshiharu had considered staying at Stout to attend graduate school until June, but the principal of Central Intermediate School in Honolulu promised him a job there, even though it was the middle of the school year.[25] He accepted the job at Central Intermediate and began his teaching career with the spring 1941 semester. Yoshiharu did not have anyone in Honolulu with whom he could live, so he resided at the Nuuanu YMCA. Established in the 1920s, this YMCA catered to the working-class Japanese and Chinese communities, whereas the Central YMCA branch was used primarily by haole, Portuguese, and Hawaiian boys.[26] At the Nuuanu branch, Yoshiharu socialized by playing games like tennis and badminton and met girls who attended Harris United Methodist Church, which was across the street. During Noako's last year of college, she often went to Harris Church after her classes to practice playing the church organ and then to the YMCA to socialize as well. It had a cafeteria where she would meet her father for lunch, and it gave her a place to play badminton.

The two young people, both Nisei and yet culturally different, met through a mutual friend, Yozo Shigemura. Naoko knew Shigemura from the University of Hawaii, and Yoshiharu had met him at the YMCA. They became part of the group of young Japanese Americans who would chat, play sports, and enjoy the company of the opposite sex at the Y. After their matches, Yoshiharu escorted Naoko home on the bus and would stay and visit with her family. After the family became more comfortable with "Ogie," he began to stay for dinner. Naoko's brother Ted remembered Ogie as being so different from the numerous "townies" who pursued his sister. The Japanese on Kauai were more agricultural, lived in small communities, and had generations of men who worked in the fields and mills while the women stayed at home, and Ogata's family fit that profile. As a contemporary newspaper reported, "The Kauai Japanese are not as 'sophisticated'—if that word may be used, or worldly-wise as those on Oahu."[27] In a conversation during the writing of this book, Naoko still mentioned Yoshiharu being a "country boy from Kauai," quite different from the "elite" Tsukiyama family.[28] The family members liked him "alright," but when considering all of her courters, they did not think the couple were a good match. The Tsukiyamas and the Ogatas demonstrated that members of a single community could separate into a privileged class that had opportunities "equivalent to those of whites with similar levels of training and skills" and an "underclass."[29] Their experiences reveal that race and ethnicity contributed to one's identity, but class mattered as well.

✼✼✼

The war affected every aspect of life in Hawaii, and its impact on race shaped generations of Japanese Americans. The Territory of Hawaii had come to define race on its own terms, as it offered an opportunity for a blending of cultures. University of Hawaii sociologist Romanzo Adams explained in 1925 that "the multiplication of contacts between Orientals and Occidentals brings possibilities of misunderstanding and conflict and at the same time opportunities for an enrichment of human life."[30] On the mainland, Americans saw increasing nativism and racism, but in Hawaii, the conflicts involved notions of culture and class, which for some overshadowed differences in race. The seminal events that affected race in Hawaii during this time arose in the plantations and the judicial arena. The elite haole businessmen (a redundant description at the time) strove to keep the local plantation workers separated according to their traditional homelands, focusing on race as a foundation for difference, and they created subgroups of Asians, rather than using Asian as an encompassing racial category. Then the notorious Massie-Kahahawai case of 1931–32 affected Hawaii's understanding of race, class, and power as it pit local Hawaiian, Chinese, and Japanese men (and their communities) against the haole military and political leaders.[31]

Locals embraced differences among themselves to define race relations in Hawaii. To many, "locals" simply meant those who were not tourists, military personnel, or recent immigrants.[32] The local population crossed ethnic lines to band together against haole planters and the merchant elite, but it still recognized a hierarchical society, with white businessmen at the top, followed by Portuguese overseers and then rankings of nonwhites by order of arrival—the Chinese, the Japanese, the Koreans, and the Filipinos.[33] The plantation labor system meant that each ethnicity had its own place in the racial hierarchy, with no "Asian American" identity or sense of solidarity.[34] Yet, a common language developed on the sugar plantations, and this "pidgin"—a creolized language that mixed native Hawaiian, English, Portuguese, Puerto Rican dialects of Spanish, and myriad Asian languages that laborers heard on the plantations—helped them form a local identity. However, the language of the elite, of the haole, remained proper, standard English, providing another way to differentiate between locals and others. Despite the acknowledged ethnic differences, a "local" consciousness arose from the plantation culture, pidgin language, and shared island lifestyle.[35]

Race may be biological, but in Hawaii, "local identity is a matter of positioning oneself in relation to power and place."[36] Building upon the nuances of this idea, then, the cultural identity of "local Japanese" can also be dissected. One's place in the economic spectrum determined one's power. Just because two people (or families) could connect their ancestry to Japan did not mean that they shared the same cultural identity. Yoshiharu and Naoko are direct examples of this.

Despite the couple's differences, they were both Nisei and consequently saw similar changes to life in Hawaii that would later affect their wartime experiences. The population of Hawaii at the 1940 census stood at 423,330, with roughly 61 percent (258,256 people) living on

Oahu. Although the Big Island was the largest in the archipelago, it held just 73,276 people, or 17.3 percent of the territory's population, and Kauai's population of 35,636 constituted 8.4 percent. No ethnic group could claim the majority; the Japanese made up 37.3 percent of the population, and haoles 26.5 percent.[37] By then, the term "haole" applied to whites whose ancestors had not immigrated to Hawaii to work on the plantations and there was no haole working class.[38] The haoles were the elite, but they were not the majority. They, in fact, were the outsiders of the larger community, foreigners once and foreigners still.

On the eve of World War II, approximately 150,000 Japanese lived in Hawaii, of which 113,000 were American citizens.[39] The combination of various ethnic workers on the plantations, the native Hawaiians, the haole minority with American ideals, and few African Americans prevented the same kind of black/white racism that developed on the mainland and instead allowed Japanese Americans to develop identities specific to the island lifestyle. The Japanese in Hawaii made their living by working on the plantations and beyond. Plantation managers regulated their laborers' lives, demanding obedience, cleanliness, and the maintenance of a class system based on race.[40] Although the Ogata family had followed this familiar path, the Tsukiyamas, like a few other first-generation immigrants, had settled outside the plantations and sought upward mobility, finding jobs as merchants and as professionals such as attorneys, architects, and dentists. The Tsukiyama family and others like them never intended to work on the plantations and never shared in that common local culture. Regardless of the differences among the Japanese, both plantation workers and white-collar Japanese identified themselves as Americans. But some mainland Americans did not understand that. They feared that the large number of Japanese in Hawaii made the islands a stepping-stone for Japan's world domination.[41] And yet, for the Japanese in Hawaii, the territory was not a pawn for Japan, nor was it simply an economic market and military base for the United States. It was home.

2   These Things I Love

Even prior to the bombing of Pearl Harbor, Hawaii's risk of being attacked was no secret. Nor was it unexpected that Japanese Americans would be targeted as tension grew between the United States and Japan. Yoshiharu Ogata, after graduating from the Stout Institute in December 1940, traveled home to Hawaii. As he made the trip from Wisconsin to the West Coast by train, and from California to Hawaii by boat, he received advice from Japanese Americans and whites, civilians and soldiers alike, all encouraging him not to dally, because the possibility that federal officials would stop him from going home was imminent. Yoshiharu later recounted that the FBI had indeed stopped him at a train depot in Utah because "[he] was Japanese; [he] was different." He noted that the FBI already knew "to be on the lookout for anything suspicious."[1]

In Hawaii, preparations for war were well under way, and both the government and civilians prepared for a possible attack. In 1939 the city of Honolulu organized a blackout, and by the following year it had an emergency disaster plan in place. The U.S. Army also planned for military rule over the Territory of Hawaii if invasion threatened.[2] The City and County of Honolulu established a Major Disaster Council, which warned, "Even though the possibility of enemy air attack upon industrial plants and public buildings in the United States may be remote, it is essential that protective organization be developed at once to guard against the disruption of normal activities." The council advised the general public to create rescue squads, fire-watcher squads, and police and medical squads[3] and went on to say: "How can we help? Incendiary bombs must find something to burn. Reduce risk of burnable material [to make] enemies less effective. Reduce common household hazards."[4] Other advice from the council included a list of emergency food items that families should store, with recommended caloric intakes per day for one month.[5] Even more notably, the Territory of Hawaii passed the Hawaii Defense Act, which gave the governor sweeping power over people and property.[6]

Private citizens undertook projects that promoted the preparations for war. Some volunteers knitted socks, blankets, and sweaters for the Red Cross. Others took first aid classes and then taught first aid to people in their communities. Adults learned English in classes that were part of an "Americanizing" program called "Speak English."[7] At Central Intermediate School, where Yoshiharu would later work, students participated in a national organization that collected blankets, old newspapers, empty tubes of toothpaste for the lead they contained, and old clothes, raising $125,000.[8] And a Mr. Ogata (perhaps Yoshiharu) donated $5.00 for the war cause.[9]

As part of the interwar generation, Naoko Tsukiyama and Yoshiharu Ogata witnessed an emphasis on Americanization as they grew up in the shadow of World War I and a time of expansion of the Empire of Japan. The informal Gentlemen's Agreement of 1907 had stopped Japanese laborers from moving to the United States (but not the Territory of Hawaii), and the formal Immigration Act of 1924 "slammed the door on Japanese immigration, isolating the Japanese in America." Suspicion toward Japanese Americans grew, as other Americans worried that they would become a pro-Japanese fifth column of spies and saboteurs.[10] Americanization efforts on the U.S. mainland and in Hawaii "sought to strip immigrants of their native customs." Americanizers, as historian Eileen H. Tamura observes, offered adults clubs, libraries, lectures, and kindergartens, as well as classes in English, civics, sewing, and cooking.

Public schools taught Japanese American children patriotism, including saluting the flag and observing national holidays—all through English-only instruction.[11] The FBI collected files on Japanese community leaders whom it considered potential threats to national security. And the 1940 Alien Registration Act authorized the government to collect background information on resident aliens, required them to report a change of address within five days, and stipulated that they confirm their address every three months.[12] By January 1941 the Honolulu Police Department and the FBI pondered what to do with the Japanese community in Hawaii if the United States went to war with Japan, and they both began questioning the loyalty of the Japanese.[13] Japanese Americans, in return, were ready to sever ties with Japan (including renouncing Japanese citizenship) and to volunteer for U.S. military service.[14] Thus, in Hawaii, the general consensus was that the local Japanese would be loyal to the United States and not to Japan.[15]

The Issei and Nisei worked to demonstrate their patriotism as well as their acculturation into American society. On the mainland the popular belief was that the Japanese would be unassimilable, but in Hawaii even the territorial governor believed that the Japanese "could and would be assimilated by the dominant society."[16] The Nisei believed themselves to be Americans, and they adopted tastes and trends similar to those of white Americans. But their physical differences were constant reminders of their ethnic background. The Japanese American Citizens League emphasized nationality over race, and developed a creed pledging to support the Constitution, to defend America, and to assume duties and obligations of an American citizen.[17] Before the attack on Pearl Harbor, Japanese Americans on the mainland and in Hawaii had their loyalties questioned and challenged, but they also lived their lives as their fellow Americans did.

In Hawaii, Americans came from a variety of ethnic backgrounds, and popular culture, rather than direct exposure, gave Naoko Tsukiyama and Yoshiharu Ogata examples to follow. As was typical of the era, they showed an enthusiasm for popular music and, in fact, structured their social lives around the radio. Nisei on the mainland and in the territory watched Hollywood movies, listened to American big band music over their radios, and borrowed lyrics from songs and quotations from movies for their correspondences.[18] Historian Kelly Schrum notes that movies played a large role in American culture, providing role models, demonstrating new attitudes toward romance, and teaching about fashion, beauty, language, and behavior.[19] Naoko and Yoshiharu both sprinkled their letters with song titles and quotations from songs and movies. Naoko, for instance, referenced the song "These Things I Love" and explained that she had the words to it, since, as she put it, "it's number one on my hit parade." She also asked Yoshiharu if he was still singing "Nighty Night," a song that tells of sweethearts parting with a farewell kiss.[20] It would not have been proper, and actually would have been quite forward of Naoko, to state that she thought of kissing Yoshiharu, but by using the lyrics of a popular song as camouflage, she could express her sentiments and desires. In response, Yoshiharu also mentioned "These Are the Things I Love," thus revealing his feelings as well.[21] These trends ran rampant in the correspondences of their white mainland counterparts, and Naoko and Yoshiharu followed suit.

Although members of the Nisei generation had the physical features of Japanese, they could still Americanize their attire and attitudes. They wore corduroys, V-neck sweaters, saddle shoes, and pleated skirts. These second-generation Japanese Americans belonged to Boy Scouts and Campfire Girls, ate Wheaties, drank Ovaltine, and played baseball.[22] In Hawaii, ethnic baseball teams formed and became rallying points for the plantation communities.[23] Baseball had in fact become a "vehicle for Americanizing Hawaii's Japanese community."[24] Tennis and badminton also captured the youth. The games' setup for playing as either singles or doubles made it easier to compete, as large numbers of players were not required. Young men and women could compete and play in acceptable settings that were still intimate enough for them to socialize.

Additionally, Nisei showed their Americanization by calling each other "dear," "sweetheart," and "honey" and by shaking hands instead of bowing.[25] Historians Beth Bailey and David Farber argue, "Hawaii is about as different from 'representative' as one can get in 1940s America. Hawaii was at the margin of American life as well as of the war."[26] But Naoko and Yoshiharu were not on the margins of either. Their lives were caught up in the war, and they also indulged in the popular recreational activities of the time. The couple's letters in this chapter make reference to movies, dancing, and dating. American popular culture affected them, just as it did millions of other Americans who came from other ethnic and regional backgrounds.

The letters below are from July through September 1941. In the first set, Naoko is living in Honolulu, on the island of Oahu, and writing to Yoshiharu, who had returned to his family's home on the island of Kauai. The two had just met that summer through their mutual friend, but then had to prepare for their jobs as teachers with the start of the upcoming school year. Yoshiharu's training as an industrial arts teacher made him a desirable hire, because public schools used vocational education classes to direct students toward plantation work.[27] But for Yoshiharu, the industrial arts became a way for him to find a job beyond the confines of the plantation. Naoko had recently graduated from the University of Hawaii. She had received domestic training and knew how to sew and cook, and she also had secretarial experience and worked for Island Homes, a real estate company. She had taken some business classes and knew how to format a letter and take shorthand. When Naoko went to college, she started in liberal arts and sciences and planned to major in business, but she ended up attending the Teachers' College, where all of her friends were. During the summer after her graduation, she worked at the University of Hawaii Business Office but knew that she would be leaving in the fall for a teaching post on an outer island.

As the two began their written correspondence, their future was uncertain. They were both teachers and expected to obtain positions in the public schools. The Organic Act, which set up the territorial government of Hawaii, provided for a superintendent of the Territorial Department of Public Instruction and a Board of Commissioners, both of which led to centralized control of schools.[28] The "D.P.I." that Yoshiharu and Naoko both mentioned in their letters stood for the Department of Public Instruction. Historian Franklin Odo describes the DPI as the "quintessential 'Americanizing' institution." It worked to transform all immigrant children into U.S. citizens. Americanization efforts included teaching children about democracy, a representative government, law and order, capitalism, and general health and hygiene. Public schools taught ideals of liberty and democracy but often still held to a discriminatory policy in which employee candidates had to show proof of expatriation (from Japan) before they could be hired.[29] The DPI expected newly minted teachers to pay their dues, teaching on the outer islands before earning a job on Oahu, the most desired spot.[30] Both Yoshiharu and Naoko awaited their placement and did not know to which island the DPI would assign them.

Worthy of note in these letters is the differences in lifestyle available on the two islands. Naoko had a pink-collar job, doing administrative work for the University of Hawaii. She filled her social calendar with church activities, movies, and sporting events. She noted both female and male companions, her Japanese American friends from the university and from her church. She informed Yoshiharu of her outings with their mutual friends, Mits Oka and Yozo Shigemura. Yoshiharu, after living for five months in Honolulu, went back to Kauai to spend his summer vacation with his family. His social activities included riding his horse, working in his woodshop, and swimming at the beach. He enjoyed solitary events, and his only companion for many of these activities was the family dog, Lulu. The social life in which the two young Nisei engaged typified the contrast between the city and rural lifestyles in which they were raised.

Kaimuki, Oahu

July 28, 1941

Dear Teacher,

Well, how is the Live Alone And Like It Society getting along? It must be The Life. Getting away from it all and living your own way. You must let me know some day of its advantages and maybe disadvantages if any. Remember I'm the one who advocates plain and simple living. I was looking at a Tourist Bureau map of the different islands, just in case you know, and Kauai looks like a pretty wet place. Lots of rivers for fishing, and rainbows in the valleys, plus Mt. Waialeale or something which is the wettest spot on earth.[31] How are the people? Maybe some day I'll find out myself. Most likely I'll get stuck out on Hawaii, so why worry now.[32] Do I worry. Only I don't like the surprise ending they are giving us. Have you found out whether you'll be here or there? I hope you get what you want anyway. Why a man or rather a teacher with your qualifications should be recognized as an asset to any high school. Let's tell the D.P.I.

Now about 'such' that I was going to write about. I have the words to "These Things I Love" now, since it's number one on my hit parade. Are you still singing the first line to "Nighty Night"? One thing about isolation, there's no progress. Yesterday being Sunday our church gang went over to Wahiawa for baseball and picnic supper.[33] Yozo asked me along and guess what, we got left behind. Mits wouldn't go to the country so we had to follow him to Ala Moana Park where the South King church was having a picnic.[34] There were two bikes and we rode all over the place, played baseball, watched the evening sun go down, had a devotional period, ate supper, listened to a radio and Mits talking, and watched stars come out.

From tomorrow I've been called again to my paid-by-the-hour job at the University Business Office. I count football and boxing tickets which is no fun, but nobody bothers me and vice versa. Otherwise I stay home and sew clothes for my jaunt to the country in September.

Goodbye now,
Naoko

Eleele, Kauai
August 1, 1941

Dear Naoko,

For the first four or five days after I got back to Kauai, I wondered how I'll ever find something to do. I have all the time—car and what else yet nothing to do—I finally figured out that fun is where you make it. Yes, make my own fun and I'm liking it. This is my "live alone" schedule.

I usually get up about 6:30 in the morning—get in shorts and make my own breakfast—usually coffee and toast. After that I usually take out my grudge and temper on wood. Cut away and dig and everything else.

Well, this usually lasts me until noon, dinner. I help my mother get some grub. Afternoons I usually go out riding. Alone too. No bicycle— but horse or car. I usually end up the day by going swimming. After supper I usually rest—talk with my folks and then tune in my radio— read magazines and do I worry? No. I sleep.

In the evening I sometime go driving. Now days especially with the moon keeping me company I like to sit and look out over the breakers and into nowhere.[35] "These Are The Things I Love" and I see to it that I get them. All the while I'm doing these things alone something seems to be lacking. I sometimes wonder if it is a feminine company that I'm missing. Perhaps she could be one that won't say anything but just let the wind blow through her hair and sit and sigh.

When I'm out with a girl especially where there are no influence of society, she's one just like me only physically not quite as capable to move about. What I mean is on a hike and things like that I'd help a girl up a bank or things like that but why over do it? I was wondering before I went out with you whether it was you who demanded that kind of response of the men or whether it was the men who did it. I think it's the latter. You're as regular as anyone can be. If you don't get along with any guy I think it's the guy's fault and not yours if you act as you did to me.

So long—

Ogata

Have a good laugh at my English—you probably won't come across anything funnier.

Kaimuki, Oahu

August 10, 1941

My dear friend,

You said you were making things out of wood. What are you working on now? I was reading in the *Reader's Digest* about a sculptor who believes that everyone should have some sort of hobby along creative lines. It might be hard for boys to find hobbies because they think they have to be skilled to make anything worthwhile, but for girls I think it would give them a big kick just to sew their own clothes or cook up a new dish even if the family has to suffer eating it.

Well so much is enough, nothing much happens around here that is much news. My friend's returning from Columbia this Wednesday, she just finished her Master's. She taught at Central last spring, and how time flies. I'm looking forward to seeing her again, the name's Doris Fukuda.[36] Maybe you'll be teaching with her some day and it wouldn't be bad knowing a person like her. You know there are some interesting women around and that's a comfort. The men must have all been drafted or something, no kidding.

My regards to your horse,

Naoko

This next section of letters addresses gender roles of the 1940s. Both men and women worked for wages, but by the 1930s, most men and women believed that women should not work if they were married. In fact, being a housewife was a woman's main duty once married.[37] Advice for proper women included "sprucing up" before husbands got home from work so that they were "fresh, clean, and kissable." An article cautioned, "He is bound to see you with your hair tousled, your face shining, and a streak of dust across your nose. But that doesn't mean you can let yourself go." Women adhered to warnings that they should care about how they looked, even if it was just in front of their husbands. Magazine articles advised women never to bawl out their husbands in public, and especially not in front of relatives. Women were to be "at least as polite to the man [they] have wed" as to they were to an "old beau whom [they] discarded."[38] Women's advice magazines clearly described women's subservient roles and all that they had to do to make their marriages successful. At the local level, students from the University of Hawaii's Hawaii Union (the debate team) held a debate focusing on the topic "Women's Place Is in the Home." "Heckling was thoroughly permissible," and the debate "ended without a decision."[39]

Japanese Americans learned distinctive gender roles that paralleled those of white America, but adjusted them to fit their own economic and social backgrounds. Japanese American girls helped with cooking and cleaning. Both boys and girls helped with household chores, ranging from taking care of younger siblings and farm animals to working in the fields. Another value that parents instilled in children was to devote time to their studies.[40] However, the extent to which children and families followed these patterns depended on where they lived. The Tsukiyama family, as city dwellers and members of the merchant class, did not have the responsibility of maintaining farm animals or fields. The Ogatas, on the other hand, worked on a plantation and had both farm animals and an extensive garden. For many plantation families, growing vegetables and Japanese-style gardens, as well as raising chickens, rabbits, ducks, and pigs, was a way of life.[41] When Yoshiharu lived in Honolulu, he lived away from his family. But with each return to Kauai, he resumed his role as a proper son and toiled in the garden and cared for the family's animals.

Education played a large role in the development of the Nisei. Their parents came to America with the importance of an education already impressed upon them.[42] The United States had opened its public schools to Japanese immigrants since 1907, and they learned about democracy through a "capitalist state bent on social control."[43] Parents worried about their children striking out on their own and carrying on their valued traditions of religion and good behavior, while the Nisei wanted their "right to an American citizen's opportunity."[44] Despite their desire for higher education, many were denied admission to colleges and universities because of restrictive quotas. Those who did earn college degrees found themselves excluded from white-collar and civil service jobs.[45] Naoko's brother Jimmy Kagawa felt the impact of this trend. Despite graduating from the Guggenheim School of Aeronautics at New York University in 1940 with a degree in engineering, he could not overcome being the first Japanese American to have earned that degree, and those circumstances discouraged major U.S. companies from hiring him. Nevertheless, a college education represented an accomplishment for him and "for the well-being of the wider collective, the Japanese American community."[46]

In Hawaii, however, education could be a way out of a plantation life, as Yoshiharu's experiences proved.[47] Hawaii's public school system opened its doors to all ethnicities, and the children of local plantation workers attended public schools, in which Chinese, Portuguese, Japanese, Hawaiian, haole, and mixed teachers taught pidgin English (Hawaii Creole English) as a spoken language.[48] One report on the Nisei noted that the public schools fostered a "wholesome spirit of inter-racial good will," as they taught students to think in terms of America and to live American ways.[49] Children of immigrants learned to accept America as their own country, the U.S. Constitution as their own government's foundation, and democracy as their own way of life.[50] They learned that all men were created equal and had inalienable rights as Americans, regardless of their race or skin color.[51] Thus, in spite of the obstacles they faced, they aspired to professional jobs in the civil service, education, medicine, law, and business—jobs away from the sugar plantations.[52]

Schools themselves served as a marker of class as well. The elite haole and Hawaiian families sent their children to private schools, such as Punahou School, Mid-Pacific Institute, and the Kamehameha Schools. White families on Oahu sent their children to English Standard Schools, which the DPI created in Honolulu in 1924. To get into an English Standard School, a student needed to pass an oral exam, and most children of immigrant parents could not gain admittance. In fact, the DPI had established most of the English Standard Schools in communities where haoles lived. The schools encouraged good speech habits and no pidgin English. The system led to a de facto private school system within the public school system and to class differentiations between white and nonwhite.[53] Having attended Aliiolani Elementary and subsequently Roosevelt High School (both English Standard Schools), Naoko was among the elite Japanese who gained admittance to such schools. She embraced the standard English they taught, and she recognized the differences between pidgin and proper English. In contrast, other local children felt conflicted. When they spoke "good English," their friends and elders paid less attention to them, seeing them as being know-it-alls and acting like haoles.[54] Overall, most Japanese American children went through Hawaii's public school system in the decades before the war, constituting one-half of the territory's students.[55]

The exposure that the Nisei had to American education and popular culture provided a contrast to their parents' traditions, occasionally causing tension between the generations. The Issei felt the conflict as parents who wanted their children to be Americans but also to embrace aspects of Japanese culture. They gave their children Japanese names, sent them to Japanese-language schools, and taught them Japanese values.[56] Some Americans believed that Japanese schools impeded the path to U.S. citizenship, because they could promote loyalty to Japan, as well as foster Japanese nationalism, Japanese culture, and Buddhism. But of greater concern was that they interfered with learning English, "the language of America."[57] The reality was, though, that as members of the second generation, the Nisei commonly spoke four languages— good English in school, pidgin among their friends, and good or pidgin Japanese when the situation called for it.[58] One study explained their plight: "To be a Nisei was to be two people: a dutiful child of Japan who honored parents and respected authority as well as an adventuresome, independent-minded American youngster who tested limits."[59] The Nisei wanted a good education to prepare themselves for participation in community and political affairs, to help solve social problems, and to be able to contribute to the moral and ethical standards of Hawaii and the world.[60] The idea of a college education was not a dream just for the Nisei. Issei parents believed that a college education would allow their children "a life of ease," but the Nisei saw college as a means to obtaining new ideas, a new standard of living, and even a new way of life.[61] Moreover, the friends they made in school affected their ambitions, needs, and interests.[62]

The entire Tsukiyama family represented the Japanese American family's interest and participation in American education. By the 1940s the eldest son, James Kagawa, had already completed his engineering degree at New York University. The next three children, Naoko, Ted, and Kazu, attended the University of Hawaii. A count of the senior classes in 1940 and 1941, during Naoko's college years, shows that Japanese American students made up 41 percent and 48 percent of the graduates, respectively (the Japanese American population in Hawaii was just under 40 percent at the time).[63] They participated in the Reserve Officers Training Corps (ROTC) and in religious organizations like the YMCA and the YWCA. They joined the University Japanese Club, with "membership limited to twenty Japanese students" and a mission that included "service to the university to the utmost."[64] "The U," as students called it, also had a Japanese social fraternity called Hakuba Kai (meaning "White Horse Group") and a Japanese social sorority called Wakaba Kai ("Falling Leaves Group"). Wakaba Kai opened its doors only to female students of Japanese ancestry, and Naoko became a member. The sorority organized rummage sales, presented a Christmas program to the Japanese Old Men's Home in Honolulu, showed a Japanese movie as a fundraiser, and exhibited dolls to celebrate Japanese Dolls' Day. The sorority also held two dances in conjunction with Hakuba Kai, whose activities, beyond those hosted with Wakaba Kai, included a dinner dance, a beach party, a skating party, and a grand stag party. Naoko noted that her membership in Wakaba Kai was for socializing; she did not see it as a conscientious decision to segregate and unify with other members of her ethnic group. Although her college boyfriend, Toshimi Tatsuyama, was a member of Hakuba Kai and the Japanese Club, Naoko did not consider the organizations as statements of ethnic alliance. Sociologists Michael Omi and Howard Winant state that although race is "a concept which signifies and symbolizes social conflicts and interests by referring to different types of human bodies," it also "plays a fundamental role in structuring and representing the social world."[65] Understandably, then, Kazu joined the University Japanese Club. Ted's social circle grew as he took an active role in the ROTC alongside other Nisei. The youngest daughter, Martha, turned eighteen less than two months before the bombing of Pearl Harbor, and she had not yet begun college. The Tsukiyama children received an education typical of the white families in Hawaii, and this formal education was evident in Naoko's letters to Yoshiharu. Naoko demonstrated a penchant for proper grammar. She had been trained in standard English at home, in primary and secondary schools, and in college. By using good English, she exhibited the trappings of a higher class of Japanese Americans in Hawaii.

The Ogatas' education, on the other hand, typified that of the plantation workers. Yoshiharu became the exception in the family by attending college on the mainland. He chose the Stout Institute because he had known another man from Kauai who went there for training as an industrial arts teacher. Yoshiharu's siblings found work in the business and service sectors and did not strive for a four-year college education. Yoshiharu's educational level and exposure to myriad cultures gave him experiences beyond the boundaries of the sugar plantations. Those experiences included living among whites on the mainland for more than three years, where he earned the nickname "Chief" from his friends there, who thought he looked like a Native American. He did not use his vocational training to obtain an agricultural job on a plantation, although he possessed skill and talent for raising plants and animals. His letters describe him working in the garden, building lamps and furniture, raising chickens, and doing general handiwork.[66] Instead, he used his education to gain a professional occupation. English became his primary language. His writings reveal his struggles with grammar and his use of pidgin English, but his formal schooling is evident. His English was much better than that of many of his sisters and brothers, but in his letters to Naoko, he admitted his self-consciousness about how his writing skills compared with Naoko's.

In their letters, the young couple also addressed their differences in terms of high culture. In a letter dated August 17, 1941, Naoko wrote about the joy she got from listening to Beethoven. She explained that some people listen to classical music "so they can say things like that," and that "they get all 'cultured' on the outside." But, she argued, she saw beauty in sunsets and her surroundings too and believed that "symphonies are made for those who don't have the real things or the eyes to see them in their natural surroundings."[67] Yoshiharu's response to her commentary was, "About the only time I'd really enjoy reading poetry or listening to symphony is when I'm in bed with perhaps a broken leg." He did not create any pretense of being interested in "music, literature and all the other fine arts." He went on to say that a person would force himself "to do it only because he is too dumb and thinks culture means to know all those things by heart and to be able to just about recite it in front of other people." He agreed with her that those who really want to see the beauty in the world could "get it from the wind, the trees and really enjoy it."[68] Throughout his letters, Yoshiharu made it very clear that people should be who they are and not put up any facade. This became particularly necessary to him as his relationship with Naoko developed. He emphasized that they both needed to reveal their true selves. Even in this early stage of their romance, he did not feign a common interest, and in fact his stated lack of interest in the fine arts demonstrated how differently the two were raised.

As Yoshiharu and Naoko prepared for the next step in their professional careers, they also began to examine their personal lives. Naoko continued her busy social schedule but wondered about the company she was keeping. She noted in one passage that a former classmate had asked her to the movies, but she let Yoshiharu know that there were only a few people "you just enjoy being with."[69] Although she did not specifically say that he was one of those few people, she did make clear that she chose not to date any other men. She also let him know that she hoped to see him again, while still revealing her hesitancy in assuming too much of their budding relationship. Yoshiharu, in response, dwelled upon his self-declared shortcomings. He recognized that her city upbringing had exposed Naoko to different social circles, but at the same time he still hoped to see her again too.

Kaimuki, Oahu

August 17, 1941

Dear Yoshiharu,

[This] afternoon [I was] watching the Asahis play a poor game.[70] They went to pieces in the 8th inning, and the better team won. Perfect coordination is what I like most, and you see beautiful throws as well as catches made as a result. A girl can't figure out all the technical points of the game, but those things can be appreciated. Oh yes, once in a while I see a tall lanky player and I love to watch them in action.

Wouldn't you say too, that there are certain people you can enjoy certain things with? If you like dancing with one, well you go out and have a wonderful time dancing. The same with seeing a movie, and you can enjoy seeing one with that person and it doesn't mean holding hands either. You can go to a concert with one you'd never think of going to a picnic with and so forth. And lastly there's very very few you just enjoy being with. Where? It doesn't matter, and you don't have to do anything in particular to have a wonderful time. You find people like that in dreams or in story books mostly, they seldom run around loose because it is better for them to stay in dreams or story books. If you don't agree you can add your own opinions to that.

Tomorrow I'm going down to reserve passage on some of those inter-island tubs. The kids (my classmates) say I'd better so I can fly off anytime. The commissioners meet tomorrow so by this weekend we'll know. I'm booking for Tues. Aug. 26 to leave for either Maui, Lanai, Molokai or Hawaii and Thurs. Aug. 28, for Kauai. Anything can happen you know so we get ready for any place. Only a week more and we'll have our futures more or less settled. You'll probably come back to town, you lucky bum, but I'd rather not stay here for a while. I'm falling in a rut, same old things, same old people and all some much on-the-surface stuff. In the country, even if it is quite peaceful, you can get closer to yourself and learn to appreciate others more. I don't know though, I've never tried it but I'm sure it will be so.

When are you leaving for the bright lights of our fair city? It would be rather tragic if I left before you arrived. Why I hardly know you! Well maybe it would be better that way, I wouldn't know. I hope I'll hear from you soon anyway. If I get to Kauai you'd better stay home, I don't know anyone else.

Nighty-night—Naoko

Eleele, Kauai
August 20, 1941

Dear Miss Tsukiyama,

Naoko, my humble complements to you. Your letters are the best I have ever received in all the corresponding I've been doing. I honestly mean this and I take my hat off to you. Of course this probably doesn't mean much to you coming from a guy like me. I'm sure that the social and cultural contacts that you had so far is far beyond that you find in me and I'm sure those people also paid you complements.

Naoko this is what I really liked about your last letter. I smiled as I read this part and the rest of the paragraph. There are two kinds of things in this world that one should know—first are the things one should know to live intelligently, everyday things and the other is the things that would be nice to know. Why stay in on a nice day or night when you are physically well and read poetry or have a wholly symphonic orchestra pounding on your ear drum.

I will be returning to Honolulu on the 29th of this month. If you are sailing for the other islands I won't get to see you. Perhaps as you said that is the best thing. When Christmas vacation comes along you will be coming back to Honolulu and I will be returning to Kauai. Well, why think that far ahead anyway, you would probably forget me by then anyway. I hope you don't think I don't want to see you. I want to, but I think it is better for you. There are many swell and better fellows than I am. I know you will meet them. When you do, I will envy him.

So long for now,
Yoshiharu

The letters continue through the end of August and into the beginning of September. By then Yoshiharu had returned to Oahu and was working at Central Intermediate School in Honolulu. Central Middle School (as it is known today) opened as Central Grammar School in 1908. It became a junior high school in 1928, and by the time Yoshiharu started there in 1941, it had been an intermediate school for nine years.[71] He later recalled that the principal of the school had welcomed him back to Hawaii when he returned from Wisconsin. But after he finished his spring 1941 term, he, like all other public school teachers, had to wait to see where his next teaching job would be. Once he received word of being rehired at Central Intermediate, he returned to Oahu and again lived at the Nuuanu YMCA.

At the end of August, Naoko started her teaching career at the Olaa School in Olaa, near Hilo on the Big Island of Hawaii. She, along with several of her classmates from the Teachers' College at the University of Hawaii, traveled by steamship, the *Hualalai*, to Hilo to begin jobs as rural schoolteachers. Naoko held a positive outlook on living away from the big city of Honolulu. Even though her family lived there and she participated in social activities in town (including a beauty pageant in which she was first runner-up), Naoko embraced the change of pace. She welcomed the serenity of the countryside and looked for the beauty in nature, just as she had said she might do. She described an appreciation for the peaceful streets, the abundant flora and fauna, and the waves breaking on the seashore.[72] Much of that seems contradictory to her city lifestyle, but she claimed it nonetheless. It is not clear how much of her expressed enjoyment of rural life was genuine and how much was simply a matter of being a good sport (or setting herself up as a prime candidate to reside on Kauai, which was also rural). Regardless, Naoko's stint on the Big Island did not last very long. She had a bad cold even before she embarked, and within a month she contracted bronchitis, so she took her leave from teaching and returned to her family's home in Honolulu.

⚏⚏⚏

Hilo, Hawaii
August 31, 1941

Dear Yoshiharu,

Here I am at a classmate's home in Hilo where they've been treating us like guests at a hotel, but with the homey touch—my 'principal' Shizue Katashima and I.[73]

We are meeting tomorrow at 10:30 with our supervisor, then we push off to the black sands of Kalapana.[74] It's 30 miles from Hilo and part of the road is full of bumps, some of the kids were teasing us so. Well we'll see tomorrow, and I'll know then whether I'll still be happy.

Everytime I think of the way we counted the hours and minutes left, it makes me smile. It all happened so fast, I didn't have time to get sad. Only when the whistle blew, did I feel momentary panic and sort of sad, but it was too exciting for me to cry about. With all this and almost heaven too, there is no need for me to feel sorry for myself. I hope.

It was sweet of you to come over and remind me of the 'last hours of agony' every five minutes. Anyway it was nice having you around, you aren't the kind to make a big fuss over things. Sometimes silence is greater comfort than a lot of noise. I kind of remember you standing there at the pier by the boxes (not beer cases?) and just being the silent observer. Thank you for those beautiful ginger leis, and I really didn't say goodbye to you again but consider it done.

Nighty-night,
Naoko

Hilo, Hawaii
September 8, 1941

Dear Yoshiharu,

I spent a lovely week at Kalapana, the more I live there the more I like it. No kidding. Talk about living alone and liking it—that is the place. Remember I had a slight cough before leaving Honolulu? Ever since I got here it's been raining and it really blows out at our seaside residence. Saturday I went to a doctor in Hilo and he said I had bronchitis. I've been teaching all week with a cloth around my throat, vicks rubdowns at night, hot lemonade and what not. Nothing else was wrong with me, in fact we were laughing at how much we could eat. So now I'm recuperating at the Kims' home for a week. They keep me in bed, bring me warm milk, Japanese food, and baby me to death. Yesterday afternoon for the first time since I left home I lay in bed and let the tears roll down my face everytime somebody said a kind word to me. When you're sick, you feel weak enough to cry about anything. Anyway it felt good, but it was a tragic affair the way it kept raining outside and inside too.

I feel more 'God' out there all over the place than I would if I sat in church a whole week. That's why people in the city have to go to church once a week, at least it makes them feel better, and they should. In the city you don't find 'God' all around, so you have to look for him in church. Sometimes it's hard to see anything, when the sermon is lousy, or the choir sings flat.

Have you found a place to stay definitely? My goodness, I won't have you sleeping here and there like a '2nd class bum.' Do it again and I'll promote you to 1st class. That's the whole trouble with city people, they live only for themselves. If you still haven't a place, just go to my house and tell them I willed you my bed. Just walk in and take it. I'll call them all sorts of names if they won't let you.

Living with people, we have to be what they expect us to be, then when something happens that we think could never be again as real as it is, we have to turn away from it because it 'isn't reality'—in other words we aren't being 'realistic.' I wonder which is the more real—being just ourselves or being the way people expect us to be. It puzzles me sometimes to figure out which is which—I prefer the first, it's the only way you really live and be happy, yet can you live and be happy without depending on people, or associating with them. So far, out here in the isolated country the more I'm left alone the more I'm really enjoying life. There's something about the wide green spaces that's friendly and comforting. As soon as cars approach and strange people come, then we begin to worry.

Well anyway I don't see why you should build up such an attitude as to say 'I don't deserve people and dates like you.' You needn't get so moody. Gosh, I could just do it all over again, that walk up the hill—the wonder and the beauty in it.[75] Something I wanted to do all my life with just the right person and you happened to be the one. If you didn't deserve it who else would? Anyway it just happened—I guess the atmosphere had a lot to do with it. Now we can say 'be realistic and don't begin something that'll have no end or future in it.['] If you think that's best and you seem to think so, I think that's a good idea.

Nighty-night,
Naoko

Kalapana, Hawaii
September 19, 1941

Dear Philosopher,
Well, this may be the last letter you'll get from me. For a while at least, because I'm coming back to 'noisy' Honolulu much to my regret by plane Sunday morning. I feel okay, but the doctor advised me to go home and rest for awhile until I'm all well. After that cold which they called bronchitis and X ray of my lungs and all that, they tell me if I don't take a good rest and build up resistance it will be too bad for me. I still

cough a little and sometimes feel tired for nothing, that's the only reason I believe the Doctors aren't kidding me. Besides the folks at home,
especially my mother, got so frantic I think it's better for me to go
home than be cared for in a hospital. So anyway I'll go home to read
magazines and lead 'a very quiet life.'

Sincerely,
Naoko

3   The Sun Still Shines

On December 7, 1941, at about 8:00 A.M. Hawaii Standard Time, the Empire of Japan bombed the military base at Pearl Harbor, on Oahu. Although Hawaii had territorial status at the time, the president of the United States, Franklin Delano Roosevelt, considered this surprise attack, done "suddenly and deliberately," as an attack on the United States. The two countries had been in peace talks, to no avail. The bombing—by aircraft that included torpedo planes, dive bombers, and fighters—came in two waves, destroying the bulk of the U.S. Pacific Fleet, killing approximately 2,400 people, and wounding around 1,200 more.[1] The date that lives in infamy drew the United States into World War II, but for the residents of Hawaii it also led to economic, civil, and social upheaval.

Through the Hawaiian Organic Act of 1900, the Territory of Hawaii was placed under martial law. In an interview, the late Senator Daniel K. Inouye (D-Hawaii) once explained that the newly assigned military officers who administered the martial law could not differentiate between the Issei and the Nisei. They considered all Japanese to be enemy aliens.[2] This military regime affected residents at every level. Authorities forbade any speech or action critical of the government. To prevent lights from serving as beacons for further attacks at night, the army ordered a complete blackout at 6:00 P.M. on December 7, and in the following weeks it even barred all private cars from the highways. Anyone caught with a lit cigarette or pipe after blackout, or even having a visible stove burner, faced possible arrest. As the United States saw increased victories in the Pacific Theater, martial law regulations were relaxed somewhat.[3] General orders from the military governor of the Territory of Hawaii called for curfews to begin at 10:00 P.M., and the curfew hours were to change according to the seasons and correspond with sunrise and sunset. They remained in effect, however, until July 11, 1945.[4] Residents could not use lights outdoors, and the lights allowed indoors had to be authorized by the military.[5] Hawaii's residents covered their windows with thick black paper or dark heavy curtains to prevent lights from shining through as beacons. Martial law also restricted assembly, with laws in some areas preventing more than ten people from congregating at one time. When the military took over Hawaii, it limited access to public spaces, and the forced crowding caused a wider spread of disease.[6] Frequent air raid alarms sounded by the spring of 1942, but the threat of another attack on Hawaii lessened with increasing American victories in the Pacific that year.[7]

The letters of Yoshiharu Ogata and Naoko Tsukiyama in this chapter span the period from January 11, 1942, until August 4, 1942, and reveal that the bombing immediately affected everyone in Hawaii, regardless of ethnicity. Officials encouraged residents of the territory to donate blood, volunteer for fire and police departments, and stand guard at public utilities. Within a week of the attack, stores closed at 3:30 P.M., pubs closed for more than two months, and the government set gasoline and liquor rations. It was not until February of 1942 that adults could again buy liquor, but it was rationed, and an elaborate system controlled its sale and distribution.[8] Adults, excluding alien Japanese, could obtain permits to buy a case of beer, three quarts of wine, or a quart of hard liquor per week. Some people would line up to receive the rationed liquor when they did have a permit for it, and nondrinkers hoarded their ration tickets, making it even harder for drinkers to obtain liquor.[9] Liquor restrictions affected Yoshiharu more than Naoko. Although both mentioned drinking alcohol throughout their correspondences, he indulged in alcohol whereas she commented on the drinking of others.

Additionally, nearly eight thousand shops closed, as they faced a shortage of products and manpower and dealt with an abundance of governmental red tape. The military set prices for food and Hawaii had its own currency, which looked similar to U.S. currency but had "Hawaii" printed on it and was either smaller or larger than regular U.S. bills. Residents could not carry more than $200 in cash, and businesses could not hold more than $300.[10] Although cash was limited, everyone was encouraged to buy war bonds. People could purchase them at banks, sporting events, stores, post offices, and theater lobbies and from door-to-door sellers. Holidays and special events became associated with bond buying, and some people gave them as gifts.[11] Japanese American families heard that buying bonds was a way to demonstrate their patriotism.

As the military continued to exert its power, martial law froze wages, established an eight-hour workday, suspended contracts between employers and workers, and did not allow for job mobility. The military authorities fined or jailed workers who failed to show up for work or protested their jobs.[12] By December 9, martial law demanded that alien Japanese give up firearms, other weapons, ammunition, bombs, short-wave radios, cameras, and maps of Hawaii. Places of amusement reopened on December 24, 1941, but martial law regulations remained in effect, including directions for garbage collection, establishment of one-way streets, regulation of bowling alleys, chlorination of water, and restrictions on interisland travel. Even dogs were subject to martial law, with requirements like being indoors during blackouts and wearing a license tag at all times.[13] The military censored newspapers, regulated night driving, controlled radio stations, prohibited enemy aliens from traveling in cars after 10:00 at night, and closed civil courts.[14] Civil courts reopened a week after the attacks, but military commissions and provost courts tried criminal cases with no juries and, sometimes, no lawyers. Under martial law, suspects went to provost courts and faced steeper penalties than in civilian courts.[15] Censors read outgoing mail and edited it with scissors or black ink or simply returned it to the sender. Schools closed temporarily, as did stores that were required to take inventory of all their supplies. Hawaii's residents had no choice but to adjust to living with gas rationed at half a tank, air raid sirens, and blackouts after dark, all of which Naoko and Yoshiharu chronicled in their letters as they commented on their daily activities.[16]

In addition to economic and civil challenges, islanders faced a lifestyle change. The army distributed gas masks on December 10, 1941, and by March 1942, adults, children, and infants had masks and instructions to carry them everywhere at all times. Gas mask drills were performed, in which everyone practiced putting on the masks. Newspapers ran public service advertisements demonstrating the way to properly put on a mask. Students even had their masks tested for effectiveness against tear gas. Using patterns approved by the U.S. Army's chemical warfare division, Red Cross volunteers and high school students refashioned the gas masks for infants and young children into "bunny masks" with long, floppy ears, to make them more appealing to youngsters.[17] People did not like carrying the bulky, ugly masks with them and often "forgot" them. Yoshiharu wrote about being caught without his mask once. Other inconveniences included having to dig trenches that could serve as bomb shelters and stop enemy planes from landing. Locals prepared evacuation kits with canned foods, blankets, and flashlights and updated their typhoid and smallpox vaccinations.[18]

Military and defense workers moved into the islands, and residents had to adapt to their presence. The army took over schools, parks, plantation fields, vacant lots, supply depots, and offices. Twenty-nine schools were used for offices, housing for troops, storage, and hospital space. Open spaces at schools, once used for outdoor classes and playgrounds, were turned into air raid shelters, first aid stations, and military headquarters. This particularly affected Naoko as she found herself teaching in basements and other makeshift classrooms. The *Honolulu Star-Bulletin* reported, "Rising to this emergency, public and private schools have cooperated with the military government to the fullest extent. Many schools have been taken over almost entirely for military use."[19] Yet, for the army, it was not all work and no play. Fort DeRussy on Oahu had swimming pools, ballrooms, parks, barracks, and a dining hall for a recreation center. When servicemen had overnight passes that allowed them to socialize in town, they often discovered that there were not enough hotel rooms to accommodate them, so residents invited them for meals and sometimes overnight stays. The United Service Organizations (USO) had operations on each of the five main islands by the end of 1942, with eighty professional employees, four hundred camp show entertainers, and two thousand volunteers.[20]

Another challenge that came during the war years was an identity crisis and constant racism. Naoko noted she was "ashamed, even humiliated" to be able to trace her ancestors to Japan. In her reflection on December 7, 1941, she had written, "I hope this will give us a chance to show we are as American as we can possibly be."[21] This sense of duty, of having to "pay for the evil deeds of their racial ancestry," became a common theme among Japanese Americans. In the United States, more and more Japanese Americans attempted to embrace their American culture. The term "Jap" became commonly used to denote anyone of Japanese ancestry and also "connote[d] a fifth columnist, a member of the Fascists Axis." Japanese Americans fell into the category of subhumans, inferior to Western whites, and were depicted as primitive, childlike, and "jaundiced baboons." Because of this trend, Nisei were more likely to stray from their parents' traditions and embrace the American culture.[22] In fact, many Japanese families stopped observing Japanese holidays and wearing Japanese apparel once the war broke out.[23] Both the Issei and the Nisei did volunteer work at the Salvation Army, the YWCA, the Red Cross, and the USO.[24] In their precarious position, Japanese Americans accepted their mistreatment, and the saying *shikata ga nai* ("it cannot be helped") grew in popularity, as many believed that they were vicariously at fault.[25]

On the mainland, Nisei college students from Hawaii were stuck on the continent, unable to return to the islands because of martial law, but both Naoko and Yoshiharu had earned their degrees before the war began.[26] For college students on the islands, the University of Hawaii offered a reprieve from the war conditions. In fact, Naoko weighed returning to the university as a way to secure permission to travel from the Big Island back to her family home in Honolulu. The large number of Japanese American students, the long-standing service of Japanese American professors, and their close relationship with haole administrators and bureaucrats kept the university in service to Hawaii's citizens—including Japanese Americans—during the war. The university reopened in February 1942.[27] Naoko's brother Ted, at that time a member of the Varsity Victory Volunteers (the VVV, primarily composed of former ROTC members), told students it was a great privilege to continue their education.[28]

⸺⸺⸺

Naoko's and Yoshiharu's experiences demonstrate that, in some ways, Hawaii was a microcosm of the rest of the country as racism reared its ugly head, but their letters also show the personal impact of war and the unique situation that Hawaiians faced. The territory stood separated from the mainland United States, had Japanese Americans as its largest ethnic group, and had whites in positions of authority. After the war broke out, Naoko had returned to the Big Island from Honolulu, having recovered there from her illness, and was once again teaching in a very rural area, at Olaa School. Yoshiharu was still teaching on Oahu and living at the Nuuanu YMCA in Honolulu. On December 7, 1941, he stood on the roof of one of the YMCA buildings and saw the Imperial Japanese Navy airplanes dropping bombs on Pearl Harbor. But by January, he and Naoko, like many people in Hawaii, attempted to resume life as they once knew it.

Like millions of American teenagers and young adults, Naoko and Yoshiharu continued to participate in quintessentially American activities, as they had before the war. In Honolulu, Naoko had combined her Japanese heritage with American popular culture as she ate chicken *hekka* (a Japanese dish of chicken and vegetables in a soy sauce base) while listening to songs on the radio like "Tonight We Love," by Freddy Martin and his orchestra.[29] She and her friends and family played "wee golf" (what she called miniature golf) in Waikiki and patronized restaurants in the area. Once she was back on the Big Island, she and her friends watched movies like *Tom, Dick and Harry*, a romantic comedy starring Ginger Rogers.[30] No matter the distractions they created, though, war affected their daily life.

Naoko and Yoshiharu, like other teachers throughout Hawaii, were responsible for enumerating and fingerprinting the residents on the islands in both rural and urban areas. Volunteers did paperwork, manual labor, and medical work for the Red Cross, because everyone, including children as young as six, had to have duplicate identification certificates, be fingerprinted, and receive immunizations and booster shots. The ID cards required of each person, often made by the Department of Public Instruction's teachers, could be used to identify bodies in case of another bombing, and the lack of an ID card could single out enemies who tried to sneak ashore and blend in with the citizenry.[31] Anyone without an ID could be arrested, and even First Lady Eleanor Roosevelt underwent the identification process when she visited Hawaii. To complete "the arduous task of enumerating the civilian population," teachers, including those who were Nisei, undertook responsibilities similar to those of census workers.[32] The field enumerators went door to door to determine how many people lived in each house, and residents who lacked the proper identification were given summonses to appear at the district registration centers. After the teachers collected the relevant information, they transferred it to cards, took fingerprints, assigned serial numbers, and handed out identification cards. The army also used teachers as members of the draft board. Some enumerators had the additional responsibility of handing out gas masks and distributing liquor authorizations.[33] Yet the DPI still required all Japanese American teachers, whom it considered "'alien' and difficult to assimilate," to show proof of expatriation before they could be put on the payroll.[34]

One phenomenon of the war was that the number of marriages increased and couples married at younger ages. Naoko and Yoshiharu saw how that affected their friends. Naoko remarked that the marriage of one of her college friends was "kinda fast," given that the woman had not yet graduated. Another set of newlyweds married without telling the bride's parents, who "wouldn't approve of their getting married so soon." The husband's station in the army allowed them only five days together as man and wife before he had to report for duty. "What the army doesn't do to them guys!" Naoko commented.[35] Additionally, she told Yoshiharu that her friend spent a day looking for an engagement ring with her fiancé, and noted it was their "last and only day together!"[36] Yoshiharu mentioned more of their friends on Oahu who were planning to get married. As the wartime romances swept up some couples, Naoko and Yoshiharu continued to test the waters of their own relationship, but Yoshiharu made clear that he had no plans to get married anytime in the near future. "As I told you before if you are in a hurry count me out," he warned Naoko.[37]

Still, one of the constant issues that the couple endured was traveling to see each other. They faced uncertain work schedules because the DPI canceled holiday breaks and required them to volunteer on weekends. Both Naoko and Yoshiharu wanted to spend time together, but with him on Oahu, her on the Big Island, his family on Kauai, and her family on Oahu, they also had to meet family obligations and they worried about being away from their aging parents. Complicating matters further was that the military had priority for air travel and determined who would be allowed to travel. One Japanese American student from the University of Hawaii described the process of booking interisland flights during the war: Passengers with reservations gathered at the airline office and waited for approval before boarding. They had to pass through security and wait for their names to be called. They boarded according to race: haoles first, then Portuguese, Chinese, Hawaiians, and Filipinos, with Japanese boarding last. Japanese Americans could be removed from the planes and replaced by non-Japanese customers.[38]

Naoko and Yoshiharu never mentioned being removed from the planes in their letters, but they did face delays and rejection when trying to make reservations. Naoko recalled that once she had waited all day in hopes of getting on a flight, and finally, with the last one departing for the day, the officer in charge announced that there was only one spot left. Most of the other waiting passengers were families, so when he asked if there was a single person who wanted to go, she jumped up and yelled, "Me!" and all of the people in the waiting area laughed because they knew she was on her way to see her beau.

～～～

Hilo, Hawaii
January 11, 1942

Dear Bachelor Man,

Guess what. I didn't leave Friday morning. When I got there they said, please take the 12:30 plane today. Some others had priority being there first and they picked up some US engineers from Maui who have first preference. We stopped in to tell my mother of the delay, then went to the U to see Ted again. It was still 10:30 so we went to play wee golf at Waikiki.

Funny I haven't felt homesick yet. I like this place too much. The air is so clean, in the morning your face and ears are real cold from sticking out of the blankets. At 4:00 AM at the Kims today, Richard's sister in law who's been awaiting the stork, had to be taken to the hospital via blackout in an ambulance. We all woke up, altho I stayed in bed and listened to the commotion. What women don't go through, but she took it in stride alright. I hope this blackout doesn't continue too long.

[My supervisor] told me that there had been a mix up and for me to report to Kapiolani Sch. on Monday. It looks to me more like my type of elementary school. But I hear the principal a Mrs. Beers is a fussy old thing.[39] Anyway we'll probably be stationed at different districts. Teaching 3 hrs. from 8–11 one group and 12 to 3 another group each day.

I had to spend the day getting things for my room. Richard K. helped me fix it up, blacked it out for me and put up the shade and curtains. He's very helpful and I appreciate his attitude very much. Strictly on the level and we have a good time talking during blackout nights, he, Shizue and myself about movies we liked best. He went back to Honokaa today where he teaches and coaches.[40]

I hope this gets to you soon because I'll be waiting to hear from you too. As usual I hate to say goodbye but I'll say so long for now.

Goodnite,
Naoko

Honolulu, Oahu
January 13, 1942

Dear Naoko,

We're still on the same job of enumerating. We will be through by this weekend though. I hope school doesn't start Mon—It would be a robbery if we didn't get at least a weeks vacation after this work. Not that I have anything to do but as you have said often, it's the principle of the thing.

Since last Friday—the night duty for schools has been canceled so I'm sleeping in the dorm—about all I do is "gab" for a while until about 8:30 or 9:00 then sleep.

I still don't have my room blacked out so I have to go to Ono's room—He and I usually play badminton after work.[41] Have supper and then talk. He seems to be getting fed up with his girlfriend. I'm wondering when I'll be.

As for the draft. I'm still out but I don't know what's coming up and how soon—My other brother passed his physical exam so that leaves only me in my family—My other brother is married and has 3 kids so that I guess [that] leave[s] him out for a while.[42]

Quite a few from this dorm here are getting drafted though. What a place this town will be after next month—I mean for the women.

Well, it seems that all your friends are getting married. What are you waiting for—Better count me out because it will be a long time. My mind is made up I'm living from day to day and taking everything lightly.

There ought to be some good men left in Hawaii in spite of the draft and work here in town. You're able so just be willing then it's all yours. Waiting doesn't always help. Sometime it's better to choose and adjust afterwards. So take my advice, if you will, put on your charm and social mask and go out—I mean it.

So long,
Yoshiharu

<hr>

The war called for adjustments among Hawaii's students, just as it did its teachers. A study on Hawaii's children found that youngsters felt the effects of martial law. Those under sixteen had a 10:00 curfew, and this led to a clash of personalities and conflicts within families that had to live in close quarters. Gasoline and tire rations limited travel by car and led to less organized recreation and a drop in attendance at commercial amusements, group meetings, picnics, camping, and sporting activities. Some students went to school only four days a week, and some chose not to finish high school. Some children smoked and gambled from as early as the sixth grade.[43] Another side effect was that youngsters neglected their religious development. The basic problem, the study asserted, was "one of psychological adjustment of life-aim and values, loss of ambition, etc."[44] In Honolulu, boredom among youths became such a large problem that the Japanese American teens who acted out were giving all Japanese Americans a bad reputation, including the "nice, decent" ones.[45]

The DPI sent out a letter to all teachers and principals that outlined their duties and stated, "Teachers must do everything to help the morale of these people [the students]."[46] The DPI also warned that schools were opening under never-before-seen conditions, as the residents lived in combat zones and contended with the effects of martial law. The letter informed instructors that their primary responsibility and role in the community was that of teachers, and that building understanding and boosting the morale of students and parents fell to them. Children of the community were their main responsibility, the letter advised. The DPI expected teachers to face the challenge of providing constructive and helpful leadership. Hoping its employees would avoid gossip and rumors about the war, it reminded teachers of the need to be sensitive of the effects of the war on their students and not to "become the bearer of tales." A supplement list added:

1. Promote feeling that Hawaii has something worthwhile to preserve in the way of human relationships.
2. See unquestionable acceptance of the idea that a united citizenry is essential to our national defense.
3. Encourage complete faith of all the varied groups in the American way of life and their absolute willingness to defend it.
4. Seek absolute confidence in the constituted authorities.
5. Seek to overcome fear on the part of all the people.
6. Develop a sense of personal responsibility to do everything possible to make Hawaii and the entire nation strong militarily and otherwise.
7. See cognizance by the general public that every loyal citizen, regardless of race, color or creed, must be given a place in the scheme of national defense.
8. Make clear that loyalty grows only when it is given a chance to grow.[47]

In addition to enumerating and fingerprinting citizens, teachers helped with evacuations and first aid and focused their lessons on citizenship, gardening, health activities, and safety. The faculty intended to help students adjust, as many school programs shifted to the war effort.[48] Both Naoko's and Yoshiharu's letters show their attempts at that.

When children returned to school, their lives seemed to be all about the war. According to the *Honolulu Star-Bulletin*, Hawaii had 187 public schools serving seventy-eight thousand students. Outer-island schools opened in January of 1942, but most schools on Oahu did not open until February 2.[49] School rules included cooperating with military authorities, obeying martial law and safety rules, conserving useful material, staying healthy, avoiding the escalation of rumors, protecting oneself through blackouts and air raid alarm systems and shelters, knowing what to do in emergencies such as incendiary bombing, knowing first aid, and being aware of fire hazards and prevention. Students could earn armbands if they did tasks for the war effort, such as planting home gardens, raising chickens, knitting items for the Red Cross, working in plantation victory gardens, taking care of babies in their own family or someone else's, and participating in the Kiawe Corps, a volunteer civilian labor battalion whose members were mostly Japanese. (It was called the Kiawe Corps because the men's main responsibility was to clear the beachfront of mesquite, or "kiawe.")[50] Students and their parents went to school campuses on weekends to help dig trenches for air raid shelters. They dug zigzag patterns with picks and shovels into the thousands of yards of ground. When back in school, the students practiced air raid drills, evacuating the schools and climbing into the trenches as they prepared for attack.[51] As public schools teachers, both Yoshiharu and Naoko had to participate in and facilitate these emergency preparations.

The correspondence between Naoko and Yoshiharu from this period continued to demonstrate their acculturation. Naoko began one of her letters by quoting William Wadsworth's "It Is a Beauteous Evening,

Calm and Free," as she admired the natural scenery of the Big Island and adapted to her rural surroundings. She also told Yoshiharu that she missed him "too much" so that her favorite theme songs were "Having a Lonely Time" and "I Get Along without You Very Well."[52] She later claimed, "I'd die without the radio, now that I have it. Music is good."[53] She also noted that she went to see Laurel and Hardy and Jack Benny, but asserted that she "never liked to see them on screen." One of her favorites at the movies was the "piggy cartoon" entitled "Notes to You," a Looney Tunes short featuring the character Porky Pig. Her location in rural Hilo, though, meant that she could not "be particular . . . about movies or anything."[54] Yoshiharu responded with a quotation from the movie *Here Comes Mr. Jordan* that epitomized his relationship with her: "It's a great discovery to find some one who is the same inside as yourself. Then nothing seem[s] to matter, what she is or what kind of work or how she stands socially."[55]

Through his letters, Yoshiharu further revealed his connections to the rural plantation life, in contrast to Naoko's upbringing. In one letter, he mentioned staying at a private family home while enumerating in Waipahu.[56] When noting that he had to take a bath while he was there, he said, "It's one of those 'tub in the corner affair' too." Although he did not specify exactly how this tub worked, it was most likely a *furo*, a Japanese-style wooden tub for soaking. He added, "I don't mind it, I grew up with it. It's only for the last 4¹/₂ years that I've been using the 'civilized' type."[57] His comments revealed his exposure to "civilization"—in this case, modern Americanized plumbing instead of what he had grown up with on the plantation. In another instance, Yoshiharu took a police entrance exam and later observed that he had felt comfortable with the math and "common sense" portion of the exam, but with regard to the vocabulary section, he said, "That's the only part I didn't know much about."[58] Even with his three and a half years of higher education in Wisconsin and a bachelor's degree, he still lacked confidence in his English and grammar.

The couple also began to deal with the complications brought on by the draft. Yoshiharu wrote, "Sooner or later I'll have to get in the army—then no telling what will happen." He used that statement as a springboard to discuss their relationship.[59] Even from this early point, Yoshiharu was adamant that Naoko not wait for him if he became a soldier. But he was determined not to join the army. In his next letter, he revealed his dilemma over teaching. He thought that he would not receive a deferment for teaching. Yoshiharu considered joining the police force and thus took the police entrance exam and physical. His belief was that if he failed the police physical, he would also fail the draft physical. But he also gained the help of his principal and did obtain a deferment.[60] Naoko, on the other hand, noted that a friend of hers from the University of Hawaii, Richard Kim (at whose family home she stayed in Hilo), was "crazy enough to ask his draft board to change his 1B rating to 1A" because he hoped to be drafted immediately.[61] Yoshiharu's attempts to avoid the draft and Naoko's comments on the soldiers and potential soldiers around her continued to be themes throughout their courtship letters.

Hilo, Hawaii
January 15, 1942

Dear Yoshiharu,

The principal has taken a liking to me because I'm 'always smiling,' but she's the most unreasonable female I ever came across. She told me yesterday that the 'Japs' are the most 'treacherous things!' (She means the soldiers.) She went on to say 'Why I hear they go around raping all the women folk and who knows when they'll come here!' She says to me, 'Why you're not safe here. I'm not safe.' I had a strong temptation to say 'Who in h——would want to come after you.'

You don't have to worry about me and my future. Do I tell you how to run yours? Then kindly refrain from telling me how to go out and hunt down an innocent victim. I don't do that for fun and you ought to know it after knowing me the way you do. So far I haven't seen anything that looks like a man here yet. Maybe that's why I feel so good here. Go ahead and laugh, you brute. Some day I'll surprise you yet. The only advice I have to give you is don't be so darned pessimistic. The sun still shines by day and the stars by night and time doesn't stand still.

So long for a while,
Naoko

Honolulu, Oahu
January 20, 1942

Dear Naoko,

I'm starting right off with a comeback to what you said. The only reason I said what I did in the other letter is because I think enough of you to tell you so. It's not because I want to get rid of you—quite the contrary—but you know as well as I do that nowadays it isn't very much what we think or want to do—it's more what is expected of us to do.

Sooner or later I'll have to get in the army—then no telling what will happen. And if anything does happen what will you get for spending your time and thoughts on me. Perhaps you don't anyway—you're too good to be left that way that's why I'm saying what I did. If you can't see it that way well that's that. Neither is it that I don't appreciate you. I do and too much—In fact it's more than appreciation it's [——].[62] Furthermore I'm not trying to ruin your future. It's that I don't want to be a cause for something you don't deserve.

This is a very uncertain and uncomfortable feeling. If everything were normal I'll do something about [it], but now [——].[63]

Enumerating in Waipahu isn't so good. The people are scattered and very uninformed—Not dumb. We expect to be through in about 8 days. Then what? I don't know.

So long–
Yoshiharu

Hilo, Hawaii
January 26, 1942

Dear you—

After the first week of getting settled and having things to get in town, there isn't anything new around here. I go to school from 8 till 3 in the afternoon, come home to my room and listen to my borrowed radio and then have supper. That's all I have time for, and these past 2 Saturdays I've been working at school for the 'High Command' there.

The town is so deserted on Sundays that I get the jitters walking down the street which is so quiet it feels like something's going to happen.

The other week was more eventful but I enjoyed it less, having crammed too much in at a time. I played tennis with my classmate Richard Kim who's crazy enough to ask his draft board to change his 1B rating to 1A so he can get drafted now. He's teaching at Honokaa now but I expect to see him in the army the next time.

God, your spelling is as bad as my writing, "take it or leave it." I just tho't of it.

I teach grade 1 from 8–11 and grade 5 from 12–3. We're located in a basement of a Chinese School building and I have a heck of a time talking to the old Chinese caretaker there.[64] He gabs away then I explain with gestures etc. and neither of us gets what the other is saying.

You lucky people—no school till Feb. 2. I hope you have a few days off so you can write.

So long for now. Period.[65]

Naoko

Honolulu, Oahu
January 27, 1942

Dear Naoko,

We finished enumerating at Waipahu on last Saturday and we've been taking it easy since then. The Central school day will be very much like before because we have all the buildings back and there won't be any other schools crowding in with us.

Today I've been debating whether to keep on teaching or not. I don't know what exactly to do. I know one thing, I won't be deferred teaching. I'm considering the police force.

Friday—

Today I went down to the police station—I was interviewed—First question was. How old are you? 22 and will be 23 in a week. He was surprised. My height was 5'8³/₈" weight 148. The next thing was where are you working. D.P.I. He looked at me—What school? I told him. I guess he didn't know whether to believe me or not. We were also given a test to my surprise. This wasn't bad though because it was mostly math and common sense. A little vocabulary—That's the only part I didn't know much about.

He told me I did alright on it. So now what remains is my physical exam. Which comes on Wednesday. If I don't pass I won't at all be disappointed because that would mean no army for me either. If I do pass that I have to hope that they take me on, although I don't think my height and weight is quite enough. So wish me luck. Maybe you think I'm nuts trying to be a cop. Well, I have my own reasons.

Periods.

So long for now.

Yoshiharu

Hilo, Hawaii
February 1, 1942

Dear Yoshiharu,

You must be going to school as usual, back to the old grind—4hr. a day snap, if I'm not mistaken. Hope you're liking it and 'living from day to day' as usual. So am I.

I had a heck of a time getting a bus back to Hilo by 11:30. Can you imagine! I had a luncheon date with the army—a lieutenant no less, and kept the army waiting.

The man in the story being Doris' cousin Mits Fukuda who married my friend 2 weeks ago when he went to Honolulu for 8 days. Remember the girl I was talking to at the U cafeteria that day everybody seems to have seen us up there. The lunch was very enjoyable mainly because I think he's swell guy and I like his wife a lot too. He wanted someone to talk to, being shut up at the airport barracks all this time.

I couldn't figure out why he up and married her so suddenly, she still has to finish her senior year at the U and he's stationed over here. But I can see why he wanted to get married and didn't tell him he was being a d—— fool. I think he got enough of it from the parents, the dopes went and done it before telling the folks. He said they knew they wouldn't approve of their getting married so soon. Anyway he has the memory of 5 days he spent alone with her at a friend's cottage but he told me that it wasn't the happiest way to get married. They got married at our church and he had to run over to the Y to get some 'casual friends' as witnesses.

So long with Love,
Naoko

Honolulu, Oahu
February 3, 1942

Dear Naoko,

Today I'm 23 and the only surprise or celebration or anything like it that I got was your letter. Thanks.

Today was the first full school day and it was very much like that in September because quite a few dropped out and many changes were made in the schedule. At the meeting last week I asked him whether we shop men were to be deferred he said he didn't think so—so I told him to count me out on as many things as he can.[66] But now it seems that we may be deferred again. The department is trying hard to get okay to get deferment for us. Keep your fingers crossed for me.

As for the police force I'm still considering it. I passed the written exam perhaps I told you that and will be getting my physical exam tomarrow.

Wednesday—

Today, I told Mr. Gordon that I was going for physical exam but he told me not to after he found out what it was for. He however, promised me he'll do anything he can to defer me. I told him that if the Department wasn't going to do that for me I was going to look out for myself and go find a job that I'd be deferred on. He thought I might be deferred on account of my parents, because they are partially dependent on me. Well, I'm hoping but not too optimistic about the whole thing.

Feb. 7, 1942

Today, I blacked out my room so now I can write to you anytime. Tomarrow, the men teachers of Central have to report to school to dig trenches. The trenches are to be made deeper by the P.T.A.[67] So that includes me. I'm going and willingly because Mr. Gordon has been very considerate as far as I'm concerned.

Today he called me to school to check upon the rest of the family and their earning capacity to see whether I cannot be exempted from the draft. He is writing a letter to my board and so is the department. So keep your fingers crossed for me. If this is successful it's Central for me for a while. You don't blame me do you?

Periods—

So long for now.

Yoshiharu

As the letters continued, Yoshiharu's artistic, creative, and handy talents became evident. His interest in woodwork had led him to become an industrial arts shop teacher. While at the Stout Institute, he joined the Arts and Crafts Club, whose members were "interested in hobbies and hobby work." These students had to have a hobby, and a minimum 1.6 scholastic average, and they were affiliated with the National Home-workshop Guild.[68] That field, he hoped, would also make him valuable on the home front and reduce his chances of being drafted. As he continued to teach, he also worked on his own projects. He used the school shop and his free time to make smaller items, like trays with more than 175 decorative pieces inlaid.[69] He also promised Naoko a lamp for her birthday and gave her advice about electrical circuits and repairing her iron and radio. To make extra money, he built furniture pieces for sale, including a phonograph cabinet and a speaker cabinet for thirty dollars. He also turned down an opportunity to teach carpentry classes to defense workers for two dollars an hour.[70]

Yoshiharu kept busy with work and play in Honolulu, and the couple's letters reflect the differences between his lifestyle and Naoko's in the rural area of Hilo and later on rural Kauai with Yoshiharu's family. Living in the city, Yoshiharu had easy access to a telephone and played badminton at the YMCA, just as he had before the war. He told Naoko that he had not "really talked to any girl since January."[71] However, his work at school and his attendance at church (though infrequent) put him in contact with young women, and Honolulu provided many opportunities for proper dates. Conversely, Naoko noted that she had nothing planned on the weekend "since there's nothing in particular going on anyway."[72] Instead, many of her letters from this period are filled with her comments on the scenery of the countryside, the snowcapped mountains of Mauna Kea and Mauna Loa, and the earthquakes that she felt resulting from the volcanoes. The two could behave as any young Americans adjusting to living on their own and working at new jobs.

Naoko's and Yoshiharu's letters show their patriotism and their recognition of racism, but Naoko displayed much more enthusiasm for the military effort than did Yoshiharu. Still, neither ignored the discrimination that the war brought. At a time when tensions were rising between the United States and Japan, Naoko's oldest brother, Jimmy Kagawa, saw that his ancestral background prevented him from getting a job on the U.S. mainland or in Hawaii. Major corporations like Boeing, Pan American, and even Hawaiian Airlines in Hawaii refused to hire him. Kagawa did not want to waste his education, so he went to Japan in 1940, but there he faced discrimination, suspicion, abuse, and hatred for being an American. His family did not hear from him for the duration of the war.[73] In contrast, Naoko's younger brother Ted served in the ROTC at the University of Hawaii and continually sought to demonstrate his patriotism during the development of an all–Japanese American combat battalion. None of Naoko's immediate family members were ever interned, but the situations of her two brothers highlight the conflicts and hardships of Japanese Americans families. Yoshiharu's family, on the other hand, continued their plantation lifestyle on Kauai, and that disengagement from larger American society contributed to Yoshiharu's opposition to serving in the military.

⚏⚏⚏

Honolulu, Oahu
February 13, 1942

Dear Naoko,
Tomarrow and Sunday I'll be helping at Central for the registration of the draft group.

Your mother is right when she said it is difficult for your brother [Jimmy] to get [a] job right now. There are many like him who is willing to work but "not qualified" according to the definition of some of the employer's around here. The kind of discrimination that is going on is bringing a greater destruction than that which bombs and rifle can bring. If this goes to far the result will last for a generation. It seems to me people have too little faith in each other. I'm not saying risk should be taken but after all being to careful about matter like this can be equally bad. After all every one has a soul and feeling. It's not that this is ordered down from the top—because men up there know what they are doing—but it's the in between—the people who hire and fire—They think they know it all. Usually this little [group] is the worst part of the people here who are not to be blamed for what blood runs through their vein. Yet, they are judged on that and have to suffer.

Periods.

So long till next,

Yoshiharu

Hilo, Hawaii

February 18, 1942

Dear Yoshiharu,

Someday I'll be living in the street if the army decides to move into this dorm and school. We've already had notice to expect it anytime, altho' it isn't very likely. Tomorrow, next week, or never is the definite intention. I hope we don't have to, as I like having my own room and the view of the big vegetable garden in the back. The men who make the volunteer squad at the fire station cleaned up all the long grass and turned it into a nice garden. I see little green rows shooting up nowdays. It takes the place of my garden at home, but so far nothing takes your place.

You're still at school I hope and no changes made? That kid sister of mine writes that she hears there's quite a killer roaming around Central. The younger generation are quite wide awake these days—nothing seems to escape their eyes or tongues. Well it's a good thing some males are still on the loose to keep up the morale. It seems the women folk in Honolulu are getting frantic over the scarcity in the male population, and I'm glad I'm not around there, to tell the truth. Nothing like avoiding the grand rush.

So long for now,

Naoko

Honolulu, Oahu
February 20, 1942

Dear Naoko,

Last Sunday I went to church for a change. I saw your sister and Kazu asked me whether somebody told me to go to church or not.[74] No it wasn't that but it concerns you. If you should decide to come home for Easter—which is only five weeks away and I decide to remain in town and I would then want to go to church with you. If this happens to be the first time I go to church for a long time it won't look so good. So this is my way of covering up things. Well, go ahead and laugh. If it doesn't work out this way then no harm done anyway.

Periods——.
So long for now,
Yoshiharu

Hilo, Hawaii
February 23, 1942

Dear Yoshiharu,

There are enough [men] roaming around here of course, but if you have your own business to mind it's hard to find time to do anything else. In Honolulu you can't help getting into society of some kind. You go to church and there's a bunch there ready to invite you places etc. Over here 'we schoolteachers' keep in among ourselves. Snooty? Well no, we're so busy during the week, and weekends we might bump into each other in town, have lunch, to a movie, or the bowling center.

Goodbye now,
Naoko

The war at home called on everyone to sacrifice material goods. The location of Hawaii in the Pacific Ocean meant that goods for consumption had to be either grown locally or brought in from elsewhere via plane or boat. The limited transportation, along with priority being given to military personnel, quickly led to shortages. Men, women, and children learned to ration goods of all sorts. Gasoline and tires, both necessary for the war effort, became scarce commodities, especially affecting rural people by hindering their movements.[75] Oil companies reduced their stock by 20 to 25 percent, but the problem was compounded in Hawaii, where gasoline had to be brought in by ships and barges. With tankers being lent to Britain and under the threat of attack, cargo space was at a premium.[76] Yoshiharu's letters from Kauai personalize these difficulties. The iconic Hawaiian-print shirts (known as aloha shirts) also appeared in this era, as material for dress shirts had become a luxury rather than a necessity. Housewives and dry goods stores quickly learned that they could make clothing out of the brightly colored fabric that covered rattan furniture. This was just one example of reusing material. Women throughout the country attended sewing classes to learn to refurbish clothing. The prices of piece goods, as well as patterns and trimmings for making garments, all increased from 20 percent to more than 700 percent.[77] Just as in past wars, American women took up their sewing needles as their war weapons.

In Hawaii, the availability of food was reduced, and the U.S. government had to ship in thirty-two thousand tons of food every month.[78] Hawaiians could grow their own vegetables to supplement their diets, but a population that based its meals on rice depended on these shipments of food, even for staples. Many people in Hawaii and across the United States supported the war effort by establishing local victory gardens, which provided produce not only for the citizenry but also for the military. Naoko had a vegetable garden, and working in victory gardens by preparing the land, planting, irrigating, and harvesting became a popular pastime for many islanders. Those who had enough land on which to do it grew sweet potatoes, Irish potatoes, corn, and beans, as well as grass for feeding livestock. Thirteen large community gardens grew throughout Hawaii.[79] As families adapted to fewer food choices, the canned precooked pork product known as Spam became more popular because it could be stored for long periods and substituted for fresh meat. Some housewives also adhered to the request to go "meatless" twice a week. Butter was rationed at a quarter pound per person per week, and rice was also rationed. Farm animals were affected too, as rationed feed led to the wholesale slaughter of chickens, pigs, and cattle.[80] Overall, the restrictions of martial law, the lack of shipping facilities, and the dangers of sea travel contributed to the shortage of food.[81] Both Naoko and Yoshiharu made note of the foods available to them and expressed an appreciation for homegrown produce, which was more accessible in rural areas than in Honolulu.

The entire population of Hawaii contributed to the war effort in a variety of ways, regardless of their location. Lei makers wove camouflage nets, the Boy Scouts served as guards at roadblocks, residents rolled bandages for the Red Cross, and men, including Yoshiharu, did manual labor like cutting trees, digging shelters, taming forests, and stringing barbed wire along beaches. The Emergency Service Committee was formed on Oahu and established morale committees on the Big Island, Maui, Lanai, and Kauai.[82] The morale committees organized public meetings and lectures, produced propaganda, and told Japanese Americans to show their patriotism by buying war bonds, speaking English, and donating blood.[83]

The more familiar story of Japanese Americans in Hawaii comes from the men participating in the military and is a tale of both heroism and patriotism. Naoko's brother Ted serves as an example of the Nisei's dedication to the United States. In 1940 the United States instituted the draft and inducted able-bodied men, including Nisei, into the army.[84] These men had attended public schools and Japanese-language schools, both of which taught them loyalty to America and to the ideals of democracy.[85] One Nisei soldier wrote, "There was no doubt in my mind that I was an American of Japanese ancestry—not a Japanese living in America."[86] Shortly after the bombing of Pearl Harbor, several hundred undergraduates who made up the University of Hawaii ROTC reported for duty. By 4:30 that afternoon, the ROTC had formed the Hawaii Territorial Guard (HTG), swearing in 35 officers and 370 men in arms. Because the university required all able-bodied male students to serve in the ROTC for two years, they had already been trained for duty. The primary duties of the HTG included guarding buildings and infrastructure like Washington Place (the governor's mansion), territorial archives, bridges, water tanks, high schools, emergency hospitals, telephone exchanges, and electric substations. They also had the duty of evicting Japanese Americans from military-sensitive areas. Still, the U.S. government worried about men of Japanese ancestry carrying guns, and military governor General Delos Emmons could see the apparent contradiction of arming Japanese Americans at a time when much of the country found them suspicious. He disbanded the HTG and discharged the Americans of Japanese ancestry (with the justification that a Japanese American in uniform would be the first to be killed), and then the HTG reorganized without any Nisei.[87] The Japanese American volunteers even saw their draft status change to "enemy alien," but some young men, such as Ted, pursued their personal goals as patriots.

Despite their dismissal, the former HTG members gathered on February 23, 1942, to create the Varsity Victory Volunteers, serving as an auxiliary organization of the Army Corps of Engineers and part of the 34th Engineer Regiment. They had witnessed the injustices and recognized their "failed idealism rooted in a romanticized notion of U.S. democracy."[88] They received a IV-C draft classification, labeled as aliens ineligible for service. The VVV, activated on February 25, worked on YMCA projects and did manual labor, including building barracks, digging ditches, quarrying rocks, assembling furniture, building child care facilities, and making prefabricated housing, and its members lived at Schofield Barracks. Their pay amounted to about $100 a month.[89] The men also performed services like donating blood and giving speeches in the community, and they participated in social activities, including gambling and dancing. The bonds that the VVV members formed with one another would connect them for a lifetime.[90]

The VVV men wanted a chance to prove their patriotism and to do their duty as citizens; they wanted to bring to life the American ideals and values with which they had been instilled, and thereby dispel suspicions based on their Japanese ancestry. One Nisei soldier commented, "How I hated the Japs for bringing this upon us!"[91] Ted Tsukiyama wrote that the VVV would appreciate and welcome encouragement and that its members wanted to "set a good and living example of what good Americans can do . . . [and] break the ice for other groups to demonstrate their Americanism."[92] The volunteers' background played into their notion of patriotism. Odo observed that the VVV members were not from plantation families or the urban poor. Rather, the men's fathers typically were supervisors, skilled craftsmen, or white-collar workers.[93] Thus, they had not been confined to the plantation communities, with their racial hierarchies and limited economic opportunities. This factor helps explain the difference between Ted Tsukiyama's reaction to joining the military and Yoshiharu Ogata's decision to repeatedly seek deferments from the draft. Men like Ted saw the promise of the American dream in their fathers and wanted it for themselves. Men from the plantation, like Yoshiharu, saw that ideals of equality and financial gain were not their birthright—their loyalties remained to their families and local communities, with whom they most identified.

Yoshiharu's letters constantly reveal his concern about being drafted, particularly after the draft heated up for American men in March 1942. The third round of the draft put at risk 17.5 million men who had registered in 1940 and 1941. Many were unsure about how the draft worked, so the Selective Service officials explained that the army would not draft men with dependents and that men who had married before the Pearl Harbor attack were likely to be deferred, unless they had married just to avoid being drafted. If a man's wife worked, however, or had affluent relatives to support her, then the man "was due to be inducted."

Passing the army's medical test meant an immediate induction, but furloughs were allowed for "draftees who just have to straighten out their civilian affairs."[94] For Yoshiharu, the possibility of being drafted felt like a threat that loomed closer and closer. For Naoko, whose brother Ted had reported for ROTC duty on the afternoon of December 7, 1941, seeing Japanese American men volunteering to serve the United States was the norm.

Honolulu, Oahu
February 26, 1942

Dear Naoko,

Yesterday, I received my classification from my draft board and I'm deferred until May 26, 1942. Classified as class IIA with a—3–0 vote for deferment. So I'll be teaching at least until then. When that comes around I'll have to try for another deferment. One thing looks good though if they are considering school term they would have deferred me until June but it's latter part of May. So maybe they'll just give me another one I hope so anyway—If things don't get worst it may turn out that way.

The liquor ban is off but I think I'll still stay "dry." It doesn't bother me at all. I guess I can make a fool of myself without being drunk.

Yoshiharu

Hilo, Hawaii
March 2, 1942

Dear Yoshiharu,

I didn't like the news from your draft board, but I guess you're lucky to even be deferred. What does the 3–0 vote mean, does it make you less eligible then a 1–0 vote? Please explain. They can't take you in when they can take anybody else for a soldier. I doubt if just anybody can do what you're doing for the kids now. It's more important for you to work with individuals who have a future before them, not with those who haven't any. Of course you ought to 'do your duty' but you can do it better in the job you have right now.

Yesterday morning we heard the air raid siren over the radio from Honolulu. I'd rather have one on here than there, as nothing matters to me over here. People here got so scared they cleared the streets and waited for an alarm here but none came. I went on washing clothes but worried like anything. It's the suspense that gets me—as I said everything I love I have at home—my dog, even my vegetables.

We went to the Chang's home for supper.[95] I nearly fell over when she had a big T bone steak for each of us, and I had to come all the way to Hilo to have one. She's a good cook, and the home-y atmosphere was nice for a change. What I couldn't forget was the kid I saw standing guard at the gate outside near the house. He was eating his supper from a tin plate while standing in the rain. It rained all night and each time I woke up that picture kept bothering me. I really never saw anything quite so forlorn.

My brother's back with the Varsity Volunteers as they call it. My, how he must love the army. He never had to stand guard like that that's why. His bunch are swell tho', and they have fun. I hope if you ever get in you get a good bunch too.

Add the periods.

Naoko

Honolulu, Oahu

March 4, 1942

Dear Naoko,

The 3–0 vote means that the board members are all for my deferment. So it's as good as it could be. Frankly, I think I'll do more good out of the army but sometimes people don't think so.

I don't believe in man's (male) superiority or anything like—To me [a woman] should be one for company advice and everything else 50/50—Of course naturally man should be the bread earner because he is more adapted physically to do so especially if there is to be a family—Agree or disagree?

So long and periods,
Yoshiharu

Honolulu, Oahu
March 9, 1942

Dear Naoko,

Last Saturday when the air raid sounded I was caught in Davis without my gas mask and did I feel foolish.[96] It seemed that everyone else had their gas mask. Learn by experience, and how true I thought that was. I'll remember next time.

I guess we won't get any Easter vacation except Good Friday off. That means you won't be home so I guess it means another two months. Perhaps this is the best.

I don't know what this will mean. When you were here and I kept on seeing you, we thought that if you went away for a while this might be a way of finding out. Now I'm thinking that if we are to see each other only once in a while for a short time it will never give us enough time. You know just seeing each other when we can is entirely different from living together. Well, I guess with the war and everything being so uncertain I suppose as I have said often it remains to be seen. We'll see how you and I feel when June comes around, but one thing promise me you won't kid yourself or me, and I'll promise the same.

So long for now. Periods.
Yoshiharu

Yoshiharu pondered the wisdom and practicality of the pair's long-distance relationship, and Naoko's status as a single woman in a rural area shows the impact of the military's presence in the islands. Her company was in demand from the officers and soldiers. As the local boys left to serve their country, Hawaii's residents saw an influx of haole servicemen and defense workers who arrived in the islands with their own hopes of protecting their nation. Seventy-four thousand soldiers had arrived on Oahu by June 1942, with 13,000 more on the Big Island and another 12,800 on the other islands. By the end of the war, millions of servicemen had passed through the territory. An additional 82,000 men and women traveled to Hawaii as war workers.[97] These defense workers became the first whites to do manual labor on Oahu. The residents saw them as "professional hell-raisers" who drank, gambled, and whored.[98] Haoles, who were never the majority, had previously been part of the elite in Hawaii; with the newcomers, locals no longer saw haoles as belonging only to an upper class. A great change came to the islands with the large intrusion of military personnel and defense workers, and both Naoko and Yoshiharu, and women and men in general, had to adapt.

Men complained that the ratio of men to women in Hawaii was 1,000 to 1. Although a more realistic figure might have been 150 to 1, the men in Hawaii, newcomers and locals alike, felt the shortage of women. Servicemen pursued women without regard for class or race.[99] By February 1942 the military was transporting prostitutes from the mainland to Hawaii. From 1941 to 1945 the Honolulu Police Department registered 250 prostitutes, each of whom paid one dollar for their license and tax. The army believed that it was inhumane to confine them to red-light districts, so many lived and worked scattered throughout residential districts, and some homes became brothels. The military was in charge of public health, sanitation, and disease prevention, issues that many people associated with prostitutes.[100] Nevertheless, vice districts arose, like Hotel Street in Honolulu, where people sold shoeshines, flower leis, pictures with hula girls, and even sex at a rate of thirty thousand interactions a day. Prostitution became a million-dollar industry, and female sex workers, most of whom were haoles from the mainland, could earn $30,000 to $40,000 a year, though they risked contracting venereal diseases. Historians Beth Bailey and David Farber note that before the war there were two doors to brothels, one for white servicemen and one for locals. This was because the servicemen were "contemptuous of the men of color" and did not want those men having sex with the same white women they patronized.[101] Yoshiharu did not mention patronizing these businesses, but his letters indicate that he was well aware that men, particularly soldiers far from home, faced constant temptation. He was adamant, however, that he would not disappoint Naoko by giving in to such temptation.

Sex could easily be bought, but friendship and companionship came at a different cost. Despite the ongoing war and the animosity toward those of Japanese ancestry, people in Hawaii saw that relationships between soldiers—who took over community halls, schools, and camp housing—and locals were amicable. They did not have the history of racism and discrimination that mainlanders did—their understanding of the racial hierarchy stemmed from the plantation structure.[102] One local wrote, "The soldiers have established friendly relations with the Japanese families." And Japanese families throughout the islands even invited servicemen into their homes.[103] On the island of Kauai, the situation was relatively peaceful. Residents generally accepted servicemen as members of the community and gave them rides when they hitchhiked, since public transportation was minimal. Some Japanese Americans considered the soldiers to be "swell" people and taught them to use chopsticks.[104] On the way home from school, students could not help but meet military men. According to one Japanese American female from Kauai, parents did not mind the socializing, but that did not keep gossipmongers from talking. She believed that talking to the soldiers was acceptable, as she knew she was not doing anything wrong and was behaving wisely. "I knew these men left their homes to come to our homeland to protect our homeland against invasion, and I knew they missed their homes and their families, friends, sweethearts, and others. I tried to make these soldiers happy and feel at home. This was the thing that the narrow-minded Japanese of my camp overlooked," she said.[105] Naoko's actions revealed that this acceptance, and even promotion, of socializing with the soldiers had become a common sentiment. Her role as a schoolteacher, however, put her in the public eye and required her to monitor her behavior.

The number of local Japanese girls dating military personnel increased, and even Naoko found herself presented with opportunities for romance. She sought to remain true to Yoshiharu, though, and did not pursue serious relationships with any of the soldiers. Not all local girls behaved as Naoko did. Some even accepted proposals of marriage from the soldiers, and parents felt "resigned to the situation."[106] The Reverend Masao Yamada of Kauai noted that 90 percent of the girls attending USO events were Japanese. Yet, at first, the girls were not allowed to participate, because of their cultural descent. The army men "demanded" that Japanese American girls be allowed in, perceiving them as "well-dressed and intelligent" and as "wholesome companionship."[107] Dances became crowded with servicemen, and the girls' relationships with them were no longer "scorned with distaste" as they had been before the war.[108] "This is partly because parental objection is not as great as it used to be," one twenty-something woman explained. She added, "Group opinion directed against such associations is not as great either."[109] Local families took in soldiers, feeding and entertaining them. A minister on Kauai, whom an interviewee classified as "very patriotic," invited the army chaplain to preach and told the local girls to sit among the soldiers. The girls then prepared lunch and invited the men to eat, before pairing off in couples.[110]

Naoko's attitude and her commitment to Yoshiharu made her more skeptical about the soldiers' intentions than were many other local women. One University of Hawaii student explained that the local Asian girls had no option but to date haoles, because men of their own background had left for college or entered into military service. The "very attractive" servicemen became homesick and turned to locals for comfort. The girls replaced soldiers' mainland girlfriends, and the local boys became the soldiers' buddies. The university student added that from a first date, "a beautiful friendship may begin." Others found that because there was a shortage of white women in the islands, it was "not objectionable" to date local women.[111] A marine who was asked about interracial dating in Hawaii replied that he went on dates with "Oriental" women and had "a grand time." He added, "I don't want, however, to get too serious with any girl here, because I want to get back home to my people and friends of my own class." He believed that if he stayed in the islands, it would be okay to have a serious relationship with an Asian woman, but if brought her back to the mainland, he would be "condemned for marrying a girl outside of [his] class" and would become a social outcast. He concluded, "I would lose my prestige and the respect of my friends."[112] A white woman confirmed this when she stated, "Too bad that our nice boys have to run around with Japanese girls." Some haole women even believed that Japanese girls were spies who used sex to get information from the military.[113] The local girls, on the other hand, did not realize that they were not considered equal or even appropriate partners. One of them stated that "servicemen accept oriental girls" on the "same level" as they did haole women.[114] As critical of interracial dating as haole women were, even more so were Japanese Americans, especially when girls as young as seventh graders became pregnant, without knowing where the soldier fathers were stationed.[115] Some parents who had heard stories of girls getting pregnant or raped tried to protect their daughters by keeping them at home.[116] Older Japanese women commented that wartime hysteria was no excuse for sexual license. Some asserted that it was "shameful" for Japanese American women to marry white soldiers, and others thought that merely dating the soldiers was unpatriotic.[117]

Young local men complained about local women's attraction to the newcomers. The interracial relationships discouraged local men from going to church, a traditionally approved place where they might meet young women. As one of the young men said, it was a "waste of time to go to church." He explained, "The soldiers get everything and we get no chance."[118] A Japanese American college student reported that the local girls went "gaga" over the soldiers because "white people are different." According to her, the girls saw "Oriental" boys as "clumsy in speech" and no match for the soldiers, thus making the girls "easy prey" for the servicemen. But meeting new people exposed local girls to a new culture and better English as well, the student observed.[119] The local men in turn lamented their "difficulties holding [on to] their girlfriends in competition with the men in uniform."[120] The local females frequently dated the newcomers, accompanying them to dinners, dances, cocktail parties, and nightclubs. Advice columns informed young women that men simply wanted someone to listen to them and praised the women for chatting with the lonely servicemen. But some females grew to hate the servicemen, who could be too pushy, too aggressive, and too drunk. Others remained conflicted about the situation, wondering if these men who fought for their country should get any woman they wanted.[121] Naoko expressed her dislike of the soldiers for disrupting her peaceful town, but at the same time she recognized a need to be patriotic and empathetic to the men who had dedicated their lives to protecting America. She also had to factor in her duty as a representative of the DPI, her attraction to adventure, and her loyalty to Yoshiharu.

Hilo, Hawaii
March 10, 1942

Dear Yoshiharu,
I was supposed to move to a house by a big pond near the Waiakea Mill with the family I've been with till now.[122] But Mrs. Beers my dear

principal, practically pushed me into this place. All the single rooms are taken so we have to sleep in a big room like a ward with so many beds. It's roomy and clean so not bad, but we have to do our own cooking. I don't mind that either as there's only the two of us. Shizue commutes daily to Olaa, because the army moved into their school cottage too.

The town's getting too full of men who seem to be too anxious to pick up anything with a skirt on. Heard this one? "They call her 'shortwave' because anyone can pick her up." Well I'm not one of them, so they'd better keep distance.

The army sure has moved in since yesterday. 7,000 of them—more of them than people here I bet. It's going to be some problem you just wait and see for this community. It makes me sick, this was such a peaceful place. I don't like the mob in town now, as bad almost as the Hotel St. area.[123] I can't see why they lifted the liquor ban, not all of them are smart like you, in their ideas about that.

Until next time,
Naoko

Honolulu, Oahu
March 13, 1942

Dear Naoko,

If you have to stay there I hope you like it. Isn't it encouraging now that there are 7000 more men around? I hope you don't think that they're all no good because they want to "pick up" women. You can't blame them. If I were in their place I probably would myself providing there are no other way of getting to meet and talk to people other than those connected with the army. I think for most of them there first intention is to have someone to talk to that would not talk the "same language." When it's all army during the week it's a relief only to have someone in other life to talk to. Of course this is simply deduction and not from experience so you can agree or disagree and I have no proof. But as you know man is the aggressor and being kept away from women makes them more desperate for women company. In most cases this is pure company and nothing more. Perhaps I'm wrong.

There are probably some nice fellows in that bunch too, white or otherwise.

Tomarrow I'll be walking around town paying taxes (territorial) shopping and what not. I hate to do those things but I guess I just can't help it. I'm telling I'm pretty lazy. Maybe the army will get the laziness out of me.

Periods,
Yoshiharu

Hilo, Hawaii
March 14, 1942

Dear Yoshiharu,

I hope you had your gas mask with you today when the air raid alarm sounded. It seems to be a weekly event for you folks, but nothing goes on here like that. Besides the shelters are so full of water with this rain, it would be mass suicide to jump in.

You know what you say about you and I not having enough of what we would like is true, and sometimes it maybe because we want what we can't have. But there are still a lot of things you can still want even if you have it, did you think of that or do you get tired of everything you have once you get it. [There are] the kind [of people] you meet just on the surface and those you don't meet—you discover from the inside. I've met lots of the former but few of the latter, just as you wrote me about. The people whom you know from the inside remain the same to you no matter what happens in the outside world. In fact they mean more to you, just like your own family. If times are uncertain you can't let even those deeper values become uncertain too, in fact people find that things like faith, hope and love are the unchangeable things that hold them together. If I had none of these I wouldn't be able to stay here another day, even if it's a beautiful place. To me it is beautiful because I still have things to believe in, if I didn't I would see only the grey skies and they certainly are grey over here.

I'm sure you see things that way too, or you wouldn't be what you are. I wouldn't keep writing to you or anything if I didn't believe in you. If you think the same way, the uncertainty of the times should not have to change. These things we believe in. If you want to know, two months from now won't make much difference. I'll still love you the same old way, so what's two months? Only a lifetime maybe, but it's better to be optimistic than not.

Periods,
Naoko

<hr />

The heroics of Japanese American soldiers have been chronicled and dissected in terms of both patriotic duty and ethnic pride, but Yoshiharu demonstrated his contributions to the war effort as an industrial arts shop teacher. While at the Stout Institute, he had been ingrained with the importance of an industrial arts education, since he was attending a college that taught teachers "in every state of the Union as well as in Canada, Hawaii, Cuba, the Canal Zone, and the West Indies." The institute emphasized that its students "acquired definitely useful skills" and that "with them into laboratories, shops and classrooms they take a thought from age-old wisdom,—that the happy life is to be found in service to others." Yoshiharu's education prepared him for "increased responsibilities" that teachers faced as "the practical arts [took] their place in the expanding program of general education" and "as new social responsibilities [became] the problem of the state." One of his activities as a member of the Arts and Crafts Club at the Stout Institute had been sponsoring a Model Airplane Club for students in the neighboring communities.[124] His letters in the section below discuss building model planes as part of the military effort and an activity for which he had been trained at school. The students traced a government-issued template onto a block of wood, cut out the pattern on the wood, then carved, glued, and sandpapered the model planes into shape.[125] By February of 1942, as part of an effort to make two hundred thousand models of various American, British, German, Japanese, Italian, and Russian planes, seventeen schools in Hawaii took on the responsibility of building two thousand models at a 1:72 ratio for the Navy Bureau of Aeronautics to use for training purposes. Central Intermediate School on Oahu and Waimea High School on Kauai participated in the project.[126] The DPI and the American Legion both joined the effort, but more help was needed, and in the next month, the U.S. Navy asked civilians to participate as well. Shop teachers had models of twenty types of planes, and school shops were "turned into miniature airplane factories" where youngsters were hard at work.[127] Navy Secretary Frank Knox believed that the planes (with the smallest having a wingspan of five and a half inches) would be helpful in training personnel.[128] Civilians and civil defense workers also used the models for learning to identify planes from a distance.

Even as Yoshiharu continued to promote the war effort through his shop classes, he emphasized that his first duty was to his family. For Yoshiharu, his traditional Japanese upbringing outweighed his civic duty as an American citizen. Thus, he contributed to the war effort in ways that allowed him to avoid joining the military. He constantly referred to his obligations to his family. As the only son left at home, he felt responsible for helping his elderly parents financially. His parents, as well as his siblings, had sacrificed to allow him to attend college on the mainland for three and a half years, and their sacrifice fostered his belief that he could not waste his education, and their money, by joining the army. He did not imply that he would dodge the draft if his number came up, but he did what he could to obtain a deferment each time a prior deferment was set to expire. Naoko tried to support his decisions, as indicated in her earlier statement that "it's more important for you to work with individuals who have a future before them, not with those who haven't any."[129] She also told him that she was thinking of going home to Oahu for the summer to take college courses and suggested,

"Maybe if you went too it would be more fun, but I know you're going home too." Pointing out that she and Yoshiharu had many more summers ahead of them, she added, "But the old folks have few. And they deserve whatever breaks they can get."[130] Yoshiharu revealed his family's financial and social position to her, noting that although his parents never showed that they missed him, they had "nobody to look after, not very many places to go and [were] living in a rather limited society."[131]

Naoko and Yoshiharu's relationship continued to deepen as they both realized how they felt about each other. They hoped to see each other during the summer, but Yoshiharu's worry about being drafted prevented him from making any commitment to Naoko. She encouraged him to go home to see his family and told him she supported his consideration of his parents.[132] They both commented on people they knew who were getting married. In one letter, Naoko wrote of a dorm-mate who had married an army doctor and he lived seventy-five miles away: "Ye gads, she's as good as not married so she lives there with her sister in law and waits for her husband to get leaves."[133] A *Time Magazine* article explained the trend: "U.S. girls, never really convinced by live-alone-and-like-it books, seemed to have decided that a soldier-husband for a few days was better than no husband at all."[134] Indeed, this seemed to be a common sentiment, as Naoko wrote of another friend who had married a man stationed on the other side of the island. His busy schedule prompted her to pontificate: "I think it's harder to be married and separated than not."[135] Such wartime conditions allowed Naoko to project concurrence with Yoshiharu's plans not to marry, despite her admission of love.

⚉⚉⚉

Honolulu, Oahu
March 18, 1942

Dear Naoko,

Thanks for the lecture and I won't argue with you. This isn't because I'm giving in or giving up, but it's because I agree with you.[136] I thought you felt that way, but you know me, I'm a pessimist. Now it's clear in black and white so I have nothing to say however until now I never knew what was going on in your mind about that. Two and a half months to summer isn't a long time, but when that is up of course I don't know where I'll be. If not in the army, I'll probably be home. Of course there is one exception—you.

My folks were counting on my coming home for Easter, but they know I can't and they will be waiting for the summer. As I said before I'll satisfy them before most anything because I won't be able to do that very much longer. My mother is rather soft hearted. Perhaps I can't blame her. After all [out] of all her nine children there is only one at home with her and must be hard to take as far as parents are concerned. When I do go home they never show that they've missed me or anything but I like to go home myself. I'm sure you feel that way about your folks too—only they aren't as old as mine and little things like going home are big events for them. Especially my folks who have nobody to look after, not very many places to go and living in a rather limited society.

[No signature]

Hilo, Hawaii
March 21, 1942

Dear Yoshiharu,

I had to go to a lecture yesterday about gas warfare by a woman, Dr. Hamre.[137] She said it's alright to them if people say they can do what they please about their own lives so if they don't want to carry a gas mask around it's their own business. But she said the catch comes if they do get gassed they won't crawl off to die by themselves. Instead the time, attention and skill of the hospital attendants, Red Cross etc. will have to be used on a person who doesn't deserve it. I got the idea that people have to be considerate in these times, it's everybody's war. It sounds like your letter where you said "Such things as uncertainty does not change me within but I think I should be more careful about getting other people involved."

I'm glad you feel you'd like to go home this summer instead of staying in town. Not that I want you to, but as you say it is nice to consider it from your parents' viewpoint. It seems to me they are blessed with a good boy, and why not let them enjoy that blessing as long as they can. I think it will be nice for you too, to get away from it all and eat all the vegetables you want at home and go back on your live alone schedule as you had last summer.

Periods,
Naoko

Honolulu, Oahu
March 24, 1942

Dear Naoko,
We did not have any air raid last week-end for a change so nothing was unusual as far as the town was concerned.

Since Monday we have been busy doing the model air planes. This is for the War Department as you may know. So Imada and I are working together.[138] We are getting along fine and getting much accomplished.

This model airplane business isn't as easy as many people thought. We are required to make scale models and they have to be just so—That is something that the student can't do well—I mean making things accurate—When completed they must pass inspection and that's another thing. Some of the kids will complete theirs but to have them excepted [accepted] is another question.

Periods—
Yoshiharu

Hilo, Hawaii
March 27, 1942

Dear Yoshiharu,

Here's hoping you aren't too cross eyed from building model airplanes to the scale. My big brother used to spend most of his leisure hours doing that at one time, so I can imagine what a job it is. Especially for the kids, but I guess they'd feel important if they knew it was for the War Dept. Gee, what is education coming to these days, but it's good fun isn't it.

Next door are 3 girls—one who teaches at Intermediate here and of all things a friend who used to sing in our church choir. She married a doctor who is serving as army M.D. way down in Pahala about 75 mi. from here. Ye gads, she's as good as not married so she lives there with her sister in law and waits for her husband to get leaves.

They're going to start finger printing next week here, we may have to help all or part of the time.[139] The kids may have some vacation, but none for us. This place is so over run with the army we can't go anyplace without bumping into them. Some are decent and miss their families, I tell my kids to talk nice to them. Teacher does too if they seem nice, but not too much they'll follow you home.

Periods and ditto,
Naoko

Honolulu, Oahu
March 30, 1942

Dear Naoko,

It's ten o'clock and tonight I've spent most of the time making a model airplane. I started my second one to-night and have it I mean the body completed. It actually takes only about 8 hours to complete one, but I'm not to enthusiastic about making models. These are made only as a source of interest for the kids. They asked me to open the shop on Saturday and Sunday which I did. They were nice though, since they couldn't bring any 'apples for the teacher' they brought me some bananas. This of course was for my overtime.

Today I had my injection for typhoid and the vaccination. Neither is bothering me. I have the first in my right arm but I'm still able to write to you. I wouldn't use this as an excuse even if it hurt me a lot.

Periods and more.

Yoshiharu

Hilo, Hawaii
April 1, 1942

Dear Yoshiharu,

Today my friend Toshi (whom we met <u>that</u> day at the U) came to see me with her Lieut. husband.[140] She arrived today and plans to stay till Tuesday. He drove in from Kau side where he's stationed now and they're driving back tomorrow.[141] He had only a 24hr. leave so they couldn't stay in Hilo. He gets one or two free hours a day, so she'd rather go way out there to be near him. It's quite a life, and I think it's harder to be married and separated than not. Everybody I know seems to be in the same boat, some worse off than others.

So long with love,

Naoko

Honolulu, Oahu
April 4, 1942

Dear Naoko,

This week I've worked in the school shop with some of the very much interested kids. They are all doing alright. We have about a dozen planes completed. Couple of them already finished three of them. I made three of them myself but I think I'll quit for a while and do my own work. Only one other teacher made a model so far. He made one and the other two teachers did not make any. So I can command respect. They think I'm good in model making—As long as they think so it's okay with me.

One day a week ago I saw your mother at the "Y" cafeteria. I sit there every day now that the school lunch is terrible. I can't hold out until after school if I eat there. Well, I saw her and about all I said was hello. Last week I saw Kazu drive by in her car. I called her, but I don't know if she recognized me—she probably didn't like it anyway.

I had my typhoid shot last Monday but I was well enough to play badminton every day. Vacination didn't work.

Solong for a while—periods
Yoshiharu

Hilo, Hawaii
April 8, 1942

Dear Yoshiharu,
We're beginning enumeration tomorrow. I won't go from house to house yet since we're taking all the Filipino workers from Waiakea Mill at one station for the next few days and they come to us. Maybe I'll find my dream man yet. By the time this and the next registration for men is over I'll be speaking with a Filipino accent anyway.

Every week something new happens, never a dull moment. Now they're taking over the Intermed[iate] School for a hospital, but my friend Shigeno who is librarian there is going to stay there with all her books and the Army.[142] Honestly they're all over the place, some nice some fresh—but give me Hilo in the good old days when we could walk down the street and everybody would mind his own business.

Goodbye now—
Naoko

Honolulu, Oahu

April 12, 1942

Dear Naoko,

I hope you are finding enumerating a pleasant thing to do. For a while it was for me but after a while like most things it got monotonous and very tiresome. If you do start going around I hope you have a good partner because that helps a lot. Perhaps you can get some young men teacher to go around with. Then "poor me."

Mitz asked me to teach defense workers class in carpentry for 4 hours a week 2 hours each night for $2 an hour but I'm too lazy so turned it down.[143] I don't need the money now. I have enough to eat so I want time to do what I want to. So far I have much time to my self and enjoy it very much.

Periods.

Yoshiharu

Hilo, Hawaii

April 16, 1942

Dear Yoshiharu,

We're behind in our enumerating, not our team but the whole school in general. Due to a lot of dumb people who try to run things.

I stayed at the station enumerating families from the mill the first 4 days and have been out in the field the past 4 days. Since we're behind, we're expected to enumerate 70 a day so Jean Okita (Mrs. Francis Okita who lives next to me) and I got mad and really took off.[144] She used to work in Dr. Alsup's office so she makes out the summons slips like a veteran, while I do the interviewing.[145] We did 86 people yesterday and slowed down to 76 today, so probably tomorrow we'll be through with our last section.

The things I enjoy most is X-ing out the plat map every nite with ink and ruler. I don't know who drew all these areas to scale but I must give them a lot of credit. I don't see how it can be figured out correctly—so many feet to an inch. I guess making model planes is mostly mathematic like that, it's beyond me how it's done. I got all mixed up last nite trying to number the enumeration sheets in advance. After working on everything over an hour I found I had numbered everything wrong. Oh well, how boring. Anyway after tomorrow we won't have to go knocking on people's doors, I hope. No weekend again.

Anyway I'm thinking of going home this summer and telling my mother to take a vacation. She needs some diversion some time, so she might as well get it when she can. I tho't of going to take summer courses at the U. but what's the use. Maybe if you went too it would be more fun, but I know you're going home too. After all we still have a lot more summers to do as we choose, but the old folks have few. And they deserve whatever breaks they can get. Anyhow I don't mind staying home for a change, altho' I almost got fed up with it a couple of months ago.

So long for now,

Naoko

P.S. Was invited to a rum party Sat. nite, but we had to enumerate Sunday so no soap. Hilo is a wet place.

Honolulu, Oahu

April 19, 1942

Dear Naoko,

Another Sunday and I think it was spent as well as I can. In the morning from 9:00 to 12:00 I went over to the shop to help the kids with their model airplanes. So far we have about 30 planes completed. In the afternoon from 1:30 I played badminton until 5:00. After playing doubles and more singles we cooked our supper in the kitchen downstairs. Lefty, Tom Hoon and I.[146] We had some meat and pork chops, with buttered string beans, [tsukemono], watercress, avocado and ice cream for desert.[147]

There are only 7 more weeks left of this school year. What will I do this summer depends a lot on several things. In the first place my deferment is good only until the end of May. I don't care especially to go home because food stuff are hard to get at home. My mother will be hurt if she can't get enough good things for me to eat when I go home. There are only three people at home and if I go home it will be like 6.[148] But if I don't go home they'll think I don't care to go home. My brother who is working down here is going home this week for a while.[149]

Solong and periods,

Yoshiharu

⌁⌁⌁⌁⌁

Japanese Americans in Hawaii found that race relations were better there than on the mainland. One Nisei explained that this was because there was no "racial tolerance" in Hawaii; rather, there was "racial goodwill." Tolerance meant one group was considered inferior by another, but in Hawaii there was a "friendly semifamily relationship in which every race and racial extraction understands and appreciates the others, or at least attempts to do so."[150] In the islands, the local residents made a distinction between "Japs" and people of Japanese descent in a way that mainlanders did not. Locals could also more easily differentiate the Asian races than could the Americans on the mainland.[151] In Hawaii the local Japanese described themselves with terms like "Americans of Japanese Ancestry," "AJAs," or simply "Americans." They did not identify themselves as Nisei.[152]

Yet, for many Japanese Americans in Hawaii, as well as on the mainland, the story of internment camps became all too familiar. As Americans, many of them had believed that the Constitution and the Bill of Rights would protect them.[153] After President Roosevelt authorized internment through Executive Order 9066, nearly 160,000 Americans of Japanese ancestry, of whom only 35,000 were classified as aliens, were forced to leave their homes, businesses, and property to live in communal housing in isolated areas.[154] Those who were American citizens understood the contradiction between democracy and internment.[155] But for the Issei whose traditional Japanese culture ingrained them with attitudes of fatalism, acceptance of adversity, and bowing to authority, internment further emphasized the concept of *shikata ga nai*. Many Japanese Americans on the U.S. mainland saw Executive Order 9066 disrupt their lives and their families, and parents lost traditional control over their children as the military's demands usurped parental authority. However, internment camps were not as common in Hawaii.

The islands' proximity to Japan and large Japanese population made it seem logical to relocate people of Japanese ancestry to internment camps. President Roosevelt and Navy Secretary Knox hoped to remove all local Japanese from Oahu to the outer islands. The ones the government designated as most dangerous would then be sent to internment camps on the mainland.[156] Still, the government established five internment camps in the islands: Sand Island and Honouliuli on Oahu, the Haiku Internment Camp on Maui, the Kilauea Military Camp on the Big Island, and the Kalaheo Stockade on Kauai. People of Japanese descent made up 37.3 percent of the population in Hawaii, and of them, 23.6 percent (the Issei) were not citizens. The Territorial Office of Defense recognized that it could not remove the entire Japanese population or prohibit their "economic activities," because that "would mean that over one-third of the territory's population would be immobilized."[157] However, the FBI continued to detain anyone whom it perceived as "doing espionage activities," considered suspicious as aliens, or believed had questionable contacts or sympathies with the enemy, and some of these people were sent to the internment camps. The Japanese population in Hawaii also witnessed the closing of Japanese-language schools, teahouses, Shinto shrines, and Buddhist temples.[158] The closing of the temples had an especially large impact on Japanese American communities because the temples were their primary gathering places.[159] Still, most Japanese in Hawaii remained loyal to the United States.[160] Even the military governor of Hawaii, General Delos Emmons, argued that the Japanese were "absolutely essential" for rebuilding Pearl Harbor and that interment of all local Japanese was unnecessary and nearly impossible.[161]

One study asserted that 99 percent of Japanese Americans simply went about their usual business. Logistically, Japanese Americans provided the manpower needed in Hawaii, and the territory did not have the supplies necessary to build detention centers, nor did ships have enough space to transport all of the local Japanese to the mainland.[162] Instead, the authorities heavily regulated Japanese Americans' businesses and relocated 4,000 Japanese and Japanese Americans who lived close to harbors or military areas. Everyone who worked on defense projects had to wear a badge, and the badges worn by Japanese workers were black, to identify their ethnicity.[163] The Issei could not travel by air, change their residence or occupation, or move from place to place without written permission.[164] In addition, hundreds of suspicious persons were arrested, 1,500 were interned without trial, and countless others underwent frequent strip searches and were denied contact with their families, simply because of their ethnicity.[165]

Despite seeing that "prejudice against people of Japanese ancestry in Hawaii was not comparable . . . to that of the West Coast," all Japanese and Japanese Americans in Hawaii were "on the spot." Japanese Americans in the islands had demonstrated their loyalty to the United States, and their high percentage of the population allowed them to "make a cohesive ethnic community." Japanese plantation workers had organized and gone on strike in the 1920s, showing that they could push back against authority and gain a bargaining position. Furthermore, their identity as "local" made them similar to their Hawaiian neighbors of other ethnic backgrounds.[166] Discrimination in Hawaii had been heavily built on social and economic status, not on race as was the case on the mainland.[167]

Thus, internment did not hit as close to home for Naoko and Yoshiharu as it did for many others they knew. Naoko wrote of the internment of Mr. Shinoda, the former principal of a Japanese school. She believed that if the army would take away a man like him, it "might as well take [her] dad too."[168] It remains unclear why Naoko's father,

Seinosuke Tsukiyama, was never interned. His Christian background and connections, the fact that he spoke English, and his friendship with influential men like Kanemi Kanazawa (who was described as "a tall, handsome young man with a university education." The Honolulu Police Department recruited Kanazawa as a police intelligence officer to question the Japanese community for "hints of possible espionage or sabotage"[169]) may have saved him from such a fate. Naoko emphasized her father's Christian connections as one of the primary reasons he was not interned.

Even though local Japanese in Hawaii did not face the same kinds of hardships and internment as those on the mainland, they too could not escape the toll of war. The young adult Nisei in Hawaii, having reached an age of independence, found that their freedom was curtailed by the requirements of martial law. Naoko and Yoshiharu both detailed their work enumerating, and as public school teachers, they were expected to give their time freely and to actively show their patriotism. They grew frustrated with the mandatory work and with requirements like taking first aid classes. They, as well as other teachers, claimed to be willing to work during the summer if required, but the general consensus was that they also wanted a change from the typical paperwork routines. The couple still faced the problem of being on different islands, apart from each other and from their families. Without a clear schedule set by the DPI, they could not make plans for the summer. The monotony, the hypocrisy, and the uncertainty began to wear on them. "But damn this war anyway," Naoko wrote.[170]

～～～

Hilo, Hawaii
April 22, 1942

Dear Yoshiharu,

Haven't had 2 weekends and this weekend I think I'll have to spend it talking to old men between the ages of 45 to 65. I've forgotten what a movie could be like, but really don't miss them. But damn this war anyway.

Mr. Shinoda, at whose home I used to stay was interned by the Army the other day. He used to be a Japanese school principal but if they take a man like him, they might as well take my dad too. We spent last night at their house, only his wife and the kid at the Intermediate School is left home. Their daughter just got married the other week to a swell guy only he's Portuguese and that was tough on the parents. But last night they were there, we had quite a party. We were rather serious in our conversation last night tho', and slept early. I was still feeling dumb and sleepy from a typhoid shot. This is the second day after I've had my first shot and my arm feels like I played 19 sets of badminton left-handed.

Maybe I'll go to business school this summer just to be doing something. My kid sister works at my dad's now and I think she can be his office secretary as soon as she finishes business school. Anyhow I think I'll stay home and keep my folks company. My heart turned over when I heard Japan was bombed. I don't think I'll ever see my brother again, but there's a lot of people worse off than we are.[171] Anyhow it's pretty awful, that's why I think a lot of my folks more than ever now.

So long and love—Naoko

Honolulu, Oahu

April 27, 1942

Dear Naoko,

I suppose by now you are back to teaching. Enumerating isn't too good a thing to be doing—Is it? I didn't care too much for it. Especially with so many people around that don't know what the're doing. All they want to do is tell people what to do. Well now you know what it is like. You can tell that to your grand children in 1980.

Well, I have one more month of official liberty that I know of. After that I don't know what will happen. So far there hasn't been any more call for the army since February 7 so I don't know if the government wants us. Furthermore many of the ones who were supposed to go in Feb didn't at the last minute. So as things are the chances for another deferment is very good.

This summer I'm quite sure of going home very early. My mother have been having high blood pressure attacks quite frequently lately. I guess all the things that has happened and are happening are getting her down. So I've made up my mind to go home this summer as soon as I can and stay there as long as I can. If I can get a job on Kauai I'll stay there also.

So long—periods.
Yoshiharu

Hilo, Hawaii
April 29, 1942

Dear Yoshiharu,

Sorry to hear your mother isn't well these days. Especially her type of illness isn't very good in these times. I hope your going home will make her feel much better. I guess I don't mind it so much then—she still has priority.

For one thing, I'd rather stay here than go home back to the city life and ways. Nobody bothers me here, I just go to visit friends if I have time and if I feel like seeing them. In Honolulu, people are always coming in and out whether you like it or not. And of course I have to be sociable, to some extent. I've got to do what others do when I'm there.

I've got to take a First Aid course and like it. My principal requires all her teachers to, if they haven't already. A lady lectures & demonstrates & we read the first aid book for homework. Anyway just come to me for cuts, wounds, or any 1st aid treatment and watch me do my stuff.

So long for now and periods,
Naoko

Honolulu, Oahu

May 1, 1942

Dear Naoko,

As for the summer I don't know what I'll do. As you may know by now, the D.P.I. is expecting teachers to put in time this summer with the kids. If I'm required to stay here I guess I have to. If that's the case I may go to summer school because that is one way of getting out of doing something for nothing. I don't mind if all the teachers are to put some time in but it will most likely be only some. To me it appears that those people are going to be the "suckers." I'll go to summer school and take 6 credits even if I flunk all of them.

All in all, where I'll be—or when I'll go home I don't know and I won't know until about the last week, so don't count on me. If the environment suits you over there perhaps you should stay there. I guess I better stop here or else I'll start the same thing I did when you first went to Hilo. You know—not wasting your time on me and what not.

I may sound conceited, but seems like I'm doing quite well with the model building stuff. This week Mr. Hood the head of Vocational Education came over to my shop and told me I was doing the best of all the schools here.[172] Today they called me up and told me to be ready to have some pictures taken for the Star Bulletin on Monday and also for some models for the Honolulu Academy of Arts, for exhibits.[173] Looks like I have to go there after all. To date I have about 92 models completed. I'm trying to be wanted enough by the department so that they will get deferment for me. Perhaps I'm thinking too much for myself—?

Periods,

Yoshiharu

⸙⸙⸙

Naoko and Yoshiharu found that the circumstances of war conflicted with their American ideals of freedom. They had attended American schools and learned about liberty, democracy, and equality. And as teachers, they taught these tenets as essential elements of an American education. But as the war dragged on and they lived under martial law, they saw that freedom and equality did not come to them automatically. And while they accepted that being in love in wartime meant sacrifices and changes from the norm, they became weary of the war's hardships and inconveniences. They did not have the freedom to travel between islands, and their vacation time was reduced. As teachers away from their families, they could not visit loved ones as they had hoped to over the summer, unless, in Naoko's case, she were to take unwanted summer school classes at the University of Hawaii. All that uncertainly led Yoshiharu to decide that he and Naoko would be better off ending their relationship. Perhaps he felt that his relationship status was one of the few aspects of his life that he could still control. Unlike many of their friends, he was in no hurry to get married, and he did not want to join the army or be drafted. During the war, one could certainly hope for normalcy, but for Naoko and Yoshiharu, martial law affected practically every aspect of their lives.

Hilo, Hawaii
May 4, 1942

Dear Yoshiharu,

Earlier this evening I wrote to my family to blow off some steam. I'm finally hearing the awful truth about little or no vacation for us. The only way we can go home is to sign up for summer school at the U it seems, and of all the useless things to do at this time. Talk about equal rights, democracy, and whatnot—why don't they practice it, first if they expect us to preach it. It gets me so darn mad the way these schools are run by female dictators who think patriotism is saluting the flag and singing the nat'l anthem every morning—I could wash my hands of this whole teaching business and tell 'em where to go.

I can't see why they don't try to give teachers a break sometimes. We work extra time for the public like during enumeration, then after school closes on June 5 they want us to help with immunization. We've only been counting the days till June, then they go and extend that. Well what's another month to them—I guess they think we ain't human or some thing. Now we're supposed to report back by Aug. 15 for curriculum work or something, so Shizue and I are saying darn if we will. We aren't that important to the D.P.I., and if all the fuss and work were worth the time spent okay. But teaching as we do in basements and hit or miss conditions, both teachers and kids need a good vacation. But do we get it after all this—no!!

It looks like you and your class are really going to town on those plane models—now they must keep you for the entire summer. "Mr. Ogata is just the man we need for this type of work," etc. etc.[174] Anyway you are doing a swell job all around, I've got to hand it to you.

No, I won't count on seeing you much or even at all since nobody knows what's going to happen next. That's the hard way but as you seem to think, it's the best. Damn stubborn, too. Before we go at it again—just let things happen and see what happens, but don't let any part of me cramp your style in anything you do. And the same goes for me too, as we said before. As far as that goes I haven't changed any and I'd like to know if you have.

So long for awhile—and periods.

Naoko

Honolulu, Oahu
May 7, 1942

Dear Naoko,

Well, to the latter part of your letter all I can say is do as you please. I'm nobody to be telling you what to do and you know very well that I'll do as I please.

Nuuanu [...]
Honolulu T.T.
May 7, 1942

Dear Naoko,

Well, to the latter part
of your letter all I can say
is do as you please. It's nobody to be telling you what to
do and you know very well
that I'll do as I please—

Not that I care for or
anything like that. It's just
that I expect to remain
as I am for the next four or five
years. I set my minimum
at 36 and that's three years
away. I don't expect anybody
to wait. And you being older
than I am and being a girl
that's a long way off. So hereafter
I think its best that you think

First page of Yoshiharu Ogata's letter of May 7, 1942, which eventually states they should "call it quit." Photo in author's collection.

Not that I care less or anything like that. It's just that I expect to remain as I am for the next 4 or five years. I set my minimum at 26 and that's three years away. I don't expect anybody to wait. And you being older than I am and being a girl that's a long way off. So hereafter I think its best that you think of me just as a friend. If you think of me as less well, I have nothing to say—Reasons I've talked with you and wrote to you. I['m] beginning to think that we shouldn't let things just happen. You will remain as few of my worthwhile memories but who am I to expect more.

I still think a lot of you and wish that it could be otherwise (but time and circumstance do not permit.)

In short let's call it quit. You'll do alright anytime anywhere. I know you'll do much better with men than I could ever with women. I just don't get anywhere—But perhaps sometime someone will be crazy enough.

If you do answer this and you may if you please—don't expect one from me—I'm not promising.

It may be for the last time but I like of your taste and many things about you—very much so. Honestly. Even the little things please me a lot. But I guess I'm no good and know it so that I won't spoil your life. So. So long and periods to last a long time.

Yoshiharu

P.S. One thing you can be sure it's not any other girl. Maybe I'm drunk.

Periods again,

Me

Hilo, Hawaii
May 13, 1942

Dear Yoshiharu,

As for your last letter, there isn't much to say on the subject. Either that or too much, but as you've often said you've got a mind of your own and I am not in the position or place to tell you otherwise. You've got your reasons, and I can see what sort of position you're in which involves other people. There's one thing I've been learning more since this war's been on and that is it's very easy to become selfish in these times and have things your own way. Then on the other hand people are learning to take things with much courage and it comes easier than in normal times.

Anyway if you think it's better to just keep on a friendship basis, I shall make arrangements with my secretary to keep it as such. If it's for the better I do hope you're getting results of some kind. I mean really going back to your 'live alone and like it' way of life. Not that I'm saying I intruded that much, but it should make a difference if we do this at all. And I think you can get along the way you say, much better than most men I know. That's why when all the rest of them are trying to jump into matrimony to avoid something or the other (foreign wars maybe, but they get the domestic ones finally) you can still be very casual about it. Maybe if you get a taste of the army it might change your views somewhat, but I hope not, for your good. With the attitude you have, it will be helpful when you do have to join up. However I think you're pretty safe because I know a fellow classified 1A and hasn't been drafted yet. If you do get 'an invitation,' my brother always says it's a better gang in his Varsity V squad and it's up to anyone to join there.

As for me I'm pretty sure I won't join up with the D.P.I. again. I'm lucky being in Hilo and all that, but I'd rather earn only half my 'enormous' salary and be happy than be a hypocrite to keep this job. Honolulu isn't as home-y as this town but at least I can live the way I want to without 'a dictator' bothering me. And I'll miss hearing from you and writing regularly, but it's not the kind of stuff for you. I'm wondering what you're made of, iron man? But I hope you'll condescend to write occasionally, all my friends still do and you are one of them. If you don't choose to write back, okay but there's no reason for going that far I think. After awhile, if you feel that you get along very well and nothing could be better, I'd like to know it first if you don't mind.

So long for now,
Naoko

⁂

Necessary to note here is that after Naoko's letter of May 13, correspondence between her and Yoshiharu ceased until July 17. Yoshiharu had stated that they should "call it quit" and Naoko responded, "you've got a mind of your own and I am not in the position or place to tell you otherwise," in what seemed like might be their last exchange. Although her words implied that she would not try to change his mind, evidently she did. (Later, Naoko was not able to provide details on what happened.) The timing indicates that after the semester ended, she returned to Oahu to stay with her family and Yoshiharu remained on the island until July. At some point during their overlap, they must have worked out their differences. They spent time with each other while she was at home visiting her family and he stayed in Honolulu. But later that summer, he left Oahu to return to his own family on Kauai, and then the letters resumed, the couple having reached a new level of commitment in their relationship.

These next letters also show the lifestyle differences of the bustling city of Honolulu and the rural environment of Kauai. Naoko jumped into the whirlwind of activity in Honolulu. She took a summer job in downtown Honolulu, doing office work, and compared herself to Kitty Foyle, Ginger Rogers's character in the movie *Kitty Foyle: The Natural History of a Woman*.[175] (Foyle became the symbol of a hardworking young woman in a white-collar job in the 1940s.) Naoko also wrote about her opportunities for socializing, ranging from visiting with friends to going to dances with military men. Yoshiharu had to adjust to the slower pace of Kauai, and the responsibilities that came with living with his parents. As soon as he arrived on Kauai, he had trouble with transportation. On

Oahu, he commonly found buses and taxis, but Kauai did not have abundant public transportation. The sugar plantation camp of Wahiawa (adjacent to Eleele) was home to the community of Japanese and Japanese American plantation workers. It had wooden houses with corrugated iron roofs and outhouses. Within their plots, plantation families planted gardens and raised animals to supplement their food supplies. It was a far cry from what Yoshiharu had gotten used to in Wisconsin and in Honolulu.

Yoshiharu had to demonstrate his patriotism amid the prying eyes and wagging tongues of his small community. Both the Issei and Nisei populations felt shame and humiliation that their ancestors traced back to the country that had attacked the United States. Just eleven days after the bombing of Pearl Harbor, the Public Morale Division of the Territorial Office of Civilian Defense attempted to create a more positive atmosphere for the Japanese who lived in Hawaii. The goals included serving as a liaison for the army and the civilian community in matters relating to public morale and working toward maintaining a unified and cooperative community.[176] Yoshiharu joined the Morale Committee on Kauai, and it had a fourfold mission. First, it created, at the army's request, the Kiawe Corps. Chaired by a Mr. Ishii, this volunteer organization was established on June 7, 1942, and not only sang patriotic songs but also intended to have three hundred civilian men clear the mesquite trees and shrubs from the beachfronts, making it harder for the Japanese to sneak onto the island. It set another goal of obtaining assistance with clearing and preparing civilian areas for occupation. This goal targeted the Japanese only, and they participated in it every morning, motivated by the fear of seeming unpatriotic. The Morale Committee volunteers put in fifty-eight thousand man-days clearing brush and doing community service.[177] The committee also sent a confidential survey to the Japanese community, and the residents answered questions about religion, education, and bond purchases. Its last goal established an educational drive, under the guise of gathering the elderly to discuss matters, though no specifics were provided.[178] One record shows that from January to March of 1942, the Morale Committee had 6,923 volunteers, with Japanese Americans constituting 6,719 of them, and Filipinos the rest.[179] The Kauai Morale Committee provided annual reports to update the army on its efforts, specifically mentioning ridding the island of Japanese-language schools and churches, checking on the welfare of detainees, providing educational campaigns to show why building morale was necessary, and developing social organizations.[180]

Yoshiharu found himself dealing with obligations to his country and his community, as well as to his family and his fiancée. He continued his civic duty through volunteering with the Morale Committee, but he also expressed his dissatisfaction and, at times, disgust with the expectations and attitudes of those around him. In his personal life, his relationship with Naoko had developed to the point that he needed to tell his parents about it. He hoped to gain their approval but realized that their traditional Japanese attitudes would allow them to reveal very little about their feelings or opinions. He also had to deal with the backlash of having a fiancée who was not his high school girlfriend, Etsuko Hayashi. He emphasized that he and Hayashi were not a couple, but to their small community, their high school dating had indicated a serious commitment. Another issue that arose involved his teaching career. His return to Kauai meant that he needed to register with the government and consult with the Department of Public Instruction. The combination of adjusting to Kauai, living with his family, figuring out where he would be teaching, and revealing his plans to marry created many complications for Yoshiharu even before factoring in the impact of the war.

Eleele, Kauai
July 17, 1942

Dear Naoko,

Yesterday I got home and without getting sick either. I even fell asleep on the plane. The bus took me until Hanapepe. So I had to take a taxi until Eleele which is only one mile at the longest. Imagine that guy soaking me 50 cents for that. From Eleele I still have about mile and a half to come home so I had to take my brother's car. When I got home my mother wasn't home so I had to cook rice and get something to eat.

Everything here is quite okay as far as we're concerned. Mother was quite down hearted for a while because she didn't hear from my brother in the army on the mainland, but now that she did and I'm home she's quite happy. Dad was kidding her about my coming home and her getting a letter from my brother saying that not only my eating is going to increase the food bill but that she's also eating double her usual amount.

Periods,
Yoshiharu

Honolulu, Oahu
July 19, 1942

My dearest man,

I went to the office of Island Homes and the Am[erican] Savings and Loan to see if I could pinch hit for a week on that desk job. Met the secretary and boss Mr. Christensen.[181] They both said I would do and to come Friday afternoon to catch on about the job. He asked me how much salary I expected but I wouldn't commit myself. If I state a certain amount then I'd have to be worth it, which isn't my idea of taking a job like this. I answer phone calls, type a little, pay bills and make out checks for him to sign, and keep files about homes they sell. I keep a scrapbook of all the classified ads on house and lots for sale. If I come across one I like I guess I'll put a kapu sign on it.[182] Anyway it's interesting.

Monday

Had a nice time being Kitty Foyle today. Office jobs are really routine in nature, but now I find it interesting because everything I do is new. The boss and one of the salesmen found out I'm a teacher and they're surprised to find I'm _still_ pleasant, so they were teasing me. They have a vacancy there so I'm almost tempted to ask for it in case you will still be at Central. At least then I can have lunch with you every day, if that is the least. I'm always thinking about eating.

Doris came home with me and we listened to records. The guy who recently joined the VVV's asked me to their dance at the U but I told him I was spending the afternoon with Doris.[183] Nevertheless my 2 sisters, Doris, Martha's friend, and I all went about 4 o'clock in time for refreshments. I had the last 4 dances with different friends of my brother's. I missed dancing with somebody tall—you for instance.

Sincerely—with periods,
Naoko

Eleele, Kauai
July 20, 1942

Dear Naoko,

Here I am back in the old groove again. It is very much like last year only not much joy riding, leaving a certain girl alone and know how a certain girl feels about me. Last year only with two dates with this certain girl I didn't know what to think, but now I know—I hope.

As for you I haven't said anything yet. I'm observing and listening for the right moment. It seems that my folks made quite a thorough investigation of this girl [Yoshiharu's high school girlfriend] after I left Kauai last summer. Their objections were that she was too pale: well, she isn't exactly pale but she is very fair—more of a hot-house flower than you are. That she was too thin, but she weighs about as much as you do. The last thing was that her mother said something to the effect that I wasn't good enough for her. As for the last part—guess the feeling is mutual because my folks think that I should find a school teacher wife. As for me, I don't care what they found out or what they say. Just because I let them say these things to me it doesn't mean that they are going to pick out a wife for me. Furthermore I don't think that it is the intention of my parents to tell me who to marry but they sure seem to be concerned over whom I shouldn't marry. I'm being agreeable about what they say about this girl because it really doesn't matter to me. I figure why make a fuss and be disagreeable over something that really doesn't matter.

From the conversation that goes on after supper, I think that they are expecting and want me to get married soon. Dad even said that if I should find someone desirable and I don't have to get in the army I should get married. I couldn't say anything then but what I thought was if he only knew. Well, that is enough for that.

Monday I had to do a little chasing around to get a matter concerning my personal identification card straightened out. Some people thought that I had to notify some people here. It happened that Reverend Yamada of the Hanapepe church is the head of the some kind of committee that takes care of such matter so I went to see him.[184] He told me that I did not have to if I had a return ticket and wasn't staying longer than two weeks. So now everything is okay and I'm sure of going back in two weeks, in other words about a week from today.

Wednesday, I had to go to the Rev's home to help with some tabulation sheets. The facts we were tabulating were from confidential sheets of the Japanese families in Kauai. And they kept on talking about the religion of most of the people here. As if it was a crime to be anything else but Christians.

Solong and Periods,
Yoshiharu

Honolulu, Oahu
July 25, 1942

Dearest you—
Right now you can join the D.P.I. and see the Islands. I hear they make changes as soon as they're asked for—provided you don't ask for Niihau [or] Honolulu.[185]

Which reminds me, did you find out about that Waimea Hi[gh] job? It seems it will be easy if I want a transfer to the beautiful Garden Isle,

I've always wanted to see the scenery. From the looks of things however, I guess I'll qualify best as a schoolteacher—especially with your folks.

I'm glad to hear that your folks are beginning to think they wouldn't mind having more grandchildren. But don't forget they want it legal, isn't that right, dear man? That's what all the squawk is about with parents, but they have their rights too. That's why I do hope you aren't keeping them too much in the dark, especially when they are expecting something of you. I wouldn't feel I was doing them much justice, if they didn't know. They think a lot of you no doubt and I would rather have them approve of this that means so much to them. I don't care either what they may think of me because I'm sure that if they had a fair chance to know what I'm like, I would respect whatever conclusions they might have.

So long and periods too,
Naoko

Eleele, Kauai
July 29, 1942

Dear Naoko,
On Monday I went to get my return passage. I planned to go back today or tomorrow but the plane is full until Sunday. I guess I'll get into town around noon time.

As far as the teaching position goes—I'm quite sure I will be teaching here on Kauai. Everything here is okay all I had to do was to write a letter asking for the transfer. I more or less received a verbal okay from this end of the job but am waiting for a formal okay from the Department. If you decide to come to Kauai I hope it is on the west side because then I won't have to travel too far. Because if you come to Kauai and live in Hanalei or Kilauea it's going to be pretty hard for me to get around because of the gas situation.[186]

Yoshiharu

Eleele, Kauai
August 2, 1942

Dear Naoko,

When I didn't show up yesterday I suppose you felt like calling me all the names that you could think of. Well, I don't blame you but there wasn't anything I could do about it. I went down there this morning all packed and ready to go, but when I got there the guy at the desk tells me that I couldn't go today because of priority.

The best the guy could do about a booking for me is Friday the 7th. So I guess I have to wait around till then. It seems like I'm always running into transportation problems. Of course if this happened on the other end of the trip I wouldn't have mind it at all, but over here I'm just wasting five days. In one way it might be better that I'm staying here as far as my parents are concerned.

Yoshiharu

Honolulu, Oahu
August 4, 1942

Dearest—(you big so and so!)

I got your other letter last Friday saying you'd be over on Sunday "so be at home I'm going to call you as soon as I reach ——." So I had a nice time waiting for Sunday and since I wanted to, I went down to the airport instead of going to church. See what I get for not going to church—it was disappointing to say the least but I knew you had a good reason for not coming.

You're not sure yet about teaching on Kauai. The way they're stalling, it looks like Mr. Gordon loves you too well. As for me, it depends a lot on what you tell me when you get back. Especially where your parents are concerned. Personally, I want to be there if you are—very much. When I think of these past 2 or more weeks I really don't see how I can face a year away, but that is from a selfish viewpoint. I really want to know how your parents feel about this. Unless I'm sure they favor it, I wouldn't want to plant myself right under their noses unless I had a right to. If we were married it would be different, but to others I really have no claim to make such a move. I hope you'll agree with me on this.[187] If your folks didn't mind and were anxious to see what sort of person I am, then it would be better for me to teach there if possible.

Most likely I'd get West Kauai as there are the most openings there from what I hear. You know, teachers especially in the country are more or less regarded as inhuman, unemotional and what-have-you creatures, incapable of any other feelings except for the kids. As far as I'm concerned I can go back to Hilo for another year if it is more favorable from your family's viewpoint, because I know how you feel. It may mean no vacation in between either and chances of our getting together, if the airways are so congested by these——! priorities.

Periods,
Naoko

4   If You Still Want Me

In 1942 the Pacific Theater of World War II was in full swing. Japan had made great inroads and possessed 1.4 million square miles that had formerly been "white" countries and were inhabited by 128 million people. But the Allies, with the United States leading the way, halted Japan's advances with the multiday, multipronged attack known as the Battle of the Coral Sea. Japan's next hope, then, was to compel the United States to negotiate after luring American forces away from Hawaii by attacking the Aleutian Islands through Midway. Despite the "grossly inferior" aircraft of the United States, it "accomplished one of the most brilliant victories in the history of naval warfare," and many considered the Battle of Midway, in June 1942, the turning point of the Pacific Campaign. After that, the residents of Hawaii rested more easily, as the threat of another attack on the islands had been greatly reduced. The last big battle of the Pacific came at Guadalcanal, after which Japan abandoned the island and the Allies gained a pathway to Japan.[1]

Yoshiharu Ogata and Naoko Tsukiyama renewed their letter writing in the fall of 1942, after spending part of the summer together. This chapter, however, contains only letters from Yoshiharu. Naoko continued her correspondence with Yoshiharu during this period, but her letters have not been preserved and thus could not be included here. Yet their story is easy to follow from just his letters. Yoshiharu was on Kauai, where he taught and lived with his family. There was little excitement regarding the war, but his activities included volunteering for the Kiawe Corps, as part of the Morale Committee, and teaching his industrial arts classes. He also remained concerned about being drafted into the military. Naoko was on the Big Island, teaching again at the Olaa School.

Details about the couple's previous relationships become evident in this set of letters. Both families knew of the budding romance between Yoshiharu and Naoko, and gossip about the couple spread throughout both communities. Yoshiharu and Etsuko Hayashi, his high school girlfriend, had drifted apart when he went to Wisconsin, and according to his letters, he believed that their relationship was over. As word of his relationship with Naoko spread, he found that although he and Hayashi had come to a mutual understanding, others in the community had not accepted the breakup as amicably. Naoko, on the other hand, had a succession of courters, and the one described in this section of letters seems to have been the most persistent. Yoshiharu gave Naoko's former suitor the nickname "One Dozen Roses," because of his romantic and flowery sentiments as he professed, repeatedly, his feelings for Naoko, even though she and Yoshiharu had discussed getting engaged in December of the previous year.

Yoshiharu's letters in this section also chronicle his adjustments to living and teaching on Kauai. By March 1942, gas stations on the islands had limited their hours, and motorists endured rationing of gasoline.[2] Yoshiharu's job at Waimea High School meant that he had to commute to work each school day, and the round trip between Waimea and the Wahiawa plantation camp where he lived was about twenty miles. Because he had access to a car, he transported students from the plantation camp to school with him. As Yoshiharu recounted his daily activities to Naoko in his letters, he was also preparing her for life on Kauai.

Eleele, Kauai
September 16, 1942

Dear Naoko,

I'll be teaching two classes of Shop metal and one class of Mechanical Drawing. These things are right down my alley so it's okay with me.

Right now I'm not certain of transportation. My brother sold his car so I don't know whether I'll drive one to school. We have a car but it eats so much gas that it not worth driving also tell Doris I may not be able to take her to Kilauea because I can't use our car for that long drive. I was expecting to use my brother's. She can stay at my house over night or so with my sister if she wants to.

I'm thinking of you quite a lot. I miss you but. I guess I can't do anything about it.

Solong for now—Periods
Yoshiharu

Eleele, Kauai
September 20, 1942

Dear Naoko,

These last few weeks the army has been clamping down on cleaning up the plantation camps. So the last few days and today I've been cleaning up the yard. We can't put anything under the house so that had to be cleared and clean. Imagine, 20 year's collection of junks and dust. Along with cleaning up there is a regulation that wood cannot be piled on the ground it must be two feet above the ground. I had quite a bit of lumber. So today I had to make a rack to pile them on. This was a real job. No "play stuff" like cleaning window.

Yesterday I went to Makaweli to visit the girl I told you was getting married the Friday before I came home. She was the same old girl that I knew in High School. She went back to town today. We went there about 1:30 P.M. but she wasn't home. Since the other two fellows with me were my high school classmate and she was my "Old Flame" I mean Etsuko Hayashi.[3] We thought we'd visit her to kill time. I wanted to see her since I didn't since last summer. Reason—not because I'm going back to her but to see how I'd feel. Well I felt very much like myself visiting any other girl. I've often wondered how I'd feel if I did come home to Kauai. So it's you as I've always told you. You're different. She has always been my girlfriend from the time I began to know her in High School. Well, many people here think she still is but they'll catch on after a while.

At church today 5:00 P.M. I saw her don't worry—Believe me—There was a social after church but I didn't go since there were only about 5 men civilians. The rest of them were women and army guys. The army preacher gave a short sermon. Instead of Reverend Yamada. His sermon was based on the hymn "We've a story to tell to the nation."[4]

I showed my mother your picture and receive no comments. This is a good sign because my folks never say much when they agree. But if they don't like it the'll let you know about it.

So solong and many periods,

Yoshiharu

The toll of war and the lack of social activities on Kauai provided Yoshiharu an opportunity to demonstrate the skills he had learned and refined while studying industrial arts at the Stout Institute. When he and Naoko first began their relationship, he promised to make her a tray and a lamp. As they moved toward marriage, he explained that he would build much of their household furniture. Although he did not finish that task immediately, he did build the furniture that the family needed throughout their lifetime. He also made other handy machinery, such as a chicken coop that slanted to instantly separate and collect eggs, and an apparatus to crack macadamia nutshells. His other crafts included ceramic pottery and gardening. As he and Naoko became more familiar with each other and prepared for their life together, he detailed his expectations of married life.

He also made clear his understanding of proper gender roles. His duties as the husband, he asserted, would be to fix the house, and Naoko's job, as the wife, would be to clean it. He expected her to be the cook, but he had already indicated that he had some skill in the kitchen. Having lived on his own in Wisconsin (where he learned to eat cheese on his apple pie and hang bottles of milk outside his window to keep them cold) and in a male dorm at the YMCA, Yoshiharu had picked up a bachelor's survival skills. He also addressed his beliefs about proper interaction between men and women. Living on Kauai provided for less socializing than did Honolulu, but he still attended dances, went to movies, and flirted with women. He cautioned Naoko on proper behavior, whether the situation was her going camping with soldiers, or her former boyfriend trying to rekindle their relationship. Yoshiharu knew of the temptations that the influx of soldiers brought, and he recognized the baser instincts of men, so he wanted to be sure that his future wife, a schoolteacher in the public eye, behaved appropriately.

ᗡᐯᗡᐯᗡ

Eleele, Kauai
September 28, 1942

Dear Naoko,

Going back to school again. We start at 8:30 and end 2:45. Of course that means I leave home 7:45 to get there by 8:15. I'm driving my old car to school. It's 9 years old so you can imagine. Anyway one can't go fast on the highway now days anyway. There are six other kids riding with me. Everything seems to be fine. Looks like I'm going to like this place except for one thing. And that too will be taken care of before next school year. Then I guess I'll be a contented old school teacher in the country. Until then although I miss you more than everything else (even beer).

Solong and periods again and again
Yoshiharu

Dear Naoko,

I have one more thing I have to do before I can start my carving and that is build a chicken coop. Right now we have twelve laying hens and about six months old ones. These are at present kept about 50 feet from the house. According to regulations I have to move them two hundred feet. Since the land here is so rocky the chicken coop cannot be moved but must be broken carried and rebuilt. So this Saturday and Sunday I'll be making that. Yes, I'll be home doing that and not roaming around Hanapepe or anyplace playing wolf. The idea of you thinking that I have to be watched. So far I didn't do any playing. The nearest to it was going to church. I haven't been swimming, playing tennis nor badminton. Don't worry I'm not getting fat. I'm still the same. I have enough exercise anyway. You know, I've never been this good for a long time. No fooling around, no drinking, very little smoking, go to bed early and get up early, looks like I'm getting ready to be a good husband. By the way you better let me know what the size of your third finger left hand is. Of course, that is if you still want one. Right now I don't know where I'll get it but I'll find one. I hope you don't think I'm kidding or I won't keep my promise.

I think nine months is about as long as I'll stand living without you. After that it will be with you or the army. I prefer the first but maybe the latter can't be helped.

Yoshiharu

Eleele, Kauai
October 5, 1942

Dear Naoko,

Everything in school is progressing very satisfactory as far as I'm concerned. We are short of materials but who isn't. Anyway I think I manage to keep the boys busy and at the same time teach them something.

What you are reading in my letters of my day to day doings, will be the kind of life you'll be living "if" we should get together. I like to work around the house taking care of the lawn—raising vegetables a few chickens and have a shop for creative work. So you see I'll be one that will be constantly improve things around the home and thing that I can do. So things like walks—visit—movies—and just sitting and thinking would fill in the gap for resting and new ideas. New ideas make routine work more interesting. To me to have somebody who will help me and like and understand the things I like to do means half of my life. To me you're inspiration—I don't know why but you make me feel that the things I like to do are really worth while doing. Perhaps I should say you have a way of flattering my ego. And I don't know you're doing it. These things together with the things required of a woman to do you do very well, as far, as I'm concerned. To me these little things or perhaps I should say routine things are most important.

Don't be too brave with men I might take it differently. I'm a jealous guy you know.

Periods,

Yoshiharu

Eleele, Kauai

October 7, 1942

Dear Naoko,

Today I received plans for making airplane models. So I guess we leave our regular course and go ahead with airplanes for a while I guess this won't take very long though, a month at the most. I really don't mind it I hope the students won't. I think we'll manage. We're getting to be pals. I know the'll do most anything I tell them to do. I hope you're students are swell to you. They should be if they know you.

Well, it seems you have men around your place. Anyway that's good. Maybe you find out that there are lots of guys like myself. If you are going to change I'd rather have it now than later. So let your heart take it's course. You'd have probably felt the same toward me as you do for the guy there if you thought you had somebody. When I met you you probably didn't have anyone in mind—so you figured you'll be fair to anyone so even I had a chance. Now maybe you think you're mind and heart is set so you're not giving this guy any chance so you feel irritated when he is around. Well, perhaps I have you wrong. Anyway things like these are your own worry. However, you should see this guy as he is and not how he compares with some one else. Of course don't think I'm flattering myself and saying you think I'm the only kind that you think is any good. There are people who are entirely different from me and be swell guys. They might smoke some other brand of cigarette and still be nice. Ha—. Well, what I'm trying to say is there are many different types of nice people and lots of them are good looking at the same time and furthermore they won't let the draft stop them. I'm not encouraging you to do anything. Perhaps this is my way of covering up jealousy.

So will you make up your mind please. When? It's up to you I don't see you for Christmas and if you still want [an engagement ring] then I can send it. If you don't like that and rather wait. It's okay by me. Well, anyway let me know how you want it. Of course I want reasons too, to know what you're thinking.

Yoshiharu

Eleele, Kauai
October 14, 1942

Dear Naoko,

Today I got a letter from your mother. She writes interestingly and her post script was "Naoko get a kick out of my spelling and English."

Maybe she got a kick from mine too. She also said she didn't think I was lazy, but it seems I wasted a lot of time coming out to 17th Ave. [where the Tsukiyama Family lived]. Also she said that as she often told you "very sensible person can turn nuts (excuse me) when caught by epidemic of high fever." Well, I don't think I waisted any time. I figured I'd rather spend one summer doing nothing by [but] see you than make a hasty decision and regret it all my life. As it is I know for sure. I hope.

Solong for now and periods.

Yoshiharu

As the war effort on Kauai continued, Yoshiharu's letters reveal more of the educational adjustments that the war encouraged. The U.S. Office of Education's Wartime Commission wanted to graduate high school students in three years instead of four, after having them attend for either six days a week or for longer school days. But it also worried that, particularly in rural schools, instructors would quit for better-paying jobs.[5] Leaving the teaching profession (other than through the draft) was not a concern for Yoshiharu, but he did see changes to his teaching schedule. The army had forced the high school boys (over sixteen years old) on Kauai into civilian service, and it required those over fourteen to labor on the plantations in the place of those who left for war duties. The departure of the male students meant that Yoshiharu would have to teach girls instead. As he made that adjustment, he also provided advice to Naoko. "Here is a short lecture on painting for you," he wrote, as he explained to her that girls and housewives "like to paint and do over their furniture quite often," and that they should paint for "beautifying, preservation and for cleanliness." He then went on to describe the proper way to clean painted surfaces and paintbrushes.[6] As his teaching now required him to work with female students, he also took the opportunity to teach his future wife the skills he believed she should know for their life together.

Eleele, Kauai
October 17, 1942

Dear Naoko,

Well, now I've got it clear what to do about the ring. If you think my judgment is good enough here it is. To tell you the truth I don't have any money because we just bought an electric range $320.00. My Sept. pay check went today and so will my Oct's in November. So I guess you'll have to wait. Nov's and Dec's I guess I'll have to use half to pay my income tax in January. I'm not trying to make excuses but it's easier for me if it's later. You say it doesn't make any difference as far as your self goes. It would be nice to have and all the other social advantages (?) probably but if you say you can wait. I guess I'll break my promise. Don't worry I'll make it good if nothing happens until then.

Well, last week was broken up by—fee collecting and vision test. Beginning sometime next week the boys over 16 years of age of Kauai Hi[gh] and Waimea Hi[gh] are going to work full time for the U.S. Army for a period of at least one month and not more than one semester. So next week will be spent for readjustment of my shop schedule again. I'll have the same classes but will have the enrollment cut to almost 50%. I'm not kidding. It's a break for me. Let what may come, come along I don't mind. Anything satisfy me now days except not having you and nothing else will substitute or satisfy.

Periods
Yoshiharu

Eleele, Kauai
October 21, 1942

Dear Naoko,

Something new is coming up in school again. It is possible that we may have school for only four days a week. They are planning to eliminate Friday as a school day [so] that the students may go out in the fields to work since there is such a shortage of plantation workers. As far as I'm concerned this suits me fine. We will make up the extra time by having school one hour longer each day. This means 3:35, however, I still prefer to have a whole day off by putting in an hour extra each day. Anyway this is just a possibility but I hope it materializes.

Yoshiharu

Eleele, Kauai
October 27, 1942

Dear Naoko,

Well, yesterday we started our four day week schedule. We have classes from 8:30 until 3:30 and therefore no school on Friday.

The plantation needs labor so the kids over 14 are going to work for it. The other change effective next Monday. The boys 16 years and over are going to work for the army full time for an indefinite time. This later one cuts my metal class in the morning to 18. My Mechanical Drawing class to 14 and my afternoon Metal class to 21. My 4th period study hall (all boys) is reduced to 5. I guess I'll have to take care of some of the girls because the girls' study hall class has an enrollment of 55.

Well, I read the letter from one dozen roses. Perhaps I don't deserve what he said about me.[7]

Solong periods
Yoshiharu

Eleele, Kauai
November 3, 1942

Dear Naoko,

About what your brother said about it being more difficult for a women to find a good man. I don't know I guess it usually ends up such that a person gets near what he or she is. That is of course if it isn't too hasty.

Sometimes some people don't give anything any consideration. As for me I feel that it's easier for women to get near what they want providing they have a little bit of looks and intelligence because of man's sexual weakness. Even History shows in great men. It sure must occur in the average.

Periods and Solong
Yoshiharu

In these next letters, Yoshiharu demonstrates ideas of loyalty and patriotism, but his letters also reveal the frustration of living under martial law. On Kauai, the Morale Committee and the civilian population were not always on the best terms. The Morale Committee used Rev. Masao Yamada's Hanapepe parsonage as its headquarters. Although the men in charge of the Morale Committee seemed to have had good intentions, particularly to ease the fear of alien Japanese, they were not always popular. Charles Ishii, the chairman of the Morale Committee in 1943, argued that the Japanese community should be grateful for the way the United States had treated them, that the local Japanese were "taking life too easily," and that they "hardly realize[d] that there [was] a war on at all."[8] Teachers had the responsibility of carrying out the Morale Committee's mission, and some shunned the work. But a teacher who stood in opposition to the committee risked public censure, reproach, and even the loss of a job.[9] Ishii blamed Miss Hundley, the supervising principal, for the lack of help from the teachers, as they "hid" behind her and avoided their responsibilities.[10] Another interviewee on Kauai, listed as Captain Fallon, claimed that Miss Hundley "has hated anything connected with the Japanese since the war," that she "didn't want anything to do with . . . the morale committee," and that she scared the Japanese teachers away from the program.[11] On the other hand, at least one person held a negative opinion of Yamada. She wrote that she suspected that his secretary did all of the real work, and she wanted to know where the money came from to pay his secretary's salary.[12]

As Yoshiharu Ogata felt forced to volunteer for the Morale Committee, he expressed his dislike and disrespect for Yamada. He and others complained that they were tired of the monotony of doing the same work every Sunday. He also admitted laziness, and in fact, one of the biggest complaints from the Morale Committee was that too many young Japanese men liked to "loaf around." The Morale Committee claimed that its "sole interest" was in helping out the local Japanese and "our country" in the war effort, but Japanese Americans and other locals criticized the committee as being "stooges" for the FBI and the army.[13] Despite their complaints, the civilians continued to participate.

Yoshiharu left room to question his dedication to the war effort, but he made clear his understanding of familial obligations. He worried that Naoko's family did not approve of him. He was certainly a different kind of suitor than her previous courters—both because he was from Kauai, and because he had grown up in a sugar plantation camp. He also took Naoko's advice to inform his parents of the seriousness of their relationship. He explained how hard it was to discuss "this kind of stuff" with them because of his upbringing, and he also worried that he was indebted to his family for sending him to college.[14] He hoped to balance his desire to fulfill the wishes of his fiancée with his ingrained sense of duty to his parents.

Eleele, Kauai
November 7, 1942

Dear Naoko,

Well, two days of our second three days week end is over. On Friday, I have to go to Rev. Yamada's place to help fool around with the Morale Committee stuff. This I'm doing on request of the principal because we teachers do not want to be criticized. Meaning of course that in a small place like this the public would think we let the kids off on Friday so that they work and we play an extra day. The women teachers are supposed to be helping with the red cross.

You know sometimes your mother makes me think that she doesn't care especially to have you going with me. I sometimes interpret that "If you'll be happy with him that's all that matters." as a last resort phrase. Maybe it's because she can't change your mind that she says that. In other words she might be saying that after thinking with all the other good prospects that you had and can have if you still want me. Maybe I'm wrong but think it through. I'm not saying this and holding anything against your mother. It's just that I think it's fair for me to let you think about satisfying your parents since I bring mine in when it comes to my end of it. And further more as I said before no one is good enough to a mother's son or daughter.

Periods
Yoshiharu

Eleele, Kauai
November 17, 1942

Dear Naoko,

Well, as I told you before many people that know me automatically [attached] Etsuko's name to mine. This as I've told you is because of what happened in High School. This was not anything more than any boy and girl in any high school in any town. After high school I left I wrote to her while I was on the mainland. Well, as I said we decided not to be serious—and remain just friends. After I came back in September I saw her once as I told you in one of my previous letters when two other guys and I went to visit another friend. Other than this I bump into her off and on because this is a small place and anyone expect to see someone else once in a while. Now that I have to help with the Morale

Committee at Reverend's Yamada home I see her there some times but am to her as I am to any other girls. Well, that is that for what goes on in me concerning her. I told you just about what people would be saying around here. As far as you're concerned I have nothing to hide. I know I haven't played "rat." There was a little over lap when I was about to quit her and when I first knew you but then you and I weren't any[thing] too definite.

Well, about Christmas you do as you please. If you think people will talk you can stay clear. I'm actually flattered that people are so concerned about who I go around with. As I've always said you've got a mind of your own so do what you think best. If you won't die because you don't see me for a length of time neither will I. As for my folks. They won't believe me if I told them that I had a girl and was serious. The only time they'll believe it is when they hear it from someone else or see actually. Just like this Hayashi girl they heard it was serious—I told them it wasn't and they wouldn't believe me until I came home and stayed home every day.

Here's one more thing concerning about the Hayashi girl. Even the Reverend Yamada think we were serious. He used to kid me about it. Every time I told him it wasn't he'd kid me more because he though[t] I was trying to deny it.

However last week he finally began to hit the right note when he said "how come are you giving up with the local girls?" I told him you don't know me very well do you?

Solong
Yoshiharu

<hr style="width:15%"/>

As the men did their military and civil duty, women played their own role as patriots. By the end of 1942, the Kauai Morale Committee had a Women's Auxiliary that held socials and provided sex education. It told girls to "uphold the American standard of womanhood," but the committee report did not go into detail about what that meant.[15] Adults became aware of an increased problem related to "sex morality." The influx of a large number of soldiers, combined with local girls who were either "fast" or acting as "patriots," led to unwed mothers. Even if the men had wanted to marry local girls, they would have faced a challenge. Wartime marriages of soldiers required the approval of the army commander, who automatically denied them if the spouse was an enemy alien, a person of doubtful loyalty to the United States, a prostitute, or anyone who was "obviously unsuited." One War Department memo succinctly stated that a marriage between different races was not valid, and another stated that the men were not allowed to marry women of "Asiatic descent."[16]

For Japanese American men and women, their ideas of propriety became even more complex as they stood at the intersection of shunned traditional Japanese culture and increased mainstream American culture. Japanese American women learned that they should be "strong and be a fighter," that they should be "a woman of the world!"[17] Etiquette columns told men not to walk down the street with a girl on each arm, "like a gigolo," and that excessive gum chewing was unattractive. Men heard that they should avoid sprawling on a couch and honking the car horn (an appropriate behavior would be to go to the door instead). Japanese American women, like many Caucasian women of the time, received mixed messages. They should avoid telling white lies, be good sports, and conceal their intelligence.[18] Much of this advice could have benefited young men and women of the time regardless of their ethnic background, but Japanese Americans also faced the burden of traditional Japanese culture, as Yoshiharu's letters show.

Eleele, Kauai
November 24, 1942

Dear Naoko,
Your letter about me asking my parents. Well, this much they know—that I have somebody definite. Other than that I don't think they know

anything more. However, they might soon the way some things get around. Of course, this I'm saying only after what you told me. I'll tell you why again—the reason I don't ask my parents. First, because it is very difficult for me to discuss this kind of stuff with them. This you will never see how difficult [it is] because you never did experience it and never will because of your bringing up. As I told you before you are fortunate you have parents as they are. I know you'll say you see why, but yet you don't see why it should be so difficult. It is——.

Another thing is, if I should start stepping out on my own life by getting married. I think that the'll think that it isn't quite fair. This because not what they (my parents) spent on me but what my brothers helped. I know that according to what's right—There isn't anything wrong if I should go out on my own. Yet, somehow it bothers me to think that I'll do what I want when I want after I gained something on someone else's expense. If it's only my parents it's different. It is more or less a duty for parents to see that their sons and daughters get ahead in the best way they can. What they get in return is depended upon how they brought up their child. In other words the test of their latter half of their life.

Well, as far as they go. I'm willing to do what I can when my father isn't able to do any more work to be self supporting. As far as security— it's all tied up in us—their children. I don't think they co[u]ld have done otherwise. Of course they could have deprived us of a lot of things and saved no doubt. Lot of families saved with less income.

Well, you'll probably think why worry about my brother. Perhaps I shouldn't. If he doesn't want to get married that's his business. Well, it is. Yet if I should get married and if my father should stop working. Naturally they won't turn to me as far as it goes they won't turn to anyone. They'll accept help only from unmarried children of their own. Well, if we got married I know we'll be in a pretty good position to help either parents if there should be a need of it. And if they won't take any help then from me who would be the most logical one to get from it'll hurt me more than if I spent some time thinking about the whole thing. You don't know my folks. Stuff like this has been drilled into us for a long time. I'll admit I got the least of it. This is one reason why my brother is working in town. He never told me but I know it. He stuck around long enough and tried to be what my folks want him to be. Well, I stick around and be good only as long as it's a fifty-fifty bargain. In other words they're going to okay some of my doings if I'm going to suit them—I haven't asked for anything yet. It isn't time yet. But when I do I know the'll come through with it. The'll find out that I'm grown up and that I think too. If you should have the slightest idea that this is an excuse for me to say I don't want you you're all wet. Of course, I don't intend to make you wait forever—But what I think is the reasonable time is what I've told you before providing nothing else interferes. Don't worry, I won't make it last minute stuff. They'll have enough time to think. They won't need much time to think.

In the meantime if this doesn't suit you well, I can't do any better. This is the way I do these things. If I'm not up to your expectations maybe you did make a mistake. Maybe you don't know me very well.

If you think I'm making promises and not keeping them, I'll even make a down payment and get you a ring—if you say it. If you want it in a Via-air mail—$10 down and $5 every month—style of engagement ring I'll get it.

I don't care what people say about my past. I'm not ashamed of it. I don't have a guilty conscious or anything. Even if no one else knows the truth about the who[le] thing the two people involved knows it. Etsuko does and I do. I didn't ditch her nor did she. We just came to an understanding. We know it so what people say doesn't matter. Furthermore I don't think she'll be hurt. She knows what's what. If anybody tries to sympathize with her she'll stick up and tell the truth. Not because I've got anything over her but because she's that kind.

Periods

Yoshiharu

Yoshiharu's relationship with his family members may have demonstrated traditional Japanese values, but his friendships proved his Americanization. He played cards, drank highballs, and reminisced about college with both men and women. He celebrated Thanksgiving and went to the movies. One movie that he mentioned was *It Happened at Flatbush*, asserting, "It was fun for me the typical Brooklyn fan the show brought out."[19] He also continued to use popular culture to make references to their relationship. For instance, he reminded Naoko that he had seen the movie *Lydia*, in which a woman reminisced about her romantic interludes and realized that they were not as ideal as she had remembered.[20] He noted that he did not care to see a movie unless he was with her, and the mention of this particular movie was a subtle way for him to reassure himself that Naoko was still committed to him. His discussion of the ideal versus the reality of relationships could give her a chance to confirm her feelings for him. In another instance, he detailed a *Good Housekeeping* article entitled "Miss Laurie Will Be Late Tonight." Writing that he liked the ending of the story, he added, "Especially the last sentence and it goes like this 'I was thinking how you could lose a ring, a locket, or a picture, But I couldn't lose the memory of Miss Laurie. I would carry it with me wherever I went, because it was inside me, in my mind and heart, and I could never—never lose it—even if I died.'[21] I'm quite sure you agree with it. I do. I always feel that way about you."[22] Popular culture also helped Yoshiharu broach the topic of sex with Naoko. After summarizing an article entitled "Do You Remember" for her, he used it to explain that men could be tempted with sex outside of marriage and even though they might fight against temptations, it was the women's responsibility to satisfy their husbands.[23] The army, he believed, put men in a situation that prompted more sexual freedom, and he did not want to jeopardize his loyalty to Naoko.

Yoshiharu continued to avoid the draft, often asserting that he could make a better impact in the war effort by continuing his work as a shop teacher. His letters regarding the model plane building do not convey great patriotic fervor, but perhaps he felt as though he was doing his duty. His sentiment was not an uncommon one. Although the idea of arming Japanese Americans and conscripting them into service gained popularity, and "virtually every physically fit man between the ages of eighteen and twenty-six had been inducted into the army,"[24] some Japanese Americans claimed loyalty to the United States but would not enlist, as they were "not going to be suckers." These men believed that society would treat them poorly and consider them "as merely Japanese after the war," so there was "no use" in offering their service. The men said they would provide military service if drafted, but they would not enlist.[25] Some men who evaded the draft or took deferments faced being treated as "wimps,"[26] but in his writings, Yoshiharu never said or hinted that he had been treated that way. Like many other men who did not serve in the military but still supported the war effort by working in war-related jobs,[27] Yoshiharu continued to be both a public servant and a volunteer.

⚬⚬⚬

Eleele, Kauai

November 27, 1942

Hi–

Well, I don't know if you'd feel any happier but I thought (keeping up with the world situation) I'd open a second front and I did. Meaning what? Do you remember what you wrote in the last letter about telling my folks and make it soon and not a last minute stuff. Well, I hope you didn't think by the last letter that I just read your letter and don't consider your opinion. I told you I consider other people's opinion good or bad. My other answer to your letter, I suppose, made you think I'm stubborn and won't even listen right or wrong. Well, if that was the case your wrong.

I wrote a letter to my brother. You remember me mentioning my brother in the other letter and how my parents would bring him in and how I brought him in as a point for consideration. Well, I figured that if I told my folks first and they said what would he think about it I would be stuck. I don't know right now whether he knows that I've been going around with you—so I let him know and asked him to say what ever he pleases. I told him if he cared to find out about your family's background go ahead and let me know. Also that I know you're not perfect but that every thing seem okay to me and all in all that I think I'm the luckiest one (I am!). Of course, I also told him what your father and everyone else was doing.

Well, if I know him he'll tell me he'll rely on my own judgment and never give it much thought. But the main thing is when I tell my folks I can speak for him also and every one will be considered.

So please don't think I care less now. In fact I care more.

Another thing tomorrow is your birthday—This will be late but Happy Birthday. Feel older—From Tomorrow you shall be considered and old maid or was it 27? Well, don't let that bother you if anyone should say that tell em' you got me just where you want me and I'm coming heart—mind—body and soul.

Solong and periods
Yoshiharu

As Naoko and Yoshiharu developed their relationship as an engaged couple, ideas of propriety and of premarital and extramarital sex came into play. During the war, an unprecedented number of females entered the labor force, as good pay and patriotic sentiment lured them into wage-earning jobs.[28] But the changes in politics and the economy led to a change in morality as well. One contemporary textbook explained, "When women work, earn, and spend as much as men do, they are going to ask for equal rights with men. But the right to behave like a man meant [sic] also the right to misbehave as he does. The decay of established moralities came about as a by-product."[29] Morality had faced a challenge in the 1920s as the New Woman expressed herself sexually, and the high unemployment rate and low wages during the Great Depression had made doctors' visits and treatments an unaffordable luxury, increasing the spread of infectious diseases.[30] Nevertheless, by 1940, the market for female contraception was four times that of 1935.[31] This, combined with the influx of men and the looming possibility of death, set the stage for rampant sexual activity during the war.

The ideal woman during World War II made guns to win the war and was also supposed to be "a vision of love and beauty" that men would find when they returned from the war.[32] Society told her to stay "pure" for returning veterans, and the military told men to avoid single women, whom it viewed as responsible for spreading diseases. At the same time, though, women's increased economic and geographic freedom, compounded by their wanting "to please a member of the armed forces," whether by dancing with the men at USO events or by sitting next to them at church, made extramarital sex a greater temptation.[33] Yoshiharu was not a returning veteran, nor did he hope to be a soldier going off to war. But he was aware of the loosened morals that the war facilitated. He made clear in his letters that he hoped to not hurt his fiancée, but admitted that the circumstances of war could not be ignored.

During the war, the army had the challenge of both curbing its soldiers' desires and treating their ailments. Of each 1,000 men in the U.S. Army in 1940, 42.5 had a venereal disease. The army attempted to combat this trend with distractions such as athletic events and movies and with warnings about sexually transmitted diseases. Yet, to a man risking death by heading off to the front lines, gonorrhea seemed as inconsequential as the common cold. The army's prophylaxis program included a kit with three condoms for ten cents, and the slogan "If you can't say no, take a pro." A military study noted that 53 to 63 percent of all soldiers engaged in sex during the war, a proportion that included 80 percent of unmarried men and 50 percent of married men. The May Act of 1941 declared "vice activities" near military installations a federal offense. In 1943 the discovery that penicillin could be used to treat syphilis and gonorrhea led to wider availability of the treatment by the next year. Yet, as immoral as many felt the situation was, doctors still recommended prostitution as "an outlet for uncontrolled and uncontrollable sexual drives," considering it a better option than homosexuality, seduction, or rape.[34]

The bulk of the immoral activity in the Territory of Hawaii occurred on the island of Oahu, particularly in Honolulu. One war worker reported that Honolulu was one of the "dirtiest" towns and that the people there had "disgusting" morals. This could have been due in part to the large increase in population. During the war, the civilian population on Oahu grew by ninety thousand people, many of whom were defense workers from the mainland. Locals saw the newcomers in lines for the theaters, bars, and brothels and observed them speaking obscenities, drinking too much, and chasing women. Honolulu's population had allowed for the development of a vice district since the late nineteenth century, with both plantation workers and navy personnel as patrons. But with the large influx of men during the war, a vice district unlike anywhere else in the islands arose in Honolulu.[35] Legal houses of prostitution did not close until 1944.[36]

The servicemen did not limit their recreational activities to the vice districts, however. The USO hosted hundreds of events by the fall of 1942. Even the *Los Angeles Times* commented, "The paramount problem in the islands today is the entertainment of the armed forces and the vast number of civilian defense workers."[37] Social and romantic liaisons during wartime could be fleeting, but that was not always the case. A *Time Magazine* article noted, "U.S. girls, never really convinced by the live-alone-and-like-it books, seemed to have decided that a soldier-husband for a few days was better than no husband at all." In 1941, marriages in the United States increased by 15 percent, and more couples married in December than in June. The article also predicted that at least one-third of the marriages in 1942 would be to soldiers. Wedding ring sales increased by 300 percent, and bridal gown sales went up 250 percent.[38] Although neither Yoshiharu nor Naoko a lived in Honolulu for the entirety of the war or joined the military, they felt the wide-reaching impacts of the changes that came with the war.

⚜️

Eleele, Kauai
November 29, 1942

Dear Naoko,

There is another good one from "Do You Remember." Read the story. It tells how men could differ from women. I believe it the way the story goes. Only this guy is fortunate as in most story to see it and check himself before he is too late. That is why as I've told you often if I'm to join the army I'm going to skip the whole thing. It takes plenty to feel and act like the guy in the story if one is to be going out to the front. There is one line there that I like especially to explain men's behavior. "Women never make a distinction between temptation and sin." Well I wouldn't put it so strongly, but girls who are faithful to their husband won't make the distinction of temptation and sin when it comes to sexual satisfaction. Decent women can't see it that way. But for men it's different. Most men can make the distinction and to them it is a temptation and not a sin. Of course in the eyes of the public it is a sin to them too but in their own kind of crowd it isn't. Because every normal male has that temptation. And this is something. An ordinary guy wouldn't stop to think whether it is a sin or a temptation. If he can satisfy him self and get away with it, well and good. If he is one that stops and considers he can hold out until he is married or until he is pretty sure anyway. It takes plenty however to live a life with a wife and then try to live alone fighting down the temptation. I believe this. You might say that it is the same with women—I don't agree—If it were—there would be just as many women chasing men as visa versa and not for security either. I know there are many women after men but it's there instinct for family and security rather than for sexual satisfaction. There are exceptions no doubt but in a nutshell, there are more men out for mere satisfaction rather than for life long companionship then women. You still don't agree with me.

The kind of women that can make the distinction between temptation and sin, referring to what I'm talking about, and practice it would be one of those public "punch boards." They may as well hang up a sign and go into business. There are some that can make the distinction for themselves and men and not carry it through. These understand but they would if it concerned themselves or their husbands. It's alright if it's somebody else. They'll pass it on by saying I don't blame him or it's none of my business. Don't you believe me? You—I would put you in the last case. If you knew that I did—that is if we were married and I was away you would forgive but it would hurt and I don't think you should be hurt that way. You deserve me genuine from the beginning to the end. All things being normal I think I can be to you but right now it isn't. Opportunity in the army is too much for most guy's temptation. I may not be able to stand it myself.

To a real wife sexual satisfaction goes along with her heart and soul with one man but for men it doesn't work that way. It should according to principles of society and whatever code you may have yet it would be fighting against nature, nature very often wins. It could be harnessed to a certain extent but not completely.

I may as well say it now since I'm on it. Some women can be a perfect wife in all but one respect. They aren't smart enough to satisfy the husband. This is why they go out to other. In many case like these to the man she is the one and only in all respect except one and whose fault is it? It certainly looks like the man's but it isn't. But how many people especially the wife would see it that way.

Well read the story and see if you think it out this way. I hope you see why men usually don't want to get married and leave their wife. If they think anything about the wife they are going to leave behind they won't get married.

You say it's worth it even if I didn't come back. Yes it might be—for five years—ten years maybe but it will wear out.

Well, don't think too much it isn't as bad as all that yet. Thanks to your father for thinking I'm worthy of you.

Solong and periods

Yoshiharu

Eleele, Kauai

December 6, 1942

Dear Naoko,

Thanks, for telling me about my grammar—I know it's bad. One of the things I don't like to do among many other is to reread my own letters. I don't seem to care to do that. So if you see some spelling mistake or wrong words used I hope you don't think I'm actually that dumb. If I try and take the time to read my letters over I know I can make it better. If you insist I will. So say so.

Solong for now and Periods

Yoshiharu

Eleele, Kauai

December 12, 1942

Dear Naoko,

As for your vacation. I'm not the one to tell you what to do but if you want to come to Kauai your welcomed. Since you'll be here for only three or four days I don't think people would see much. As far as it goes you can stay at my house. I'll even buy you ticket. I want you to come in the worst way, but of course it isn't just between you and me. You have your folks to consider so you make up your mind. As far as Kauai goes you won't be in anyone's way or anything.

Thanks for your opinion on the stories. Really if two people could be sure before marriage that for the wife—she won't hold it against the man if he should be different in a men-without-women world if he still feels the same about her and the man can be sure that he won't be any different—that she is the one and only for everything under any circumstances then it would be all right to be married now. But who is sure of this.

If I were to put myself in this situation—I mean supposing we get married. Then I wouldn't act free even in a place where no one would know me. That is what I think now. Of course, what I can't know now and what no one can know before they are married is how will they act after they sampled married life. If you can stand it and say we forget about that part of my life—It's well and good, but everything doesn't work so simply.

Well, what's the sense. Skip it. If I'm not drafted soon I'm not going to wait to much longer that is if you'll still have me then. I think we gave most things enough thought. So when we get together and decide to do something and if we both feel that it is what we want to do we[']ll do it. Okay?

Solong and Periods,
Yoshiharu

⁂

As the couple progressed toward planning for their wedding, they ran into several obstacles. The biggest was that they were on two separate islands, neither of which was where they planned to have their wedding ceremony. Another was that they had not seen each other since the previous summer and were not certain that they would be able to during their Christmas vacation. Naoko planned to return to Honolulu, but Yoshiharu was spending the holidays with his family on Kauai. A third issue revolved around a common theme that they had previously experienced—a conflict between traditional values and popular culture. The couple decided to spend some time together on Kauai during their break. That would allow Yoshiharu's parents to meet Naoko and become more comfortable with her as their future daughter-in-law.

That then led to the problem of where she should stay. Yoshiharu maintained that staying with him and his family would be proper and his parents would act as the chaperones. Naoko believed that it would be more proper for her to stay with her friend Doris. Her parents agreed and allowed her to travel to Kauai, with the understanding that she would be staying with her girlfriend. However, once she got to Kauai, Yoshiharu persisted with his point, and his father thought it would be best if she stayed with them. He felt that the Ogata family should be responsible for her. The couple ultimately decided that it would be more "practical" if she stayed with the Ogata family.[39]

⌁⌁⌁

Eleele, Kauai
December 15, 1942

Dear Naoko,

I guess you're luckier than we are since you are having a ten days Christmas vacation. Ours begin on the 24th at noon and lasts only for the weekend. In other words it is only half day better than our usual week end. However, I'm not complaining because we did have a 10 days vacation last week due to the flood. The Board of Health order the school to be closed because of the water being impure.

I guess you're quite set on going home and staying there. I sure hope you would come to Kauai. Not only to see me but also to see my folks and visa versa. You can stay with Doris or if you want you can stay at my house. Do you think I'm being too forward to ask you to stay at my house? If you could get home by Christmas and be here on Saturday or Sunday it sure would be swell. I'm just suggesting it and not telling you so do as you please. I guess I won't have to tell you how much I want you to come. You don't have to worry about hurting my reputation or anything like that. In fact, it would do me good. It'll wake up the people here who think I still go with Etsuko. Don't worry about hurting her either because I'm quite sure she would like to have her name cleared off mine too. So for the good of her and my folks and myself if you can make it please come.

Of course, if you decide to come you better arrange your passage back to Hawaii before you leave for Kauai. I suppose you'll take all those precautions however I thought I'd mention it.

I renewed my liquor permit and got a bottle mostly for the reason you mentioned (social). I like to have something for people to drink when they come around.

Periods and solong
Yoshiharu

Eleele, Kauai
December 18, 1942

Dear Naoko,
According to your last letter I'm expecting you to come here. Of course what day you'll get here I don't know and I don't expect you to know until you get to Honolulu and get your ticket. That is if you can get it. However, I hope you'll try to come here on Christmas day so that I can be around to get you and furthermore I can have best contact with my relatives on that day. Some of them will be coming to my house and those that won't will be home and not working.

Periods
Yoshiharu

Eleele, Kauai
December 23, 1942

Dear Naoko,
Got your letter today. As for your decision to stay with Doris—Frankly I think it is more correct for you to stay at my house. Don't get me wrong—not because I can do what I please. Socially I think it is permissible and

if you can't find that in Emily Post's book she better put it in. Feeling the way we do and what we expect to do it is alright. Furthermore, I think according to social code, if there is such a thing, parents are supposed to be respectable chaperones and I think so too. One thing I don't like about having you stay with Doris is because people will get the idea that we are trying to keep things away from my parents. I think that if there is anything my folks don't like is getting things second handed concerning their own children. Of course I'm not saying that if you stay at my house there won't be any buzzing. There will, it seems that, that is one thing really hard to avoid.

If you stay at Doris's it will be very inconvenient for me. I have to be going back and forth. One other thing is next week we have classes three days. I get back at 4:30 that leaves exactly you know how much time. Consult Emily Post also if I were you ask your folks. They may have something to say. If I'm wrong and it should be the other way okay, so it will be.

Well, solong hope you can get here soon.

Yoshiharu

5   A Dream for Two

In January of 1943, the United States began another year of war. The war in the Pacific Theater saw great numbers of casualties as the navy and the marines increased their efforts to quell the Japanese expansion throughout the Western and Central Pacific. Also in that year and the next, the Allies improved their efforts in Europe, destroying German factories, railroads, and civilian areas.[1] The Allies took Morocco and Algeria, foreshadowing the Axis defeat in North Africa.[2] Although no additional attacks occurred on U.S. territory, the country underwent a total war effort. The federal government completed construction on the Pentagon in 1943. At the Casablanca Conference, British prime minister Winston Churchill and U.S. president Franklin Roosevelt committed to attaining the unconditional surrender of Germany, and at the Tehran Conference later that year, the United States, Great Britain, and the Soviet Union committed to launching an invasion of Germany by crossing the English Channel and then moving through France.[3] The fighting continued overseas, while Americans at home continued their patriotic duties.

The war took its toll on Japanese Americans on the mainland as well as in Hawaii. They realized that the Constitution of the United States was not protecting them.[4] By the end of 1943, the U.S. Army officially opened the selective service to Japanese Americans, whether they were living outside internment camps or were interned. With the announcement of this new official policy, some Japanese Americans believed that they should refuse to take physicals or even register for the draft until all Japanese Americans were afforded their constitutional rights. In fact, some even asserted that Japanese Americans who did cooperate with the military were in collaboration with the government to deny others their rights.[5] Some mainland detainees encouraged the Nisei not to volunteer.[6] In Hawaii, Japanese Americans were often the last hired and the first fired. When they did find jobs, those jobs were usually not in managerial positions, in territorial or county civil service, or at Pearl Harbor.[7]

Yet, Japanese Americans continued to represent the people of Hawaii and the United States in military service. By late January, the men of the Varsity Victory Volunteers had become an auxiliary branch of the 34th Engineer Regiment at Schofield Barracks and Hawaii's military governor, General Delos Emmons, created a new regiment that allowed these volunteers to demonstrate their heroism and patriotism. They formed the Purple Heart Battalion, the first combat unit in the U.S. Army to be composed exclusively of Japanese Americans from Hawaii. Over 3,000 Nisei volunteered, including more than 1,400 men who had served in the Hawaii Territorial Guard.

The men of the battalion faced numerous challenges that came with being citizens of the United States and sharing a cultural ancestry with the enemy. Ted Tsukiyama, in a letter home to his mother, explained that about 70 percent of the men were in favor of going into combat for their country, but they needed to consult with their parents first. He asserted, "It's the best thing in the world that could happen to us."[8] Some of these men had family members affected by Executive Order 9066, the federal mandate that had placed their families into internment camps, and their feelings of guilt by association motivated them to join the military. The men had had a taste of independence by living away from home as VVV members, and they had already done manual labor to prove their patriotism. According to Ted, they would not be able to continue with their education or to focus on business amid the ongoing war. Instead, they traveled from Honolulu to San Francisco, where they were renamed the

Ted Tsukiyama at Schofield Barracks in 1942. He is wearing his Varsity Victory Volunteers denim work uniform. Photo in author's collection.

100th Infantry Battalion (Separate). In addition, by March 1943, the newly organized 442nd Regimental Combat Team had more than 12,000 Japanese American volunteers among its ranks. The next month, 2,686 volunteers from Hawaii and 1,500 from internment camps traveled to Camp Shelby, Mississippi, for combat training.[9]

The 100th Infantry Battalion included men from rural areas as well as from Honolulu, and they soon gained exposure to the myriad cultures of the South and the military installations there. While in the South, they acquired a greater perspective on racism. They witnessed discrimination against blacks, and they also saw the extent of racism directed toward Japanese Americans who lived on the mainland.[10] Even though the "kotonks" (as Hawaiian locals called the Japanese American mainlanders) had seen their families interned, they still volunteered to risk their lives for the government that denied freedom to their families.[11] The 442nd deployed to Italy on May 1, 1944, and the 100th Infantry Battalion joined them. They battled on the frontlines in Europe, and some men used their language skills to do military intelligence work in Asia and the Pacific.

Yoshiharu Ogata's writing offers a view of Japanese Americans that stands in contrast to the model minority stereotype. He declared his patriotism to the United States and gave no signs of being loyal to Japan. Yet his staunch refusal to join the military contradicts the ideal of Japanese Americans sacrificing all to serve their country. His concerns aligned with traditional Japanese values, primarily the obligation of taking care of his elderly parents. As the only son at home, and one who had deserted his family first to go to college and then for his first job, he now shouldered the responsibility for supplementing his family's income. He understood what his family members had sacrificed to send him to college, and he believed he had a duty to pay them back. He did not state that his attempts to avoid the draft would bring dishonor to his family in any way—rather, he viewed staying at home to support his family as the more honorable option. Again, Yoshiharu's background came into play here. He did not attend the University of Hawaii and participate in its ROTC program. His upbringing on Kauai, in a rural, plantation setting, affected his view of America. His parents were not living the American dream; they were not economically successful, they were not Christian, and they did not speak English as their primary language. They were not mixing with larger society. Thus, Yoshiharu did not feel the same peer pressure to join the military that the "city boys" from Honolulu did. The war was much closer to them, whereas Yoshiharu could live his life with a semblance of normality and still contribute to the war effort.

Yoshiharu was not alone in his decision to avoid joining the army. A *Time Magazine* article, for example, reported that a twenty-five-year-old man had taken Benzedrine sulfate tablets so that he would fail his medical exam and be deferred.[12] Some Japanese Americans simply refused to volunteer or be inducted, at the risk of being looked down upon by some in the Japanese American community or even imprisoned.[13] Yoshiharu did not take drastic measures and, in fact, attempted to do his duty. He wrote of his participation in clearing the beachfronts of brush as a Kiawe Corps member on Kauai and of his volunteer work for the Morale Committee. But he seems to have been most concerned about leaving a wife at home if he went off to war. The threats he would face, ranging from death to infidelity and diseases, all played into his decisions, and he clearly did not want to be drafted and would not volunteer for the army.

⚹⚹⚹

This last set of letters, from January to June of 1943, follows the couple after they had just seen each other over their Christmas vacation. The first letter is dated January 3 and continues the couple's story after Naoko had visited the Ogata family on Kauai. By the time that letter was written, she and Yoshiharu were officially engaged and were in the midst of planning their wedding, which they intended to have in Honolulu. Yoshiharu was to travel from Kauai to Oahu when the spring semester ended, and Naoko expected to leave Olaa and her teaching position there. She would then move back to her family's home in Honolulu until she married.

A necessary editorial note is that Yoshiharu's letters are dated 1942, not 1943, for months into the year. The transcribed versions that follow simply say 1943, because retaining the discrepancy would have been confusing. The reason for the incorrect dating is unknown, but the corresponding information, as well as his location, indicates that the year was 1943. Naoko's letters do not resume in this volume until February 4, and at that point they provide a complete correspondence. The letters follow the lives of Yoshiharu and Naoko as a young engaged couple, but Yoshiharu remained on Kauai and Naoko on the Big Island of Hawaii. She continued to do her duty as a schoolteacher, educating her students and entertaining servicemen. Yet propriety and image became concerns for the couple, primarily for Yoshiharu, as Naoko's activities with the servicemen could have been construed as improper to some, including her fiancé. The two worked through their differences and planned their "American style" wedding as they contended with traditional Japanese ideals, as well as with being islands apart.

The couple's discussions of their wedding preparations reveal contradictions between Naoko's Americanized, urban exposure and Yoshiharu's more traditionally Japanese, small-town (or plantation camp), family-oriented background. Yoshiharu made clear that he was not interested in the details of planning the wedding, but he was concerned about doing what was proper according to his family and of conforming to the social etiquette that he believed the Tsukiyamas demanded. Yoshiharu's family (he mainly mentioned his brother-in-law Yoshio Inouye) wanted to carry out the proper duties of the groom, including having a family representative and giving gifts to the bride's family. His father did not want the new family member to move into the house in July, which was considered the month of the dead.[14] Naoko's family, on the other hand, dove into wedding preparations, discussing ushers and bridesmaids, and proper dresses and suits, as well as bridals showers and honeymoon plans.

Many of the ideals when it came to wedding preparations may have come from the experiences of the couple's parents. The Ogata family had preserved fewer documents regarding its history. Zenzo Ogata, Yoshiharu's father, was born in 1883 in Fukuoka, Japan. Yoshiharu's mother, whose name was Jyo, according to family records, once testified that her maiden name was Ojo Ohashi. In testimony to the Territory of Hawaii, she said that she had been born in the Aichi Prefecture of Japan and had married Moichi Inouye, but later she married Zenzo Ogata after her Inouye deserted her soon after their arrival in the islands. Another record states that she testified in 1928 that she had been married only once, to Zenzo Ogata, and had migrated to Hawaii with him in 1899.

Yoshiharu's sister Momoe once explained that Zenzo and Jyo Ogata married in Koloa, Kauai, in 1902, but she also found records in the Miyanojin Village Office (in Fukuoka, Japan) of their marriage in 1911.[15]

Naoko's parents had roots in both Hawaii and Japan. Her maternal grandfather, Kinshiro Kagawa, farmed pineapple in Wahiawa (on Oahu), and his daughter and Naoko's mother, Yoshiko Kagawa, was born in February 1895, in Hiroshima, Japan. At the age of four, Yoshiko and her mother left Japan to join Kinshiro in Hawaii, and they lived in Honolulu above the family's store, which sold Japanese goods and hats. Yoshiko went to English-speaking schools and also attended Christian Sunday schools. At the age of eleven, she went back to Japan to attend a Baptist missionary school and then Ferris Seminary, from which she graduated in 1913. She said that she "became a Christian" after one year in Japan. Returning to Hawaii at age eighteen, she worked at the family's hat store, while her father attempted to make a living at various farming ventures.[16]

Naoko's father, Seinosuke Tsukiyama, had relatives—"the prominent Isoshima merchants"—in Honolulu, where they owned and ran a store called the Gift Box.[17] Needing additional assistance for the store, the Isoshimas requested help and the Tsukiyamas sent Seinosuke from Japan in 1911.[18] He worked at the Isoshimas' main store on King Street in Honolulu, the Isoshima Shoten, which sold Japanese art pieces and hats. Although the store had Japan-themed products, most of the customers were haoles. It helped the business that Seinosuke and most of the Isoshima family could speak English, and the business evolved to attract a wider clientele. Japanese business owners socialized with the white business community as well as with government officials, and by doing so, "Japanese businessmen became an elite of a sort, interacting with *haoles* in many ways that Japanese workers did not."[19]

Tracing the family tree implies that Yoshiko and Seinosuke both claimed the Isoshimas as relatives. Naoko's parents were not related by blood, however, and although their families knew one another, theirs was not a love match. "We were really not in love in a romantic way but had no objection to . . . marriage," Yoshiko recounted in her memoirs.[20] Seinosuke also noted that the families "thought it [the marriage] would be suitable for the future of the Isoshima Shoten business," and since "there was no love affair involved," he "had time to observe the situation with very cool insight." After the family decided that the couple's firstborn son would keep the Kagawa name, the two married in a Christian ceremony at Harris United Methodist Church in Honolulu. Yoshiko's upbringing was a Christian one, and Seinosuke had been baptized at the age of eighteen. When he moved to Hawaii, he brought with him a letter requesting the transfer of his church membership to the Japanese Methodist Episcopal Church at River Street in Honolulu, and he became a member in 1911. The couple were among the founding members of the Harris United Methodist Church (built in 1924).[21] Though they were Issei with strong connections to Japan, their wedding in Hawaii was a Christian one. Their daughter's wedding would be no different.

✿✿✿

Eleele, Kauai

January 3, 1943

Dear Naoko,

Saturday after I left you I went to Lihue and guess what I have to go back again. Can you imagine that. They talk about not traveling and yet they tell you to come over and over. They asked me about myself and whether I wanted to fight the case [of a speeding ticket] or not. That I don't want to do. So the guy told me to come Tuesday morning 8:00 A.M. and to be safe to bring about $20 to buy a bond or something. So it won't be bad, of course, I have to face the court and catch hell probably.[22] So I won't worry about the whole thing.

I hope you write me a long letter about everything [your parents] said—every little thing too. As for my side no comments. That's good because as I told you before "no news" is good news here at my house.

Anyway they told you to come again and my folks don't say those things if they didn't mean it. All the chickens and other things for your folks were brought up by them and not me. They suggested those things to me. All these things put together—things that you noticed but I haven't amounts to that my folks think quite a lot about you.

Yoshiharu

Eleele, Kauai
January 5, 1943

Dear Naoko,

Today I had to go back to Lihue because of the tag as I told you in the last letter. I was fined $15 and all is well. I had to take time off to go there. Mr. Grisworld was nice about the whole thing.[23] He even asked me jokingly how much I was fined when I came back.

You said your father was writing me a letter well I still didn't get it. As soon as I get it I'll discuss the whole matter with my father. In the meantime my brother will have met your folks and his comments can be considered also. When all these are put together things can be acted upon. Well, things will go on more or less the way we planned but as your folks said and also mine did we have to take care of some of the formalities also. Anyway have faith in me. I'll see that everything comes out alright and on time. You don't have to worry—only keep your health and be okay when summer comes.

So long and periods
Yoshiharu

Eleele, Kauai
January 8, 1943

Dear Naoko,

Today a letter came [from my brother Yoshitaka]. The letter which I also read, was very much like the one he wrote to me when I told him I was going with you. Of course, he mentioned meeting your mother and father. He said that he was surprised to hear them speak English so well. Of course, his comments concerning your family were all favorable. Dad told me that this asking him first was a matter of formality but now that it is done and okayed that's that. Since my sister was also here at my house I took out the letter that your father and mother wrote to me and let her read it and explain to dad. Now that dad knows how your parents feel and how everyone else concerned feels he told me okay and go ahead as I see fit. He even asked me since it's "haole" style how about the ring for engagement.[24] Considerate, isn't he? Now that everything is okayed I don't know my next move. What I mean is things before engagement, and announcement of engagement, etc. Do you know what I'm to do next?

Well, he just came into the kitchen and we talked some more about our plans. Perhaps you better keep the first page [of this letter] to yourself for a while because he think that we should let our relatives know before the public. There has already been some backfire. My sister-in-law says that we're keeping things from them. This is because people are telling her and my brother that we are engaged. I guess we aren't yet. Anyway Sunday father is going over to tell them and let them know first handed and that we are going to announce our engagement. Anyway the whole idea is make it as fool proof as possible and leave no point for criticism. Things like these to us may seem a humbug but since my folks have been living in this neighborhood and kind of society it has to be done this way to be proper according to the people here. I guess you understand these things.

Yoshiharu

Eleele, Kauai
January 13, 1943

Dear Naoko,

During the early part of this week I wrote a letter to all my relatives telling them of what to expect. I didn't tell them I was engaged but to[ld] them that I will be very soon. I also wrote to your Mom and Dad telling them that everything is okay and that they could announce the engagement anytime they please.

When I wrote to your folks I also told them that the wedding will be in Honolulu so to do the planning as they see fit. Of course, they'll ask you what you want. Anything is okay with me as long as I don't have to put on more than a suit and if it's private. It seems quite a long ways off but you people can discuss it through your letters. I don't care especially how it's done. What I'm interested in is that we get married.

So long for now and Periods,
Yoshiharu

Eleele, Kauai
January 17, 1943

Dear Naoko,

This morning I didn't go to the Kiawe Corps because my brother-in-law came from Waimea.[25] I had to go over to Eleele to get them since the bus brings them only until there. Sometime last week I let them know of our plans via a letter. So today he came to talk with my folks. He is a particular guy. Only thing he isn't saying much except listen because I told him it was going to be "haole" style. This he doesn't know anything about. For that matter neither do I. Do you know whether there should be anyone else seeing your parents after I ask them. Do I have to get somebody to ask your folks too. The American way I don't think so but if you think otherwise let me know.

So long for now—Periods,
Yoshiharu

Yoshiharu and Naoko quickly learned that their personal lives as a couple were a matter of public discussion. The large Ogata family and their close quarters on Kauai meant that good news traveled quickly and scandalous news traveled even faster. Naoko, having grown up in Honolulu, was an unknown quantity on Kauai. Yoshiharu's classmates and neighbors knew of his relationship with his high school sweetheart, Etsuko Hayashi. Although they were not a couple by the time Yoshiharu left for college, many of their acquaintances were unwilling to accept that. Yoshiharu made clear to his friends that Hayashi knew that they were not a couple, and that she had no problem with that. But his male friends, who saw how hard it was to find a local girlfriend during the war with the influx of military personnel, did not share in Yoshiharu's enthusiasm about finding a fiancée on another island. As he wrote about Hayashi's situation, he provided a glimpse into her family life. The Hayashi family's war experience was not an unusual one for Japanese and Japanese American families on Kauai. Her father was interned, and yet that did not stop her brother from showing his patriotism as an American and serving in the war effort.

⚓⚓⚓

Eleele, Kauai

January 20, 1943

Dear Naoko,

If you think we should be deciding about the date I'll tell you what I'd like but that doesn't mean it will be or it has to be it—I may not be able to get to Honolulu as soon as I want to after school is out. I guess we'll have school until the 11th or somewhere near that date. I'd like it to be in June but maybe it won't be in our power to make it so. If you ask me the sooner the better. Not because I want to get it over with but because I want you for myself. I'm selfish concerning you.

I was talking to my father and he doesn't think that is it very proper for me to go to Honolulu to get married and bring you home and stay there too long. He doesn't object very much to this, but he says that according to custom July is the month for the dead and it would be better if I won't be bringing home an addition to the family then. Don't get me wrong—He is saying that if it can be done outside of the month of July do so. If it has to be July well it can't be helped.

Well so long for now honey and Periods many,
Yoshiharu

Eleele, Kauai
January 24, 1943

Dear Naoko,

On Friday as usual I went to [Reverend] Yamada's to put in my hours. For a change we did something different. He told me that we were going around to deliver some pamphlets. First, we went to Port Allen.[26] There was an Army truck there—we loaded about 15 boxes of pamphlets each box must have weighed two hundred pounds. We delivered these from Kapaa to Waimea. I rode around in the army truck from about 9:30 until 2:30. The Rev., Walter and I sat in the back of the truck and talked most of the time.[27] Well, Walter talked most of the time. Anyway he isn't enjoying Kauai and the girls here. Kauai girls are rather fussy because they get so much attention from the soldiers. You know country girls—a little flattery goes a long ways. Well, many of the soldiers aren't so dumb. They make the most of opportunities. They take opportunities when it knocks. So it goes, most of the girls can't waste time on local boys. This is what he said.

[Reverend Yamada] doesn't like to have me get married to anyone else but Etsuko. You see he knew we were going together and the two families are very friendly. He likes to get his fingers into anybody's business, but I don't ask him for advice nor do I take any from him except a blank yes, yes, to avoid argument. When he asked me about Etsuko and me, he didn't get anything out of me so he finally said she can't get married now anyway with her father interned, one brother in the army, and her mother not working. Well anyway I hope he finds out soon that he can't make me and that he better take me for what I am and not what he hopes to see me.

Well so long and periods–
Yoshiharu

Eleele, Kauai
January 31, 1943

Dear Naoko,

I suppose by now you've heard or read about calling for 1500 volunteers of Japanese Ancestry for combat service. Well, here it is. I don't know what you're thinking about the whole thing but I guess I will have volunteered by next weekend. Put yourself in my place and see what you think.

I don't know exactly whether that's the right thing to do but circumstance make it almost impossible to do otherwise. According to the Morale Committee they don't want to put any pressure on the young people, but to me the fact that we are second generation Japanese and since we've been more or less underdogs so far is pressure enough. In fact I think that's about a great a pressure as anyone can feel. If I get inducted you know what that means as I've told you before. I haven't changed my mind about you nor have I changed my mind about getting married and going away in the army. I know you don't agree with me. Nor would many other girls believe in what I think, but I think that is the best. In the first place even if we wanted to get married we won't have any time for that because of the short time. Well, anyway you better be expecting almost anything.

Well so long for now honey and periods,
Yoshiharu

Eleele, Kauai
February 2, 1943

Dear Naoko,

I don't know whether I'm doing the right thing but I'm going to remain a school teacher. After all I spent four years to prepare myself to be a public servant and why should I throw the whole thing over in 4 days time. The thing is if there are many shop teachers available that is different again. Please keep this to yourself but our principal thinks that our patriotism can be shown at home as well as on the battlefield. He told us that it was almost impossible to replace shop teachers, and that he won't hold anything against us if we didn't sign up. When my employer feels that way its okay with me. Perhaps I'm rationalizing. If you think so and you don't like it convince me otherwise. I've been thinking since last week and I can't decide to quit everything and leave. Take it or leave it. This is me.

One other thing is that pressure around here is getting pretty heavy. The Morale Committee members claim they [are] not using pressure but they're certainly doing it. First they pass out mimeographed forms of intentions of volunteering and ask people to sign it if they wish. But the catch is the committee members know where these slips are and they talk about the ones that signed up so you know who didn't. Of course, this wasn't enough they had to get the official form from the draft board and take it around and let people sign up after mass meetings encouraging people to volunteer. They might call it making it convenient for the ones wishing to volunteer but they certainly make it uncomfortable for people who honestly can't volunteer. This isn't all in my case, Rev. Yamada stopped me on the road and asked me if I signed up. I said no—then he hands me the official form and tells me to sign it and bring it to his house I guess he doesn't know me. I'm no yes-man to nobody. If he doesn't like it he'll know it now.

So long and periods
Yoshiharu

As Yoshiharu deliberated about his situation, Naoko was having some new experiences. World War II introduced a large number of African Americans to Hawaii, and many of the residents of Hawaii met African Americans for the first time. Although blacks had been serving the United States in its war efforts since the American Revolution, segregation still remained a part of life for soldiers. More than thirty thousand black soldiers and defense workers traveled to Hawaii during the war, and they found Hawaii to be much more welcoming than parts of the mainland. No segregated public facilities existed. Some people frowned on interracial socializing between haole servicemen and local girls, and some also had concerns about African American soldiers socializing with local girls. Naoko's family, however, had interacted with blacks even before the war, because Harris United Methodist Church had African American members.

Race played a role in military attitudes and decisions related to sex. Senior officers asserted that African American soldiers should not be placed in the Pacific Theater. They considered Polynesians "delightful people" who were "primitively romantic." Thus, they assumed the women of Hawaii would have sex with any newcomers. Children fathered by white soldiers would create a "very high-class half-caste," the officers believed, but the children of black fathers would make "very undesirable citizens."[28] The military had tried to teach racist ideas to Hawaiians, and local women feared stories of rape, especially when they heard of black soldiers pursuing women in a "rough manner."[29] Naoko later remembered that the haole soldiers also warned local women against interacting with blacks. Socializing had been a large part of life for city girls, but the war introduced new aspects of race relations and cultural ideals.

Naoko saw the impact of the military on several personal levels. Her brother Ted had been awaiting his call for duty since December 7, 1941, when he reported to the University of Hawaii as an ROTC member. Her mother expressed constant concern for "her boys," the men who had volunteered with her son for active duty. Naoko even told her principal that Yoshiharu had considered volunteering, although she knew he was not going to. Naoko played her largest role as a patriot by boosting morale. Yoshiharu never directly stated his opposition to her friendliness, but he did warn her of appropriate behavior and their reputations. Naoko later recalled that she and her friends had "army boyfriends" with whom they attended picnics, went to dances, and participated in recreational activities. It was not uncommon for respectable local girls to date officers, invite them over for dinner, and then give subtle hints to get them to leave once the evening was over.[30] In a moment of reminiscence when she was caught off guard, Naoko flashed back to the past and asserted, "But the only man I ever did kiss was my dear husband." Then she corrected herself. "Oh, no he wasn't," she said.[31] Despite the passage of nearly seventy years, Naoko refused to provide further details, and the conversation ended on that note.

〰〰〰

Olaa, Hawaii
February 4, 1943

Dearest Yoshiharu,

I've been doing a lot of thinking about things in general and you. I don't think I'll ever feel differently toward you come hell or high water, and I mean that. So even if you do volunteer and get accepted, things will be basically the same. When there's a war going on I guess you can't expect to have things come out alright just your own way all the time.

[My] mother seems to be feeling so low about Ted going I can't afford to let down on the morale. She seemed to be pretty upset about it, altho' she said it wouldn't do any good. But you know how mothers are—maybe she was feeling too sure about Ted being near home all the time.[32] She said she'd get over it and I know she will. It seems Rev. Komuro is thinking of volunteering as a chaplain for the boys.[33] I know he'd be doing a lot of good for them, but of course that's up to him. My mother seems to worry about me if you have to go, but I told her I've made up my mind not to make a fuss over something that can't be helped.

Anyway it'll be interesting to see the outcome of all this. Wonder what's going to be left. I told my mother if she doesn't keep an eye on Kazu & Martha they'll be going after the negro battalion next. It seems they've been U.S.O.ing them enough these days anyway. As far as I'm concerned I don't have to worry about what men look like—I'm only interested in one. Even the guys with families are volunteering. How have your brothers been affected? I know in smaller communities the pressure is greater than elsewhere, which is only natural, but people ought to be honest about volunteering when it involves others than themselves. It's a fine idea if it's real, but it gets me disgusted when they make an issue out of it—politics, gossip and all that trash. Men ought to fight for better reasons than that, and I guess it's up to the man what cause he's in there pitching for.

What do you suppose happened today. I recognized Kats Tomita a Hilo boy in the VVV's so I knew he had to come back to say goodbye to his family I knew he would tell me about Ted so I hurried up to him all smiles and [said] 'Well well, when did you get here.'[34] Well I looked up and there was Ted standing there in his plaid shirt, all brown, and laughing. Ted said they all flew up on a specially chartered bomber yesterday, about 20 of them from the Triple V's who lived on this island. They're leaving for Honolulu Sunday. He was lucky to get this free trip and I'm lucky to see him. I'm not looking forward to Sunday tho.' What does your dad say about your volunteering—either plenty or nothing at all, if I know him. Well, until it comes, there's no use talking about what will happen anyway or what won't happen at all.

Love,
Naoko

Olaa, Hawaii

February 6, 1943

Dearest Yoshiharu,

Saturday we stuck around Hilo because there was a public rally for this volunteer stuff in Mooheau Park.[35] My brother had to talk about the Triple V's and the part they played and what they were going to do next. Well his speech was the most sincere and natural sounding of the bunch—even everybody else tho't so. He didn't like to do it, not only because it gave him 'work' to do but mainly because he didn't want to be responsible for anything he said at such a meeting. What he said was good though—it didn't sound at all like he was boasting or making a 'pep talk' for the fellows to sign on the dotted line like one guy did.

Periods and more,

Naoko

Eleele, Kauai

February 8, 1943

Dear Naoko,

By this time I guess you're all cooled off as far as me being inducted goes. I guess anything can happen. I wrote a letter to your mother last night telling her of my decision and also tried to say something because I knew more or less how she felt about Ted. I hope I didn't hurt her. I must confess I'm not so good in doing things like that. Thanks for telling me how you felt regardless of what my decision was. I hope I'm worthy of all your faith and thoughts in me.

I hope you had a nice visit with your brother. It may not sound so good but I don't blame you if you cried when you left him. Of course, you never know what will happen but it seems that he didn't have much choice. If he should be wondering what he's fighting for tell him at the least there is one guy here who will appreciate it. It will be for as long as I can and when that's up I'll be doing it for some other guy also.

Periods

Yoshiharu

Olaa, Hawaii

February 11, 1943

Dearest Yoshiharu,

It was really nice of you to write to my mother and say what you did. I think it meant a lot to her—more than you can imagine. We all think you are deciding right in staying back. Defense begins at home I guess—not only charity.

[The principal] asked me if my brother would get accepted for his volunteering and I said it was quite certain. I knew what she was driving at because next she asked me about my request for transfer. So I told her that's what I came to talk to her about, and of course I had to tell her about your writing me and saying you intended to volunteer. So I told her how you had tho't it over and talked to your principal and that you decided that you could be of better service at home, and I told her your job wasn't an easy one for anybody to fill. She agreed to all I said, then some other teacher came in to see her so I said I'd come in again to continue the discussion.

Naoko

An issue that Yoshiharu and Naoko were thinking about was whether they would be able to work on the same island after they married. The teaching jobs in Honolulu were the most sought-after positions. The DPI expected new teachers to pay their dues on the outer islands before being able to teach in Honolulu.[36] But neither Yoshiharu nor Naoko wanted to work in the city. They planned to live with the Ogata family on Kauai after they married, and Naoko wanted to find a position teaching in Waimea or a nearby town. By this time, the government was worried about a shortage of teachers in rural areas, due to better-paying jobs that were available because of the war.[37] Perhaps because of that concern, Naoko was placed on the transfer list and was ready to move from Olaa to Kauai to continue teaching elementary schoolchildren. By April of 1943, the couple seemed certain that she would find a job on Kauai, and Yoshiharu even wrote of the high turnover rate there.

⬜⬜⬜

Olaa, Hawaii
February 13, 1943

Dearest Yoshiharu,

My mother wrote today too. She said you're calm about things like this volunteer business and seem to be so right along. She said they made quite a fuss at home thinking you might volunteer and they 'directed Ted to have a conference' with me in case. Well she said one worry is gone and she is relieved you decided to stick to your present job. She's back in the groove again because she started asking me again what kind of wedding gown she should look around for. She hopes I'll be back for Easter.

As for men at all the weddings I've seen (most of them through the mirror on the organ) the favorite seems to be white linen suits. What I liked best was one where the men more white flannels and a bluish tone of coat—the two-toned effect seemed less monotonous because the bride wore all white. Of course the men look well in contrasting colors if they're tall enough to wear that type. I think you'll look nice either way because of your height and the 'drape shape.' I guess you'll be asking your brother to be your best man, they usually do or some good friend of yours. Anyway we can hope to get such details settled at Easter, but it won't hurt to be thinking along such lines.

On my rating sheet I did ask for a transfer first choice to Waimea, then Eleele school and the next place I could think of was Makaweli.

Personally, Eleele School is more about my speed so I wouldn't mind if I don't get anywhere near Waimea. What do you think about husband and wife at the same school—there are good and bad points you know. However, I'd rather teacher under a man principal any day. These women—well you know old hens.

Bye now and Period,
Naoko

Eleele, Kauai
February 14, 1943

Dear Naoko,
Well, honey, I haven't forgotten about the ring today I talked to Yamamoto about his jeweler friend in Kapaa and I expect to go there very soon.[38] Not this month because my sister bought a sewing machine. $138.00 Bang went my check. She's working now so I guess it's okay. I hope to be in town for Easter. It begins the third week in April. In other words it's as late as Easter could be. If your folks want to or did announce the engagement it's okay but I guess it won't be exactly complete until I give you the ring. Yamada asked me last week when I was getting married so I told him I didn't know. He also knows I didn't volunteer. He's beginning to know me I think. He better take it and like. If he can't take it it's okay with me.

Well, so long again for a while,
Me, and periods

Olaa, Hawaii
February 17, 1943

Dear You,
Only last Friday I was talking to [the principal] about transferring and about visiting Waimea Hi. I told her Mr. Griswold let me visit the 3rd

grade there, and she knows him and said he's a nice fellow. She even asked me first whether you'd like to come here next year, so I said your folks were old and you had to stay with them, the same reason why you gave up teaching in Honolulu. I said you lived on Kauai, so that's why I was asking for a transfer—otherwise I would certainly ask for reappointment. She said by all means if I was getting married it was the logical thing to do, and I said there wouldn't be any point in our getting married if we couldn't live together. She agreed heartily.

Periods and love,
Naoko

As their wedding grew nearer, Naoko and Yoshiharu recognized that soon they would be married instead of carrying on a long-distance relationship, and they began revealing more about themselves to each other. Although at the beginning of their correspondence they had both proclaimed the importance of being themselves, the reality of spending a lifetime together loomed. Yoshiharu's letters established him as the head of the household, and he continued to chronicle the handiwork that he could do. He also made clear his views about housework. He knew that Naoko would be a working woman, but he believed that she should also be the one responsible for the cooking and cleaning. Being on the island and in the home in which the newlyweds would live, as well as being adapted to the slower pace of life on Kauai, gave Yoshiharu lots of time to ponder his future and inform Naoko of his expectations.

The couple's present situation, though, emphasized their differences. The large military presence in Hawaii made an impact in rural areas as well as on Oahu. Residents of Honolulu came into contact with soldiers and civilian defense workers, and vice districts prospered in the city. Yet, those who lived in rural areas were also affected by the military presence, as civilians and soldiers interacted. Naoko noted a basketball game between the military and the local Surfriders from Honolulu, a team that included Ah Chew Goo and Joe Kaulukukui, two Hawaii Senior League basketball standouts.[39] On Kauai, Yoshiharu attended a dance for which the army band provided the music. He found social activities when he could, but Naoko, as a single woman in a rural area, had a social life filled with new experiences.

Men were not in short supply in town, but as the war wore on, the shortage of goods in the Hawaiian Islands became evident in daily life. The federal government appropriated money for civilian food supplies, and Hawaii residents received imported canned goods, paper products, and even Coca-Cola.[40] Yoshiharu complained about his refurbished tires and hoped that he would be able to requisition new ones. He also had to constantly consider the amount of gas he used. Naoko had no car, so she hitchhiked to the bigger town of Hilo. Although she was not a drinker, Naoko took advantage of liquor laws in Hilo. She complained that what was available was "only 8 yr old stuff" and that twelve-year-old whiskey could be obtained in Hilo, but then added, "Only I don't believe in drinking it myself. Just like a good dress I may like but it fits better on somebody else and I rather see them wear it."[41] She expressed joy in finding tennis balls among the merchandise at the Hilo Drug Store. She thought the price of fifty cents each was high, "almost as bad as golf balls," but she felt that Yoshiharu needed new ones and she could not pass up the opportunity. She also hoped to be able to find badminton shuttlecocks, since as she put it, "Hilo has a lot of crazy stuff."[42]

Naoko adjusted to the shortage of material goods, just as she dealt with the excess of single men. She detailed a night of socializing with the some of the Varsity Victory Volunteers who had a party in Hilo. She and other female schoolteachers stayed the night at a beach house with the men. The teachers and the VVV men "sat around singing all kinds of songs with uke [ukulele] accompaniment," and the women watched as the men drank. In her letter to Yoshiharu, she recounted that some of the men passed out, some sang, and some got "happily drunk." She spent the night on the couch before going fishing with the volunteers the next day. Many of the VVV members there were friends of her brother Ted, and she expected them to leave for Mississippi shortly. Naoko called the party an "all night orgy" but was unrepentant in her detailing of the story.[43] Yoshiharu, likewise, did not react strongly to her confession; he claimed that he did not object and that he trusted her judgment. But he also added that her actions over the weekend were "okay" with him as long as she was not ashamed of it.[44] As young Americans, they had an acceptance of heterosexual socializing shaped by the war and their peers.

※※※

Eleele, Kauai
February 21, 1943

Dear Naoko,
Friday I went to work as usual at the Yamadas' place. Getting monotonous but I can't help it.

Today, Sunday, was a day off as far as cutting Keawe goes. I stayed home and fixed the sink. If you remember it was wooden and dirty. Well now I have the whole thing covered with tin. So it's nice and shinny and even a little too good for the kitchen. I'm thinking about you too you know. Or is it going to be me who's gonna wash the dishes. If you know me you better be prepared to wash. I'll help at times but not regularly. Am I unreasonable?

Well so long for now.
Periods—
Yoshiharu

Olaa, Hawaii
February 21, 1943

Dearest Yoshiharu,
Yesterday we saw two games at the Hilo Armory. The first was better because of the competition, Navy Bluejackets against local Surfriders. The other game featured Ah Choo Goo and Joe K. and team from

Honolulu against army Destroyers. Score 31–41. The Honolulu boys had better plays and Ah Choo Goo ran rings around the 6 ft. Army guys with his tricky playing. All the army boys had was height, but they couldn't get near their own basket and missed most of their long shots.

Periods darling, I love you still. (Putting it mildly)—Naoko

Eleele, Kauai
February 24, 1943

Dear Naoko,

Beginning of the third period [on Monday] we had an assembly. For this we had the army band. They did play the music we wanted so it was swell. By this I mean mostly popular songs. There were couple of band numbers, but I could hear them since they were so few. After this the Elementary classes put on plays about George Washington and Lincoln. Dumb huh? This wasn't much [but] it sure did take time. After all this we had only part of the 4th period left which is study hall for me so it was noon in no time. After that the dance. Did I have a good time and how. I can mix with kids so it was fun.

Yesterday of course was a full day and I don't mind it at all. After school I went to have my tires examined to get tires. I made requisition for 3 tires and 2 tubes. I hope I get them or else you'll have to walk around this summer.

Well so long now.
Yoshiharu

Olaa, Hawaii
February 26, 1943

Dearest Yoshiharu,

There's a lot of guys who don't have anything better to do than watch us dames go by. One of these days I'm going to konk their heads together because when they're together they can be so brave but I bet if I stopped and said boo! they'd all run. We have to practically walk thru them to get to the stores, and they're afraid to say hello till after you pass. Sometimes I wonder what they have in their heads if anything. They all ought to be drafted and be of some use somewhere. Individually I think they're all nice boys, but they just don't have anything better to do.

Naoko

Olaa, Hawaii
February 28, 1943

Dearest Yoshiharu,

Yesterday Yuki and I had to bum a ride to Hilo as we've been doing the past 3 weekends. We get ready about 9:30 after cleaning up our rooms, etc. so all the busses have gone by then. So we sit down in front of a candy store to size up all the cars because we can't ask just anybody, altho' sometimes we feel desperate enough to do so. After we paid our federal income tax (mine set me back \$123)[45] we went to get a [liquor] permit and it was very simple getting one. Yesterday was voting day here so no liquor on sale. If I'm not being too nutty, I'll get you a nice bottle of Haig & Haig and bring it home for Easter—maybe you'd like to celebrate the occasion with your own company then. Anyhow, it's rare stuff in Honolulu and I can give it to somebody else if you've re-formed, but as Yuki says (she knows her liquors from the Home Econ. angle) we might as well grab some while the grabbing is good.

And where was I last night. Still getting around, only I was behaving myself—as usual. Some more VVV boys came to Hilo and they had a party at the same beach house we went to when my brother folks came. Only this time we slept the night there. I went with the Kimuras (Sue Hokada formerly) because her husband was with the VV[V]'s before teaching Aggie out here at Pahoa. Three Hilo girls didn't stay overnite, so the rest of us were all school teachers and each 'practically married.'

'Brat' groans and says "All these wahines have boyfriends—I got no future."[46] They were all nice kids, and I guess our being school teachers and older sure cramped their style. They always had to bring that up, but it didn't stop them from taking down 2 bottles of Haig & Haig and 1 of Black and White. It seems they still sell the stuff here.

Ted says he's working for the Quarter Masters at 70¢ an hour, since they have a month or more yet. They drive GI trucks and load supplies and have fun just like before. Anyway, we came home from that all night orgy before lunch today.

Periods,
Naoko

Olaa, Hawaii
March 3, 1943

Dear You—

The principal says I'm not on her list for next year. I'm on another list where all the transfers are to be considered. It makes me very happy to know even that. However, if I weren't going to Kauai for my very own wants, I'd rather stay here next year than Honolulu even. We have enough fun living here. We go to shows off and on, we go for walks after supper which I have the most fun doing. In contrast to the classroom where I have to pretend to be 'dignified' to some extent, be dressed just so and all that—when I go for these walks I have on my worst pair of shoes, my slacks rolled up, a loose fitting polo shirt and we walk down the middle of the country road. When people are around of course that's different, but we have fun. Like last evening it was pretty late after walking but Shizue wanted a coke so we went into the village and sat on a bench in front of the store in the dark and drank cokes. Nobody's around hardly, then the show is over and about 50 or so soldiers go walking down the street in front of us, and we sit there drinking cokes and it's a[s] safe as church. It would be so different in daylight if we went by and they sat there, life is funny isn't it.

Yours with love,
Naoko

Dear Naoko,

Well, what's eating you lately. I'm surprised that Miss Tsukiyama owns a liquor permit and purchases liquor. I'm only kidding. If you were here I'd get you one too. Last week I bought a Haig and Haig too but it's not the best one. I couldn't get the one with a three cornered bottle. I had to get the cheaper one and be satisfied. I don't know whether you can take it back to Honolulu with you though. You better find out before you try it. Thanks for thinking that I may want to use. I may but it won't be for myself.

What you told me about your weekend is okay with me as long as you're not ashamed of it. All that you mentioned is okay. I don't have any objection. I trust your judgment so don't cramp your style if you think that what you're doing or intend to do is not wrong. You'd know how I feel about things that you do. I'll even tell you if you can fool me and get away with it, it's okay. I know you don't have any such intentions. I tell my kids in school that too. But there is one catch if I find out that they're fooling me than the penalty is double. So they usually behave.

As for what you do and your right and wrong, I feel that you are just as intelligent as I am and your sense of logic is good enough for me to respect. Please don't take this for a hint that I didn't like what you did. If I don't I'll tell you. It's only to let you know in case you still don't know how I may react to such a thing. Get it? I hope so.

This week and I suppose next week I'm taking a chance on the car. If you remember I told you that I had one blow out and expecting one more any day now. Well, that is it. The other [tire] is in bad shape with the side walls cut. I made a requisition for new tires but it won't be acted upon for 2 or three weeks more. In the mean time I have four tires and no spare. Of course I don't worry about it because when it blows up it will and that's that. Although I'm careful in driving, it may be any day. Adds a little excitement.

Solong and periods

Me

Olaa, Hawaii

March 6, 1943

Dearest Yoshiharu,

Thanks for your letter today. I certainly hope your car has the blow-out without any other thing happening to you or anybody else in it. I know you're a careful driver (only got pinched for speeding, over taking another car, etc. etc.) but remember there's only one of you—to me a priceless commodity rather, a necessity. And not only that, you take kids to and from school so please be very careful. I wouldn't want you to be held responsible for anybody else. But I guess I'm not telling you anything you haven't tho't of already so just play safe and I'll feel better.

Easter will be on April 25th, according to Miss Fixit—we get the Advertiser too you know.[47] I'm sure you can stay at our house then, but I'll write home just for formality. I think it's taken for granted you will. Ted has an extra bed in his room now, so it will be quite okay. How good is your driver's license for you to drive in Honolulu? Kazu's car will be at your disposal if you like, but of course we won't need it too much. I don't miss dancing even now, so I won't miss it on Kauai either. If I wanted to dance that much there's one every weekend at Pahoa or here with good army bands. Kazu said she saw & heard Artie Shaw at Civic Auditorium.[48]

Periods and love,
Naoko

✦✦✦

In their letters, Naoko and Yoshiharu still relied on popular culture as a way of expressing their feelings. Naoko copied the lyrics of "There Are Such Things," including the lines "So have a little faith and trust in what tomorrow brings."[49] She also said she liked the song "You'd Be So Nice to Come Home To," written by Cole Porter, and referred to it to tell Yoshiharu how she felt.[50] Yoshiharu, on the other hand, told her to read the *Good Housekeeping* article "The Favorite Suit." This story of a couple describes gender roles in the 1940s. The husband was the bread-winner, but his business was struggling. The wife wanted to help out but could not, because it was the husband's job to comfort and support her. It was also his responsibility to make sure their household stayed on course. Yoshiharu quoted from the article to tell Naoko what he took away from story: "Nothing in the world is so deeply satisfying as to start a good thing and watch it grow."[51] As someone who enjoyed doing handiwork and growing produce in his family garden, Yoshiharu could certainly have meant that literally. But the metaphor also represented the development of the couple's relationship as they headed toward the altar.

Yoshiharu's personal life charged full speed ahead, and his work life was about to present him with a new challenge—teaching classes of only female students. The shortage of male students meant that Yoshiharu's shop classes had dropped off in attendance. His new charge was home mechanics classes for girls. He taught the students about electrical cords and found it amusing that they could not understand the order of nuts and bolts, and he did not expect Naoko to understand those basics either. He also taught his students about iron cords, then gave

Naoko instructions on how to fix her own, including drawing her a picture of the screws and wires. Another lesson he prepared for his students was on sheet metal, which they cut and shaped into cookie cutters. Just as Rosie the Riveter had learned that cutting a piece of metal for an airplane was just like using a pattern to cut the material for dress, the girls at Waimea High School learned practical mechanical skills, but ones that were connected to the domestic duties they expected to do.

⚉⚉⚉

Eleele, Kauai
March 7, 1943

Dear Naoko,

Last week was a hell of a week for me. I seemed to have forgotten everything. On Tuesday I forgot to hand in my plan book. On Wed I forgot to hand in a report on blood typing and on Thursday I forgot to hand in my report on what I intend to do this summer. The worst part of it was that this all happened on one week. Komatsu thinks she has the answer.[52] She thinks it's <u>the</u> girl in my mind. Well she's wrong not that I don't think of you but that if she was right I would have been forgetful since 1941. I guess it was my tires that got me down in spite of me wanting to think that it'll blow up when it will. Every morning I hoped it will last until I get to school. Once I'm there I hope it'll last until I get home so it went for the whole week. If this week I keep on forgetting then something must be wrong with me. On Saturday I got my three new tires and 2 tubes. Now the car is worth more than it did in September. The tires are as good as priceless as far as most of the civilians goes. I'd make good money charging a penny to look at the tires.

Tomorrow, Monday, I'm beginning the class in Home Mechanics for girls. I don't know whether I'm going to like it or not. The'll be surprised if they think I'm not hard boiled. The boys think I am. They do what I tell them and willingly whether I [they] like it or not. They don't try to play tricks either. But girls I don't know. I really don't know how to handle adolescent girls. Grown up ones? Maybe. It remains to be seen.

Solong honey. I love you and Periods,

Me

Eleele, Kauai
March 10, 1943

Dear Naoko,

Well, it seems as though I'm getting in condition for a dance marathon. Today we had in school a surprise dance for the fellows who volunteered. As you may have seen in the papers those on Kauai gets their physical exams today and tomorrow. Since the boys if they pass the physical exam will be inducted right after that won't be coming back to civilian life. As soon as they are examined they go to the camp set up at Hanapepe. So we had to have the dance today. I did go to the dance for a very short while and danced two dances. After all I couldn't disappoint the girls. Oh no that would be too mean.

Well, as I told you before, this week I started my Home Mechanics for Girls class. The girls are pretty good at doing these things. So far they learned the in and out of lamp cord and iron cord. Some switches and fuse. Of course, they do some crazy things. Couple of them tried to put the nut on a bolt before they put the bolt through the hole. You don't get it, I know! Well, you see the bolt has to go through the hole first then the nut is put on the other end. But the girls put the nut on first, and puts it in the hole and tells me that it doesn't hold. Get it. Funny huh?

One other thing was when I had to tell them about the two piece plug. I told them the name but I didn't have the sample of the female plug. Then one "bright" girl says, "You mean the one with the puka?"[53] That was correct but some girls started to laugh, and then there was real laughing. Catch? Dirty minds huh? I couldn't help but laugh. I bet they'll never forget the name either.

So solong and periods

Me

Although Naoko was happy teaching in a rural area and expressed no concern about moving to Kauai, she did have an issue with the principal of Olaa School, a woman named Mrs. Duncan, whom Naoko frequently mentioned in her letters. Female principals were common at the time, but Duncan's actions were not. She did not like anyone of Japanese ancestry and called them "Japs." Even nearly seventy years later, Naoko still recalled the treatment she received from Mrs. Duncan. The principal read their mail before they sent it and would also read their incoming mail. Naoko remembered that one time she called Mrs. Duncan "Old Dragon" in her letter, but the principal could not take any action against her, because she was not supposed to be reading her teachers' mail in the first place. One of the letters in this section details that incident.

As Naoko dealt with her rights being violated by a nosy principal, she nevertheless recognized that she was fortunate in comparison with many other Japanese Americans. In one letter, she mentioned an article that she'd read about the internment camps. This article, a condensed version of one that had appeared in the *Baltimore Sun*, described the financial responsibility borne by the U.S. government for maintaining the Japanese and Japanese Americans in the relocation centers. The costs totaled $50,000 a day, averaging forty-five cents per person. The article pointed out that the once prosperous population had become "wards of the government and guests of the Treasury" because of their potential threat on the West Coast, and yet the Japanese populations in Hawaii and on the East Coast had not been evacuated. The author, J. P. McEvoy, believed that taxpayers should know that the internees included American citizens, college-educated men and women, employable citizens, and able-bodied men of military age. He noted that the living quarters, with barracks, mess halls, and barbed wire, were all provided at the public's expense. McEvoy concluded, "The taxpayer should insist that these Japanese be treated just as though they were Germans or Italians—potential troublemakers should be screened out, the others removed rapidly from the public trough and put back into useful production."[54]

Olaa, Hawaii
March 10, 1943

Dearest You,

You can't tell me nothing ever happens out here. It does, and plenty. When you mentioned having a hell of week in your letter, I had to laugh because the three of us Yuki, Shizue, and I are in one hell of a mess. It all started out when we three wrote a letter together to Mrs. Koga who used to live and teach with us. Well she left for Mississippi before our letter got to her, so the letter was sent back here. Nothing wrong in that is there, except our principal called 3 of us in yesterday and she had the letter opened and showed it to us.

I addressed the envelope and put just Olaa School, Olaa Hawaii for the return address without putting any of our names outside as all of us wrote it. Well, when that letter came back here it seems she opened it and read 7$^1/_2$ pages of it including the P.S. I had written at the end. She said it didn't have any name on the return address and she tho't it might be something important so she opened it. Yuki says that is a Federal offense to read anybody's mail and open it without consent.

Still I didn't get the score until she began to quote almost word for word what we had written—about her.[55] She read every word of it and took it as a personal insult, she couldn't sleep for 2 nights and so on. I told her that if she had called us in Monday (instead of Tuesday) we might have saved her a lot of trouble. Shizue had also said "the school hasn't burned down yet" and she practically called her a saboteur for saying such things.

Well, we finally got her to listen and hear that that was just our way of writing things and she shouldn't take it seriously. Whether she believes us or not is her own fault. I told her maybe she shouldn't have read the letter and she said maybe she shouldn't have, but she saw her name on the first page. That part of it gets me so disgusted really.

Periods and love,
Naoko

Olaa, Hawaii
March 14, 1943

Dear Yoshiharu,

I've just come back from church and cleaned my room. I guess I had my soul cleansed too, because the sermon was pretty appropriate. Mostly about troubles we have to bear. The new chaplain said that we don't have to make martyrs out of ourselves and look for troubles to bear, but since we have to face it sometime or other we can look at what we have to go thru as something that God gave us to strengthen ourselves with. He said it is better to look at our troubles that way than just take them as troubles that only you bear alone and nothing constructive comes of it. He said we would win out in the end—I guess he means a moral victory. In fact every war is fought for some cause like that even this war, but a lot of people take it as a person to person fight. I try to make the kids in my class look at this war as a war against selfishness, greed, etc. and not just to kill somebody because you hate him. Because I hear them say "I hate the Germans" or even when they see some picture of Japanese rice planters they want to shoot 'em down with a machine gun. So I have to stop and ask them why and if they really mean what they said. It's a slow process because they get it in their environment, everybody does. It's good when you come across people who face the issue practically, just like that article on Relocation Centers in the March *Reader's Digest*. Like my principal (there I go) she thinks it's terrible that our government spends thousands to house these Japanese, when people in the South are starving. Yet she said nothing about releasing them and giving them a chance to earn their own living.

It seems you're having your share of dancing and how. I'm glad you enjoy it tho' because I do too, and right now you can take a double share for what I'm not getting. Olaa here has a reputation from both service men and civilians as being one foot in the grave as far as socials go, or any USO-ing whatsoever. Mainly because 'the school' doesn't do much— "it doesn't think hula dancing is moral, and the way these Hawaiian girls chew gum & dance," we've never had our name in anything since the last dance before Xmas. Even that, the army sponsored. They still have their own and invite people who appreciate their dances. We can go as individuals, I guess, not as Olaa School. If we want to go we go to Pahoa, where we can dance as individuals and not representing some institution. I really don't know what the young people in this town do except go to the movies or play pool, and I think the girls get invited to other socials at least I hope so. In short, there's nothing cooking here except on your own stove and at least we can do what we please there.

Love & Periods to you,
Naoko

Eleele, Kauai
March 15, 1943

Dear Naoko,
If you see much more spelling errors than you usually do please forgive me because I was out tonight and had 7 bottles of beer. Tonight we had the Moral Committee meeting at one of the members home and we drank beer.[56] Do you think I'm having beer too often? Beer or no beer I

really think of you. I remember one night last year about this time per-haps a little later that I wrote you that letter telling you how I felt, but didn't think it was very sensible. I mean the one about us quitting. Well, don't fool yourself. I'm not going to write that letter over tonight.

Solong honey and period.

Me

⟋⟍⟋⟍⟋⟍

Concerns about finances also arose for the couple during this period. As was mentioned earlier, the Tsukiyama family never admitted to any kind of financial strain. Their store, which sold Japanese novelties, at-tracted many haoles in Honolulu as customers. Naoko and her sister Kazu had full-time jobs, as did the majority of women in Honolulu.[57] The Ogatas were more self-sufficient, raising chickens, sewing clothes, and growing produce. But it became evident that the Tsukiyamas had money to buy luxuries, whereas Yoshiharu worried about his family's finances. Adding to all of this was the Revenue Act of 1942. Effective as of January 1943, the U.S. Treasury forced employers to withhold a "Victory Tax" from employees. Anyone who earned wages above $624 annually had to forfeit 5 percent of their wages for taxes.[58] To reach the government's goal of covering 46 percent of the war costs through taxes, the Revenue Act also raised income taxes and reduced income tax exemptions.[59] The financial crunch and limited income increased the frugality and creativity of some families.

Cloth was one of the many rationed items during World War II. The Office of Price Administration told the housewives of America to "use the needle-&-thread at home to produce, remake, [and] refurbish family clothing" to help the war effort. The economic situation encouraged women to make clothing at home, as taxes and rising prices made store-bought clothing more expensive. In March 1942, the prices of "piece goods" (lengths of fabric cut from bolts) were 40 to 50 percent higher than in 1941, and the prices of patterns were 20 to 25 percent higher than the prewar prices.[60] Young women noted the difficulties of buying ready-made dresses and shoes, because they were not military priorities.[61] Yoshiharu wrote that his sister was using a new sewing machine to bring in additional income to help support the family. The Tsukiyamas, on the other hand, planned the formal attire for the groom, bridesmaids, and ushers and, of course, the bride's wedding gown. They did not express concerns about the costs of outfitting the bridal party.

Yoshiharu's obligations to his parents reveal the cultural guilt associated with responsibility to one's family. Japanese Americans, particularly the Nisei, were characterized by restraint, endurance of adversity, and fatalism. Parents emphasized education, spiritual values, and a focus on children. Nisei children grew up steeped in the ideals of patriarchy, diligence, and honesty. The possibility of bringing shame to the family, community, and race through one's actions weighed heavily on the Japanese in Hawaii and affected their decisions.[62] Family relations included a responsibility to care for one's parents. Elderly Japanese and Japanese Americans often had a minimal cash income and a chronic lack of necessities, such as clothes, shoes, and household appliances. The experiences Yoshiharu writes about demonstrated that his family fell into this category. He was ingrained with the idea of filial piety, which obligated him to service to his family. Another of his responsibilities was to show deference, reverence, duty, and compliance to elders.[63] Although these ideas came from Japan with the Issei and lessened for the second generation, they still shaped Yoshiharu's life and his actions toward his parents. The family patriarch's power on the plantation was reduced because he had no property to pass down to his heirs,[64] but the wife and children still held subordinate positions to the husband/father and then to the eldest son. Yoshiharu's father worked on the McBryde Sugar Plantation, and his mother toiled as a housewife. His letters show how his income helped subsidize the family.

Dear Naoko,

My General Mechanics class is going along swell. The girls complete a very short unit in Electricity and now on Sheetmetal. They are making cookie cutters. The students promised to bring me some of the first that they make using the cookie cutters. In my 1 and 2 second period class I have some 10 and 11th grade girls. Some smart aleks. Too bad I can't go and give them a good boot. Sometimes the[y] get on my nerve. In the afternoon I have a bunch of 9th graders and they're doing the best. Ninth grade girls are much more matured than boys of that grade and can do a lot more if it isn't heavy work. The cookie cutters the're turning out are better than any that my boys can make. In two hours the fast ones can complete a cookie cutter. Round, diamond, heart, spade, clubs are the most common ones and good too.

Here's one thing I'm telling you about myself. When you get married to me you just marrying me and nothing else. I still have $400 to pay up and expenses that's coming up. So when summer comes and all is done I'll be lucky if I'm on the level. Most likely I'll still be in the red. Don't tell me I didn't tell you. So if you want to change you[r] mind go ahead. I'm laughing so don't swallow it all. Of course, the financial end of it is true. I'm planning to work this summer so I guess we won't starve. We'll also have some clothes to wear I think. My sister's getting $117 including bonus and what nots. I sometimes wonder why I went to school. I guess it's just to say I'm a full fledge teacher. She'll be giving me some dough because I paid for her sewing machine. Our family always was flush and nothing else. When we were kids my father did alright just he alone working. Right now there are three of us working and we're still only on the level. I don't know where the money goes but it goes. I guess I have to get some scotch blood in me.

The AJA's volunteers (so the're called) of Kauai left Monday for Honolulu. There were 150 as you may know. I guess there raising the quota to

70 more. Seems though the Moral Committee of Kauai are really plugging. This doesn't mean me because I'm only a member of a sub sub morale committee. Further more if I think it's none of my business to promote some things I don't do it. This is one of the things—it's voluntary and I'm sticking to what that word means with out any modifications. Evidently, some people have a different meaning of that word than Webster has.

Solong for now
Me

As Yoshiharu had done, Naoko informed her future spouse of her expectations for married life in her letters. She, too, mentioned a magazine article that he should read: "Love Is a Man Trap," a "fun read" from *Woman's Home Companion*. In the story, George and Abby are a young couple who met on vacation and planned to marry quickly and without fanfare because of wartime constraints. They found that society (and her family) did not agree with their rash decision, so they began to delay their plans. As the months passed, George and Abby saw each other in their daily settings (rather than on vacation). They began to bow under the pressure of their friends and family, and each began to have doubts about the other. In the end, they decided to be true to themselves and married with the agreement that they would follow their own paths.[65] Yoshiharu had warned Naoko about his family's dynamics, and she, in turn, warned him of her family's influence. They both realized that their relationship, and thus their marriage, would involve other people. And this article served as a reminder that theirs were the only opinions that really mattered.

Also, just as Yoshiharu had read about her nights socializing with the VVV members, Naoko in return explained to him how she felt about his behavior. Yoshiharu admitted that he had written his March 17 letter after drinking seven bottles of beer. Naoko responded, "If ever the time comes and you have to get anywhere near drunk do it when you don't have to worry about me being around. I don't mind as long as I don't hear about it. Maybe I can laugh about other people being funny in front of other people when they're drunk, but you're different to me." Then, after watching the war movie *Desperate Journey* and reading an unidentified "American mag.," she added, "But one line I remember is this—'You don't know, but when you want someone, substitutes just aren't any good.' I guess nothing can really substitute when there's something you know you want, in anything." She went on to say that with the war going on, they had to be satisfied with what they had and had to wait for better things to come when the war ended.[66]

These letters from this period also indicate the continuing impact of the war effort on the civilians in Hawaii. Friends and neighbors were volunteering for military service. Naoko sewed for the Office of Civilian Defense Hospital and lectured her students on proper behavior and appreciation of the money that the government was spending on their education. She was also concerned about her own status. Her mother wanted to order ready-made furniture for her to bring to the marriage because "it is a custom usually followed."[67] Yoshiharu believed that there would not be enough space in his family's house for Naoko to bring too many items, and he wanted to make the furniture for his new wife. But he warned her that not all of the furniture would be ready, because tools and equipment were in short supply, he did not have a lot of time, and he was "no money man." Naoko responded that she would not mind watching him make the furniture, and that she would even help with the sandpapering.[68]

Yoshiharu's ideas of proper gender roles again are evident in the next set of letters. Yoshiharu wanted to travel to Oahu during his Easter break so that he could buy an engagement ring and present it to his future wife. However, he was not sure that his supervising principal would allow him to leave the island. "If she's humane," he wrote, "I think she'll see my point. But she's a 'Miss' you know so one never can tell." He had made earlier comments about "old maids" and still believed that unmarried women, with no suitors in sight, simply did not understand his plight. He was learning more about females, though, as he worked with the girls in his classes. At first they had told him that "they never handled tools or they don't know anything about it," but by the end of March, he had them taking apart and fixing faucets. "To me, if the girls learn to think a little about simple mechanics at home I think it's good enough," he wrote to Naoko, even as he planned to do the fixing and building around their own house.[69]

⚏⚏⚏

Olaa, Hawaii
March 17, 1943

Dearest,

[The students are] especially maddening this week. Today I gave them a lecture and I put it on thick. I told them the government spends money to educate them in schools to become better citizens, instead of using it all for the Army and Navy. And the soldiers and sailors were all fighting to make this country a better place for us to live in, and then we come to school and waste our time and fool around and think it's a big joke and blah, blah, blah—I bet they thought what's she squawking about. Well some of these kids you can be patient with till you're blue in the face and the only thing you can do is give them a good whack where it hurts. I think they're brains are connected with the seat of their pants, than with their eyes and ears. I always tell them if they were alone in my class they could make all the noise they wanted to and nobody would be bothered, but it doesn't seem to make any difference. Of course there are always some good kids and good days too, but not worth squawking about.

My mother said she was getting towels and such things for me, wherever any were on the market. She wants to know whether she ought to order a bureau or whatever it is you bring along when you get married. She says it's just a custom to have one, but she wanted to know if it would be 'too insulting' to you if she had one made. Or do you plan to make such things? Or will there be room for one. And I don't want to have your family inconvenienced by things like that. I'm even hoping to bring my piano along, after all I got it for myself and besides you haven't heard more than 1 line of "These Are The Things I Love."

We went to the next door cottage to say goodbye to the Tairas.[70] He's leaving with this volunteer group altho' he's been teaching and acting as vice-principal at the high school annex here in Olaa. He has experience as an ROTC officer that's why and is a 2nd Lieut. His wife and 9 weeks old baby will go to Honolulu to stay with in-laws. We're losing a real good guy, everybody likes him, which I think is some record for a guy in his position. One thing I know he treats everybody alike and is nice to everybody without making it seem as though he were trying. If he goes and Rev. Komuro goes too, I know my brother will be in good hands.

Periods
Naoko

Eleele, Kauai
March 20, 1943

Dear Naoko,

As for what your mother is thinking of doing. I really won't say what you should do. But this is it. I'm no magical man so don't expect all my furniture to be made over night. As far as making furniture for my house goes. I intend to sometimes sooner or later but I tell you this they won't all be made before summer. I'm not going to be pig headed and tell you not to bring anything. If what you're bringing doesn't inconvenience other people much it's okay with me. Well, you saw what we have in my house. First place there isn't much to get around here and secondly

I'm no money man. This is what you're walking into so get your mind set for it.

    Solong for now and periods

    Yoshiharu

Olaa, Hawaii

March 21, 1943

Dearest,

As to your financial status my dear, it looks very bad. I think I'll have to call the whole thing off and look for a millionaire. Ouch, think of the income tax. I guess I'll have to stick to you, you'll do, I think. We can teach kids till we're sixty or retire when we feel like it—after all we aren't in the Retirement System just to get rid of some of our monthly salary.[71] Anyhow people shouldn't marry people for what they have, in case you don't know that. I know what you are, so if there is any kick coming you would have had it long before this. Sometimes financial matters come between people because they make it matter more than anything else they both have. You'll see a good dig at this in the picture "Tortilla Flat." Spencer Tracy says "The sky is the best roof to sleep under. You can wake up tomorrow knowing it will still be there."[72] The same goes for my love, it will still be there with every tomorrow. So long for now and periods darling—

    P.S. Miss you.

    Naoko

Eleele, Kauai

March 24, 1943

Dear Naoko,

Today I gave some of the girls several faucets to take apart and study. I didn't tell them where to begin but told them to figure it out. How to

A Dream for Two   185

take it apart and what made the water run or stop. They really figured it all out. They even took the top off and put water in it to see where it started in and came out. Now they can take off a faucet and fix it. They won't forget it as soon as had I told them all that. To me if the girls learn to think a little about simple mechanics at home I think it's good enough accomplishment for a four weeks course. They're all sharpening scissors and kitchen knives now and doing a good job of it.

On Monday I wrote a short note to your brother. I told him to take a good look at people and things that mean much to him because when he's away that's what counts. I said this because memories are pleasant things. If these are strong enough in you than you won't be homesick. To me homesick is a mixed up account of your past life. When you can sort out your memories and remember the individual happenings actually it help you, and you're not homesick even if you may shed some tears over it. If you can sort out your memories then it help you to enjoy what ever is in the new environment by comparison, contrast or similarity.

Well solong for now honey and periods.

Yoshiharu

In Hawaii, the presence of so many servicemen and defense workers brought with it the growth of USOs and of local females becoming morale builders. Defense workers also found entertainment through hula shows, fishing, and tours of Oahu. But the main attraction was the USOs. Fifty-one clubs in the islands served the army and the navy, entertaining 151,433 workers. "Victory girls" dated servicemen, and mothers invited the men into their houses for home-cooked dinners. Most women saw their efforts as morale building or as their patriotic duty, while the men were looking for companionship rather than marriage. Even teachers provided "service to the servicemen" by cooking dinner for them and going to dances sponsored by the USOs.[73] Social patterns of the prewar days no longer existed, and relationships with servicemen were "not scorned with distaste" as they had been before the war. In fact, more servicemen than civilians went to the dances with the local girls.[74] The USO dances gave these "volunteers for victory," as the girls saw themselves, a safe place to "properly channel" their patriotism. Only four girls attended the first dance in Honolulu, but within a week, that number increased to sixty university girls, with their dean along as their chaperone. By 1943, women of various ethnicities, including Japanese Americans, attended the dances. Other USO attractions included libraries, writing rooms, floral arrangement classes, and arts and crafts. Some women from the mainland traveled to Hawaii to volunteer at USOs. A few thousand servicewomen also traveled to Hawaii, but they never had as large a presence as did the servicemen. The unbalanced sex ratio allowed every young, single woman in Hawaii, including Naoko, to be in demand.[75]

Olaa, Hawaii
March 27, 1943

Dearest Yoshiharu,

It must be the organ music but I can sure reminisce about the days when [the days before the war] tonight. Well, you can call it a lifetime of living since that night on the windy hill. We've even gone through a war—that week after Dec. 7th, we went through that. I remember we finally walked as far as the drugstore and had a root beer float shortly after Dec. 7th when so few cars were on the road. And you were going home that Xmas, but you never got to go. Well, what a year it was—so much happened then but I don't think I ever changed my opinion about you.

We saw all the 2nd bunch of volunteers march up the street to the induction ceremony. Waichi Takemoto, Tommy's brother was with them, carrying a uke just like he was going on a picnic.[76] I asked him if he got tired of teaching and he said oh he just joined up. Most of the other guys looked so serious, but this crazy Waichi he goes along waving his uke at people as he passed by. Well, they'll need morale builders like him too. I don't know if Ted has gone to Schofield yet, but Yempuku told me if he passed his exam he would, the VVV boys got priority.[77]

Well, today being Sunday I went to church. We're getting a choir started now and we plan to sing prayer responses and such from next Sunday. No special numbers yet because the girls aren't sure of themselves. They're more scared because half of the congregation are servicemen, and I bet some of them really know how to sing. Yuki is taking care of the social side—we're having ping pong and even badminton in the recreation room. It's a good thing I have my badminton handbook that once upon a time Professor Walter Inouye gave to me to study, so now I can see how they rule off a court.[78] So far this community hasn't anything or anyplace the soldiers can use as a recreation center so it's a good thing for the church to start something. The haole women here are supposed to head the USO but they have so much rivalry among themselves that it doesn't work. So the poor soldiers don't get anything out of it.

Yesterday we dropped in at the Inter-Island Airways office and asked the guy about Easter. He says don't worry they'll have special planes going if there's a crowd. He told us to call up from Olaa 10 days before the date we want to go. We hope there'll be a late plane Friday afternoon, so we can take off right after school closes. That's what we did at Xmas vacation. I wouldn't mind coming back late this time—I don't feel as dutiful as I used to toward 'Nosey.' It's different when you lose a certain amount of respect for the individual, but I still have respect for her position as long as I'm here. Yuki told the postmaster about what happened. He said he's surprised we didn't report her—he said it's about time somebody did.

Naoko

At the beginning of his relationship with Naoko, Yoshiharu had bragged about his "live alone and like it" schedule, but as his days of bachelorhood became numbered, he saw that his time was not always his own. He still took advantage of the simple life on Kauai, going swimming at the beach with his dog Lulu, and continuing his woodwork. He played baseball with his fellow teachers and spent time at home raising chicks. But he also volunteered his time with the Kiawe Corps and reported to Reverend Yamada for Morale Committee work. Although he still refused to join the military, Yoshiharu believed that his work as a volunteer curried favor with the influential community leader, and that this connection would help him gain passage to Oahu for Easter.

Yoshiharu also had to deal with joining the two families together. His family's ideals of "Japanese style" came up again when his brother-in-law Yoshio Inouye suggested that he go to Oahu to meet the Tsukiyamas as the Ogata family representative. Naoko responded that her family was not expecting formalities but would go along with whatever his family wanted. Yoshiharu later found out that Inouye had been recently questioned by the FBI. Inouye's ties to Japan made him a prime candidate for internment, and his travel between the islands was unlikely to be allowed. Yoshiharu also warned Naoko about more differences that she would experience once she moved to Kauai. For instance, he told her that she would have "plenty to eat" but added, "My mother's Japanese style cooking is farmer's style so it isn't as dainty as the kind that you're used to."[79]

At the same time, Naoko readied herself to move to Kauai. She explained to Yoshiharu that her training was in the first three grades and that she was "no good for 4th grade and above that." She also admitted that she had had no guidance in her teaching, had been teaching for only a year, and had had limited supplies to work with in Olaa. She thought that she could be helped out by a principal who gave suggestions, rather than by one who "pokes around in the closet to see if the broom hangs properly and how crooked somebody is sitting." She had not forgotten that her current principal had opened and read her letter, commenting, "Aren't women the worst cats! Well when I get pushed around I don't like it and I believe in doing just so much, especially when there is a person you can't deal squarely with." She expected a change professionally, and she also seems to have been preparing for adjustments in her personal life. While still single and living on the Big Island, she continued to "U.S.O" the soldiers, joining the other teachers in having dinners with them, talking about Hawaiian legends, and even going ghost hunting.[80] Naoko may have been engaged, but she was far away from the observant eyes of her family and her future husband. Still, she never indicated that her actions were unacceptable or even inappropriate during wartime.

⟍⟍⟍

Eleele, Kauai

March 28, 1943

Dear Naoko,

I was talking to Mrs. Chang she told me to tell you that she has a job for you at Waimea Elementary.[81] She referred to you as my wife. This didn't seem quite right although it will be so soon. So you can expect to ride to school with me and teach there. I don't think you'll have much principal worries as long as you do your regular school teaching. You'll take order I guess from Mrs. Chang. She's nice too so don't worry. She said she needs a good teacher and asking for you so you better make up your mind to do good.

Today I went to the beach again and swam. Right now I'm rather tired. I'm writing to you in bed. It's only 7:30 but with half day of Keawe Corp and swimming I guess I just about had enough. The waves were large today so I had a good time body surfing. It was worthwhile going out because there usually was a good ride in. I was the only one swimming but I didn't mind. There was one audience. Lulu. He sat on the shore and watched me. After a while I'd sit on the shore and throw sticks in the water and watch him go after and bring them back. Sometime we both go in swimming. Such is life for me at present.

Well, so long for now honey, and periods.

Me

Eleele, Kauai
March 31, 1943

Dear Naoko,

Today I finally got my two dozen chicks that I ordered from the Ag. Department. These came from Hilo—I got them and I hope the'll grow up okay. If they do we'll have good chicken for Thanksgiving and Christmas. It's so long since I've raised chicks I have to get back to some of my old techniques and also some new. Of course there isn't any hen so I have to be it and keep them warm. This is the first night so I've visited them 2 times so far and will once more before I go to bed. They have to be warm. I have the place where they sleep in heated with an electric bulb. Even the chicks have to observe black-out regulations. Well, anyway I think the'll grow up okay, I hope anyway.

Me

Eleele, Kauai
April 4, 1943

Dear Naoko,

Well, Honey two more weeks by the time you get this the week will be half over for me. The plane situation doesn't look so good. I won't be able to make any reservations until this Friday the 9th I guess. The office opens at 7:30 but you know how busy they are then checking the passengers and they close [at] 3:30. I'm still in school then. If I can't get it next Friday I have to see Rev. Yamada. If anything can be done I guess he can. However, maybe he'd be glad I can't go. After all the free services I'm giving her[e] I think he'll at least do that much for me. Maybe.

Today we had the Inouyes (Waimea) and Haraguchis from Hanalei so the house was quite busy.[82] They're all okay and somewhat concerned about us. Especially the Waimea brother-in-law. He seems to be quite a particular guy after all.[83] He wants things done properly. But to me his idea of properly is Japanese style so I tell him not to worry. He even suggested to go to Honolulu during Easter as the family representative to ask you for me. Well, you know where that custom comes from.

Periods——
Yoshiharu

Eleele, Kauai
April 7, 1943

Dear Naoko,

I suppose you're wondering when or whether I'll be going to Honolulu. I am but as it is it won't be until Monday the 19th. I guess I was too sure of my self. I always thought we could reserve dates for leaving ten days ahead but no for Kauai it's different it's two weeks ahead. So this is where I was stuck. Last Friday and Saturday I had all the time to go to Port Allen still I didn't. Monday I went to school and I found out about the 2 weeks. Tuesday morning I went to Port Allen 7:15 and waited for 7:30 when the office open. I was second to make my reservation but was through by 7:45. The corporal was in a good mood I guess. He asked me if I was a school teacher and didn't ask anything else. So it seems everything is quite alright. About the date I'm leaving here. It may be changed because I told Yamada about it. If all the "Yamada morale" work I've been doing so far means anything to him at least he can do this favor for me. He is quite influential around that plane reservation place so it might be changed.

  Solong for now honey
  Periods Me

Olaa, Hawaii
April 7, 1943

Dearest Yoshiharu,

Tomorrow morning I'm going to the Hirose's at 8 AM and phone in my plane reservation for Saturday morning the 18th.[84] Exactly 10 days on the dot. Do you have to go to Port Allen personally or can't you phone in your reservation? Anyway you'll get this on Saturday most likely, and you can go for your reservation then if you haven't done so on Friday.

  My brother wrote me from Schofield. The morale seems pretty high, the food not so hot, and they're still yelling at every skirt they can see. Right now I guess they don't care for either—it seems they're on their way to Camp Shelby now so I won't see him at Easter. He wrote about the 'sincere note' you had enclosed with the money you sent—he probably wrote to you by now. Ted sent me the VVV annual, which had a page or two of personality analysis of members. Was I surprised to read this of my own brother—"His wolfing expeditions were the talk of the camp. His chores were to talk about girls, talk to girls, and to be talked to about girls." What will his girlfriend think of that! What the army doesn't bring out! I'd like to know what you'd turn out to be, my 1-A man.

  Well, about your brother in law offering to go to see my folks. My folks as you know aren't so terribly particular but they do believe in proper formalities. But I think they are satisfied in having your own brother visit them and talk things over. I don't know how much of his visits concerned us, but anyway my folks aren't expecting any more formalities as necessary. However, if it will make your brother in law feel better, or your parents in any way, feel it would be more complete, then I don't see why anybody should object to his move. Your brother seems to have done alright, everybody at home is satisfied as far as I know. As far as we're concerned you and I—darling, you and I—it wouldn't change us any whether he went or not. So it's up to him and your folks as to what they say, you can tell them so that my family and us we're ready for the main event now. Preliminaries are over, aren't they.

Love and Periods,
Naoko

Dearest Yoshiharu,

It was good news to hear you're actually coming to Honolulu, even if it is on Monday. Is it morning or afternoon my dearest man? If you can't come earlier never mind about asking the "Morale Hd.quarters" to do something about it. He'll probably feel he's doing you a favor, and I'd rather have you come Monday then let him feel that way. Of course I don't know him, so he might do it just because he wants to then I'd say that would be fine.

As for me I got my ticket today for next week Saturday morning at 10 AM. So write your next letter addressed to 17th Ave please, I must get it there. I'm so glad I got that date—I phoned in on Thursday morning to get the reservation. Thursday afternoon I went in to Hilo because another teacher wanted to go too, and when I told the man I had phoned and wanted to go home on Saturday, he said Saturday was all filled up. So Sunday was the next earliest day, and when I told him my name he said "Oh, I have you down for Saturday morning." So for sure today I got my ticket for that day—17th.

Maybe you'd better come armed with a gun—men (eligible) are so scarce according to Kazu, in town—the women will be doing the chasing. I mean for your self-defense.

Naoko

Eleele, Kauai
April 12, 1943

Dear Naoko,

It's a matter of days now before I see you. Today there was slightly encouraging news. Since there are so many going to Honolulu on Friday there is to be another plane. However, this I heard today so I couldn't do anything about it. Tomarrow I'm going to check up. If the corporal at Port Allen is nice he'll change my booking for me because I told him I wanted to go on Friday. Anyway there is still hope that I'll get there this weekend. Keep your fingers crossed.

My brother-in-law won't be going to Honolulu because I asked him not to. He has to lay off work and F.B.I. has questioned him not long ago so I feel better if he sits still and not make things worse for himself.

I'll write again I guess. At least it'll be to tell you when I'm getting to Honolulu.

Well solong honey & periods

Me

⁂

The letters stop between April 14 and April 24, when the couple spent their Easter break with the Tsukiyama family on Oahu. By the 25th, Yoshiharu had returned to Kauai to resume his teaching. Naoko, on the other hand, was still on Oahu. She was supposed to have returned to the Big Island, but because of transportation issues, she was not able to return to work until the 30th. She missed almost an entire week of teaching, but that time on Oahu allowed her to prepare for the upcoming wedding and her move to Kauai. Yoshiharu had presented her with the engagement ring that they both picked out during their visit. She met with a friend who gave her fabric for drapes and covers for the cushions. Her sisters and friends organized an engagement party and she received gifts. Naoko spoke with her insurance agent about her policy and he promised her orchids for her wedding. She also looked into possibilities for their honeymoon.[85]

A big decision that the couple had to make was who to include in their wedding party. Naoko was set with Kazu as her bridesmaid and having two flower girls. Her sister Martha occasionally wrote and came up in conversation, but it was Naoko and Kazu who were closer in age, and Kazu took a greater interest in wedding preparations. Yoshiharu's problem was that his family would not be able to travel to Oahu. As immigrants, his parents were not allowed to fly inter-island, and the rest of his large family could not afford the trip. He had one brother, Yoshitaka, who lived on Oahu, though, and Ogata expected him to be at the ceremony. Naoko explained, "Emily Post says it isn't a strict rule, but if your brother is not the best man when available, it hints of a family quarrel." Yoshiharu responded, "It'll be Baker [for the best man] as far as I'm concerned . . . I don't think I'm asking too much to have my own best man."[86]

⫘⫘⫘

Honolulu, Hawaii
April 25, 1943

Dearest You,

For the luncheon, there were eight of us including Edith who came to church.[87] To announce the engagement, Kazu fixed for each two yellow chicks in a lavender eggshell tied with a yellow ribbon. The bigger chick had your name on it and the other had mine. They were supposed to put 1 and 1 together and make 2 out of it, which they did. Smart gals weren't they. When Gene opens her egg she says "Look at Yoshiharu on the top, looks like he's lording over her already."[88] Litheia begins to laugh and says she was thinking of something but she'd better not say it, so we had to laugh over the bright minds.[89] Kazu's getting so witty lately. She said something about having to be sympathetic listening to all these officers who she USO's.

Naoko

Eleele, Kauai

April 25, 1943

Dear Naoko,

Dad and Mother asked how everything was. And mother told me that she forgot to tell me to tell you not to bring too many things. Meaning dresser and what not. Father also said that. He said he won't judge your parents according to what you bring or what you don't bring. So their expecting [you] to come with only your belongings. Things that you own now. They feel that since time is as it is and we don't have a separate house it would be better not to bring too many stuffs.

Solong and periods
Yoshiharu

Honolulu, Hawaii

April 27, 1943

Dearest Yoshiharu,

Yesterday I went to see Fred Hiura about changing my quarterly payments on insurance to semi-annual payments.[90] It costs less in the long run and you don't have to bother about it so often that way. I also told him I'd be married in June so the names would have to be changed. He said he would fix that up when the time came. He told me he has a part share in the Crossroads Church cottage at Kokokahi, that's in Kaneohe Bay near Chris Holmes's island and that he would reserve the cottage for our use for a week after we get married—if we wanted to go there.[91] We have to bring our own food and bed linens, otherwise the cottage is equipped. However, you're the boss—too so let me know what you think about this. What I say never is final, not until you've had your say too—darling, darling, etc.

Another place I heard of from Shigeko where people spend their time when they want to be alone is on the other side of the island near Punaluu, called Cooper Ranch.[92] It's a country hotel with small lodges on the place which couples rent. My mother said that place sounds good, and we don't have to bother about taking anything down there. She also says then I won't have to bother about cooking, but I said what else are we going to do all the time. So I'd rather spend some time cooking <u>with</u> you not only for you. Tonight as usual we were talking about the wedding and the subject of whether you were going to kiss me then came up. I said Oh yes, in fact we wanted a rehearsal to see how long it should be. Pretty soon my mother comes back to say "Tell him not to spread the pollen too long." Some crazy family you're getting tied up with, but you should've known that by looking at me

Kazu says your brother can be best man, Baker the usher and Doris the bridesmaid. Emily Post says it isn't a strict rule, but if your brother is not best man when available it hints of a family quarrel. However, the best friend of the groom is often chosen for various reasons and that of course is up to you. It's your move about the best man.

So long for now and periods,
Me

Eleele, Kauai
April 29, 1943

Dear Naoko,
Well, it seems I'll be hearing about the wedding until it's all over. I'm not very fussy but I'd like to have my own choice for best man. Well, if people want to take Emily Post's way concerning not having the brother

be best man it's okay with me. It'll be Baker as far as I'm concerned. He has pretty good contacts and can get things very easily for me. If my brother [will] be my best man I won't have any one as my family representative. Maybe he can be both, I don't know. Further more he isn't the kind that would want to be bothered with chasing around for flower, making a party and rehearsals. I don't think I'm asking too much to have my own best man. After all he's suppose to give me moral support and see that I get through the whole thing okay. Maybe I'll get cold feet and back out and not show up if I can't have him. I don't care what you do all around Baker and me but that much will be my part and it'll stay that way as far as I'm concerned.

As for the get-away-from-it-all-plan I'd rather go to Kokokahi. After all you have to cook for me for the rest of my life what's an extra week. Furthermore I'll help you because I'll want to be with you all the time. To have my meals prepared by somebody else seems a little too artificial for me especially if I'm to have my wife with me. We may not want to eat at certain times. If you don't want to cook for that week I can live on love and can goods for that week. It'll take a lot of energy but I've enough to spare. How about you?

Me

Finally, Naoko's Easter break came to an end, and she had to return to the Big Island. She faced her supervising principal and then jumped back into her daily life as a single teacher. She continued USOing and chronicling her adventures for Yoshiharu. She told him that she "met one of the nice corporals today who came to supper once and he wanted to see the ring and wish me happiness." She also spent some time seeing more of the Big Island as she did her patriotic duty. She danced and dined with soldiers, had the opportunity to ride in a weapons carrier, and even fired a gun. She was not concerned about how it looked for her, as an almost married woman, to spend so much time with the military men. Her concern was that as a schoolteacher, she must act properly in front of the

community. She justified her behavior by explaining that there were always other girls doing the same, and she also told her fiancé, "We all
know there has to be a line drawn when it comes to duty before pleasure," to explain that they were all behaving decently and had done
nothing of which to be ashamed, and that she had done "nothing [she
had] to cover up."[93]

Yoshiharu's lifestyle on Kauai proceeded at a much slower pace. After
the local newspaper announced the couple's engagement, he received his
share of congratulations, including from his former girlfriend. His principal commented on his marrying a city girl, as opposed to one from
Kauai. Yoshiharu then added that his male high school students wanted
to know if his fiancée was beautiful. The military affected his life as well,
but for men, martial law did not bring more opportunities for romance
and fun; rather it brought additional responsibility. Yoshiharu had to
worry not only about civilian police but also about military police. Although he monitored his own behavior and never outwardly chastised
Naoko for her military dalliances, he did on occasion express his concern. He wrote of paying off her engagement ring, and then added, "I
hope you're okay and enjoying the last few days of your unmarried life."[94]

After not receiving letters from Naoko on a regular basis, Yoshiharu
explained to her what he believed was proper behavior. He hinted at his
unhappiness, commenting on the infrequency of her letters. Then, perhaps trying to make her jealous, he told her about being invited to the
girls' home economics luncheon. He also mentioned the senior boys'
dance and told Naoko that when he was a senior, he attended with a date
and "called for her in style." Next, because Naoko had implied that her
schoolteacher friends were the ones who wanted to mingle with the soldiers and that she was just going along with them so as to not be anti-
social, Yoshiharu added, "Tell your teacher friends who lead you to go
places that they better get married or the'll wear their legs out running
around at such a pace. It won't be good in their old age." He was not done
there, though, as Naoko's next letter told about dining with soldiers and

celebrating a birthday with neighbors and two army captains who lived nearby. She wrote of one, "He sat next to me a while, so I could close my eyes and see you and he'd be the substitute." That may have been the final straw for Yoshiharu, because in his next letter, he wrote, "So you see and I see too you got yourself into something. . . . I hate to have people say I am marrying a girl who used to go around with soldiers."[95]

Even though 350,000 women had volunteered for the military, Yoshiharu believed that his fiancée should also do her patriotic duty, and he had a very clear idea of what that should involve. He knew of the WAAC, members of the recently created Women's Army Auxiliary Corps (later known as the Women's Army Corps, or WAC), the U.S. Navy's WAVES (Women Accepted for Volunteer Emergency Service), and the WASP (Women Airforce Service Pilots), who trained male pilots, flew cargo planes, tested the newly made planes, and transported them to docks and advanced bases to be shipped out to the men in battle. Rosie the Riveter, a propaganda character that encouraged millions of women to work outside their homes in factories and in manual labor jobs that men once held, also demonstrated what female patriots could do. Other women pushed the boundaries of propriety by playing baseball and forming the All-American Girls Professional Baseball League. As these women expanded the roles for all women in U.S. society, Yoshiharu wanted Naoko to be one of those who saw it as their patriotic duty to marry.

<hr>

Olaa, Hawaii
April 29, 1943

Dearest Yoshiharu,

After supper Mr. Hirose drove us down to Mrs. Duncan's house. We thought we'd better face the music and get it over with.[96] They told me she's been raving like a mad bull since Monday at everybody.

Well, when we arrive at the house Yuki and Shizue sit in the car and make me go in alone. She actually stretched out her hand and looked relieved to see me. She said I was selfish. She can't call it unpatriotic or anything to me because I will be tempted to tell her that our Constitution guarantees the right to happiness and it's no sin to recognize that right when it comes. She says this is war now so we shouldn't expect to go home when we please, but she doesn't seem to realize that others travel by plane for reasons that the army would call lifting the morale, and they allow it because there is a war going on.

Bye now and Periods too,
Naoko

Eleele, Kauai
May 3, 1943

Dear Naoko,
Guess who congratulated me—Miss Hayashi. She's okay. Some other people may think about her when they find out I'm getting married but I don't think she think anything about it. I can look her straight in the face and have no guilty conscience. She's that way with me too, we're still good friends. You have to meet her when you get here.

Solong and periods,
Yoshiharu
P.S. Mr. Griswold to the unmarried women teachers, why in heck were they so slow that I had to get a girl from town.[97]
Me

Olaa, Hawaii
May 8, 1943

Dearest,
Guess where I am now, way out in Kalapana at the school cottage. We came out here with a Hawaiian policeman yesterday evening.

Mrs. Weatherbee a great big part Haw'n woman stays here with another girl who just seems to USO the soldiers out here.[98] Yuki, Shizue, myself, and another girl, Shigeno came out here. I just got through playing volleyball with them and really got hot playing out in the sun.

Kalapana is as quiet and I still like it as I did before, only now there's barbed wire up and a bunch of men stationed very close by. Most of them make this their home and call Mrs. Weatherbee Ma or Mom, and she treats them like her own boys. They seem to be nice fellows but they aren't as nice as those 3 we know at Olaa. These guys seem to be more rugged and it sure looks like water is scarce around here. I do feel sorry because they're in such a remote place but they act quite civilized in spite of it. This afternoon we're getting permission from the Lt. to go for a swim, he said we could. Not even the natives here are allowed to go to the beach. I don't care for this place with the war atmosphere and what comes with it. I guess you've met enough haoles on the mainland to know the different types. I get a kick just trying to figure them out from the way they talk and act. Some of them are kinda dumb if you ask me.

The army car called a weapons carrier took us up [to a waterfall] and since the driver had to go that way again at 5 o'clock with chow for some men, we took a second ride with the driver and the Lt. While we were waiting for the chow wagon to come back, the Lt. was looking for mongoose to shoot. He had a small 25 caliber gun and he told me to try to shoot a post nearby. The darn thing made such a bang when it went off I closed my eyes, so I didn't know where the bullet went. I hate to touch guns even toy ones, but I thought there's nothing like trying a thing once. It was great fun riding on that high car too, we certainly got bounced up and down.

Periods and Love to you from,

<u>Me</u>

Eleele, Kauai
May 9, 1943

Dear Naoko,

Last week I got only one letter from you but I guess you were waiting for mine to answer them. Perhaps you are too busy USOing. Well, I hope you think of me as the ring and since three is a crowd [——] [——]?[99] No, I'm only kidding. I'll trust you because I think I know you pretty well, maybe?

On Thursday I went to Lihue with Baker. We went all over the place Manpower office—O.P.A. Board of Health and several other commercial houses.[100] I went to the manpower office to get a permit to leave this island during the summer. I told him I was getting married and he thought that was a very good reason. Anyway he doesn't care if we go as long as we return.

I also went to Kapaa to pay the jeweler. So your ring is all paid for. We got to Lihue about 11:30 and got back here at 5:00. Baker told me that he got tagged sometime ago. He had to pay $25.00 though. Nowadays the civilian cops and MP.s travel together because the MP's cannot arrest civilians and civilian cops cannot arrest army people. Well, he (Baker) can get away with most cops in Waimea and Kekaha but not the M.Ps. So he had to get the tag. This happened at Kekaha.

Solong
Yoshiharu

Olaa, Hawaii
May 11, 1943

Dearest Yoshiharu,

Well, we survived Kalapana alright. We got up before 6 A.M. Sunday so we could come back with the policeman. We had the dance the night before in the school basement. We went back to the cottage around midnight, followed by about 5 guys who still wanted to sit around and talk. Sounds bad, but Mrs. Weatherbee was with us all the time and those men were nice fellows just wanting different company for a change. I've had about enough of this khaki-wacky business, but we came back to Olaa and here we meet our old friends who want to know just what happened at Kalapana. Nothing really, but it makes a good story.

The other two guys we know well here are called Botch and Gay—both last names, only Botch has more on it. I think they're regular fellows and they seem to like our company, just talking and visiting. I guess, they just want company other than the guys they see every day. They talk about home. Their families, girl friends, and anything else. They're the decent sort, and it never worries me when they're around or what they say. The only thing I object to is that we meet them too often—accidentally on the street, and they start talking or walking along with us. I don't mind it once in a while but this is a small place, and pretty soon I know we'll be hearing things. Nothing that I have to cover up, but I still feel that as teachers here we have to outwardly behave properly when people see us. Of course it's just enjoying somebody's company in a perfectly harmless way, but people can make it seem worse. If I'm the only one I can put my foot down, but if I start being anti-social it would seem very obvious just like I was so selfish I wanted my time to myself, when the others don't mind. Oh well, it may not be as bad as I think—I'm always the chaperone I tell them so we all know there has to be a line drawn when it comes to duty before pleasure. Maybe it's because of the way I think of you and know you think of me as being, I have to think things out this way. Anyway I want you to know what I'm doing and thinking about too.

Love and Periods,
Still love you—Naoko

Eleele, Kauai
May 12, 1943

Dear Naoko,

I hope you had a good time at Kalapana and with the soldiers. I mean it although I'm wishing I could be there instead. After all you won't have much chance to be doing that after this summer.

The senior boys are all excited over the banquet and dance like I was when I was a senior. Way back in 1937. I had a date then and drove the car and called for her in style. I hope the guys feel the way I did. I guess they will I was just an ordinary senior and I don't think the seniors today are much changed. Maybe the speed is a little different here on Kauai today. If you ask me the girls today seem much more matured than the boys. The boys just can't keep up with them. Maybe it's the influence of the army and permanent waves. Girls can look more matured than they are by the way they dress and paint up but boys can't do much about those things. They either look it or don't. It's six years since my banquet and dance and I hope I enjoy it. For a change the're pro- orchestra [in favor of an orchestra]. It won't be so bad.

Solong for now—and periods
Me

Olaa, Hawaii
May 14, 1943

Dearest,

I don't think we definitely decided about 4 men who should help with the ushering in of guests, etc. Is there anybody in particular you would rather have, or shall we ask the guys like Kenneth Kawamoto, Yozo and the like who are familiar with the church?[101] My mother also asks me what I want for wedding gifts, because her friends all ask her what I need. I can tell her we need anything that's practical rather than fancy. I suppose we won't need to use anything while we live with your folks. We're just going to be one of the family are we not? Of course I'll have enough towels and sheets for our use if we need them, so I guess your mother doesn't have to get ready in anyway because we're coming into the house.

As for USO-ing, we haven't seen the guys since the beginning of the week. However tomorrow, we're celebrating Shizue's birthday with a sukiyaki dinner and a couple of those GI men are coming.[102] All nice fellows, so it's okay. We're inviting Mr. and Mrs. Hirose and the 2 cute boys over too. We'll have a mob from the looks of things, but I'm not running the things so I'm not worrying.

So long and love,
Naoko

Eleele, Kauai
May 16, 1943

Dear Naoko,

I got your letter about the soldier boys and their extreme sociability. To me that's nothing unusual and for you it isn't either but as you put it under the circumstances you wouldn't want it so—not too much. The soldiers before they were soldiers, were most of them regular guys who used to go around with girls. Walk with and talk with girls when they met them on the street or wherever they may be. I don't think most of them changed although they wear uniforms so to them it's nothing wrong and only natural. However, many people have the idea that soldiers are devils socially. And you being a teacher (a public employee) people like to talk about and criticize. So you see and I see too you got yourself into something. Of course it isn't serious, however, I think it would be worse for you than the other two girls, because you're engaged. If it were Kauai it sure would make a lots of difference. If I were you I'd talk to those guys in one of the sessions that you may have together. If they can't take it or understand they aren't worth your company. I say so. It's just that people don't understand things in the same way. I hate to have people say I'm marrying a girl who used to go around with soldiers. People have a tendency to exaggerate things and talking to and walking with a soldier may be interpreted as such. As far as I'm concerned I trust you and I'm quite sure you know when and where you [have] to draw the line. But I'm telling you all this just so that you can know me better. If you knew that I thought this way than this proves you're knowledge of me is correct. Well, anyway it's not life or death so don't worry too much about it.

I don't go around with the WAAC's and WAVES.

Solong–

Me

<hr />

As the wedding day drew nearer, the hardships of war worsened. Yoshiharu decided that war bonds would be the most practical wedding present. The war meant there was shortage of material goods in the islands, so the couple may not have had access to what they wanted. Furthermore, with all of the pressure that residents had to buy the bonds, it was a way that the couple could benefit and their guests could demonstrate their patriotism. Naoko's mother, who had been heavily involved in wedding preparations, became distracted by the efforts of the 442nd. By May of 1943, she had lost communication with her oldest son, Jimmy, in Japan, and Ted had shipped out for training. Ted's letters were sparse, and the ones that she did receive were edited by military censors. Yoshiharu's parents also felt the harsh reality of wartime—they could not travel to Oahu to see their son get married. Yoshiharu also had a new worry: his deferment was about to expire and he had I-A status, making him eligible for conscription into military service. He still held the hope of obtaining another deferment, but could not be sure that he would receive one.[103] The biggest problem that the couple faced, though, was arranging for them both to be able to travel to Oahu for the big day.

⚋⚋⚋

Eleele, Kauai
May 19, 1943

Dear Naoko,

It's the 19th of May. Next month tonight you'll be Mrs. Ogata. Does that sound okay to you. I hope it'll be with no regrets.

As for wedding gifts. I can't see what material thing we can have. What we may want isn't on the market. So as far as I can see war bonds are the best thing. It'll help in making our house when we get ready for it. They'll be killing two birds with one stone. Maybe people don't want to spend that much I don't know. I'm not saying that's what I want. It's that if I were giving I'd do that. There isn't much glamour in it but it's practical, up to date and patriotic. What more do you want. They can give what they please.

Solong now and periods
Yoshiharu

Olaa, Hawaii
May 19, 1943

Dearest,

My mother doesn't write to me so often now since she said she'll be so busy writing to 'her boys' at Camp Shelby. I haven't written to my brother yet—I have to really sit down and write a volume to him. Martha actually wrote and she's still talking about the wedding. I hope they'll let me be in it somewhere.

Bye now and periods
Naoko

Eleele, Kauai
May 23, 1943

Dear Naoko,

As far as my folks are concerned they're leaving the wedding to your parents and us. Not that they don't want anything to do with—just that there isn't much they can do about it. They told my brother to tell your parents that.

Today, believe it or not I went to church. Reverend Yamada is going into the army as chaplain with a 1st Leui rank. Lucky guy. Today was his last service here at the Hanapepe Church. For once the church was crowded.

I suppose you read about the draft. I really don't know where that puts me. Mr. Griswold said that Miss Hundley is going to get me a deferment but I hope they make it fast.[104] I got my 1A card about two weeks ago and Mr. Griswold told me that last weekend. This is one of the things I can't do much about. We'll see in a week or so. Don't worry about it though you're supposed to be able to take these things. Can't you?

Solong and periods
Yoshiharu

Eleele, Kauai
May 30, 1943

Dear Naoko,

Well last Friday Baker and I went to the Ticket Office and got our reservation. I'm coming down on the 12th of June Saturday. Well, after we got there one of the students who was attending Waimea High until about a month ago, came over and introduced the corporal to Baker and me. This girl works over there. Well she told him what I was going to Honolulu for and boy did that work. I could practically ask for any day I wanted. I'm going on the 12th and Baker on the 13th so that he can get his business for the week completed.

You referred to ushers, I don't know what you mean except what you mentioned about Yozo and Kenneth. Well, as I told you or if you didn't get that letter I think you should write to them. Yozo by all means and tell him he is responsible for this because he introduced us. If you're not going to ask him send him an invitation at least.

Solong and periods honey–
Me Yoshiharu

Olaa, Hawaii
May 30, 1943

Dearest,

Guess what, you'd better take an aspirin and sit down. I can't get back to Honolulu in time for the wedding even, unless the Military comes thru with the appeal I made. When I went to the Airways office I saw all the teachers looking so downhearted, so I got prepared for bad news. It seems that they're so filled up, all they can do is take your name down on a 'waiting list' that looked pages long and that means till the end of June or July. Well, I knew it was no use talking to him so I asked the girl if they were giving any priority for other reasons besides summer session, and I told her mine. She said the best thing for me to do was to see the Military Controllers office for Travel. So I went up to the Federal Bldg. thinking up every argument I could think up in case they wouldn't consider my reason. I was even going to tell them about you being 1-A and so time would mean something, otherwise I wouldn't bother them about personal matters. Major Bryan was out and so was his assistant Lt. Copeland but the aide told me I could speak to Capt. Allan who works in the same office. I told him all the plans were made for the wedding to be on the 19th, and that you were coming down from Kauai. I said it looks like everybody's going to be there but myself, and he chuckled and said it wouldn't be so good would it. He didn't see why I couldn't get home by then because they can't reserve anybody till 14 days ahead of their departure anyway, and he couldn't see why there should be any waiting list so long. Capt. Allan calls up the Sourpuss at the office to see what could be done. Evidently Sourpuss was too busy to be in a good mood and I don't think the captain handles plane traveling alone, so he said he would take my name and phone number down and he would talk it over with Major Bryan and let me know how it turns out. Anyway he might remember me because at least I hope his eyes opened up when I came walking in with that red flower print dress on which I just happened to be wearing yesterday. It might've helped a little, but I wouldn't wear it for any such purpose if it weren't for the fact that it would bring me home even a day sooner. If he doesn't let me know by Weds. or so I'm going to see them again. I'm going to try very hard to get back on time, especially when it will upset a lot of other people's plans. As far as I go the wedding plans are a formality that comes secondary to what you and I have together.

So long for now,
Naoko

Olaa, Hawaii
May 31, 1943

Dearest,

What wouldn't I give just to have you here now. I'm not asking for much am I. Well, maybe just let me borrow your shoulder. I need it. I have such a weight on my mind, mainly because I don't know when and if I'll ever get home. I've only been counting the days and looking forward to everything, and now I don't know how it'll turn out.

[My principal] just told me this Easter that this is war and we have no business traveling for our own desires. It seems we can't live our own lives anymore—not even when vacation comes around. Then I have to write plans to make more democratic situations in classroom teaching, and stay up all night doing it when they won't even let me go home to my own home when vacation comes. Not only that—I can't even get married, it probably isn't important enough. The only thing I can do is see the military authorities who have a say in the matter, and at least they'll listen and be nice about it.

Love and Periods,
Naoko

Olaa, Hawaii
June 2, 1943

Dearest,
I went to get a plane ticket since my super. principal sent in my release, but they said a release isn't any good because the planes are full. Unless I go to summer school. So I asked if my reasons weren't good enough because I said you were getting passage from Kauai on the 12th. So the guys says see Lt. Copeland so I went. I talked to him a long time but the outcome was this—I have to wait till next Thursday and see him then. He said they may have special planes by then, but now he can't guarantee it.

You'll have to decide this. Will you and Baker come down anyway, because if there is no special plane I can't get home till the end of June about June 27th. Shall we take a chance and wait till next Thursday to find out—even then I might get bad news, or shall we postpone the wedding so we can have it when we can relax about everything. I'd hate to do that tho', it means the end of June or July and all our plans will have to be changed. You can imagine how I feel about the whole thing, but I'll take it if it has to be so. Shall we just leave things as they are and hope I get back in time to get things ready, so we won't feel too rushed. Only I hate to have you and Baker stick around town not knowing when the date would be—especially Baker he has his business. The fact remains that I don't know whether I'll be home in time or not, and I have to wait another week to find out. My family will have to wait, and everybody else concerned.

Love darling, and periods–
Naoko

Dear Naoko,

I got your letter Saturday afternoon but couldn't do anything about it because no mail service between Kauai and other islands [until] tomarrow morning. Well, it seems as though you'll be late, of course, I'm not blaming you. As I see it now the best thing is to wait until Thursday and find out for sure although you seem rather pessimistic about the chances of you getting an extra plane. I should think one week would be long enough time to have your friends and mine know about the changed date. After all it's not entirely in our power to decide when. Anyone who would feel hurt because they couldn't know sooner isn't worth giving a thought. As for me I'm going down on the twelfth and no later because I'm taking no chances. As for Baker I haven't seen him yet. I think it will be okay with him but the whole thing should be as soon as possible. Don't worry about us. It's okay. He's okay when it comes to stuff like this. He might kid you about it later but won't make a fuss over it. I don't know what your parents think but I'm going to write them a letter also and tell them what I told you. They can make their own decision. As far as I'm concerned it is that we get married as soon as possible.

Well, today was a full day for me. I went to the Keawe Corp. this morning and worked quite hard. We worked near the airports. The Inter island plane came three times today. Can you beat that? Even on this little rock. Maybe there will be an extra plane for you to get in.

Solong and periods
Me

Olaa, Hawaii
June 5, 1943

Dearest Yoshiharu,

Yesterday I got a letter from my mother and she says "What's this I hear about not getting plane passage. Well, just hop on a plane anyway and tell them it's urgent." I'd like to know what she thinks I've been trying to do for the past 2 weeks. It isn't that easy you know, and they seem to expect me to come home anytime I feel like it.

One thing that is on the bright side is this. I went to see the doc yesterday and told him that I was getting married in 2 weeks so I'd like to know what I should know and to see if everything is okay with me. I was glad to hear him say that everything is in good shape and that there is nothing the matter to keep us from having a normal married life. He also drew pictures so I could see what it was that people wanted to prevent from happening—all very scientific, and what to do about it and what he thought was the safest way.

Please give my regards to your parents and sister. I'm sorry they won't be able to come to the wedding, but I'll be seeing them soon.

Periods darling and goodnite,
Me

Olaa, Hawaii
June 7, 1943

Dearest,

Just pull yourself together my darling, because I've got good news for a change. Today I went to Hilo after school and got my plane ticket for Tuesday June 15th, just like that. The morning plane which will probably get to Honolulu after 12 noon, so come with a stretcher. I think we'll land at Maui again. But one can't be choosy, I'm so relieved we don't have to postpone the whole thing.

Monday
June 7th.

Dearest,

Just pull yourself together my darling, because I've got good news for a change. Today I went to Hilo after school and got my plane ticket for Tuesday June 15th, just like that. The morning plane which will probably get to Honolulu after 12 noon, so come with a stretcher. I think we'll land at Maui again. But one can't be choosy, I'm so relieved we don't have to postpone the whole thing.

Just before I went into the Airways office I met a girl friend coming out and she said they've changed the system and they're taking anybody as they come, regardless of the previous waiting list. So I asked her when she got plane passage for and she said June 21st. Well, I didn't want to go in there again for that, but I met Mr. Hirose there too and he told me the Mr. Bush he went to see said he wasn't in the plane traveling dept. any more since March so he couldn't do much but he would phone in for me. So I thot I'd better go in myself and ask the guy Peter again. He

First page of Naoko Tsukiyama's letter of June 7, 1943, with the good news that she would make it home in time for the wedding. Photo in author's collection.

216

Just before I went into the airways office I met a girlfriend coming out and she said they've changed the system and they're taking anybody as they come, regardless of the previous waiting list. So I asked when she got plane passage for and she said June 21st. Well, I didn't want to go in there again for that, but I met Mr. Hirse [Hirose] there too and he told me the Mr. Bush he went to see said he wasn't in the plane traveling dept. any more since March so he couldn't do much but he would phone in for me.[105] So I tho't I'd better go in myself and ask the guy Peter again. He was still in a teasing mood and I have a strong hunch he had my name on that June 15th page before I asked for it. Otherwise I would have gotten June 21st today. He said since Saturday the Army made some new regulations, giving the office more control over their own affairs so the whole set-up was changed. After I told him I was never going to come in for plane passage again, I asked him if I would really go on Tuesday's plane. He said he's the guy to call out the names from the list to get on the plane, so he'd take care of it.

Periods Darling & love.

Naoko

6 I Am What I Am

For Japanese Americans, as well as the rest of Americans, the hardships of war continued through the summer of 1943 and beyond. In May, German forces in North Africa surrendered, and in September, the Grand Council of Fascism overthrew Benito Mussolini, followed by Italy's unconditional surrender to the Allies. The Allies also made headway elsewhere in Europe. The Soviets, under the direction of Joseph Stalin, focused on the eastern front as Hitler concentrated his efforts in the west. Poland, Prussia, Lithuania, Romania, and other eastern European countries fell to the Soviets, and by the end of 1944, the Soviets had swept the Germans out of their territory. On the western front, the United States began its raid on Germany in early 1943, and by May of 1944, it had eight hundred thousand Allied combat troops in Britain, poised for an offensive. The D-day invasion of Normandy on June 6, 1944, dealt strategic blows to Germany through France. Germany suffered further blows, and Hitler's suicide on April 30, 1945, led to Germany's surrender a week letter, on May 7.[1]

Emperor Hirohito of Japan did not surrender as easily, however. The war raged on in the Pacific until the fall of 1945. The United States increased its presence in the region in October 1943 with its campaign to retake Burma, and dealt the death blow to Japan's naval power in October with the Battle of Leyte Gulf.[2] The Battles of Iwo Jima and Okinawa, from February to June 1945, ultimately gave the United States a base from which to invade Japan. The United States, in the meantime, worked up to successfully detonating its first atomic bomb on July 16, 1945 and then, under President Harry S. Truman's order, dropped an atomic bomb on Hiroshima, Japan, on August 6 of that year. Another was dropped three days later on the city of Nagasaki. August 14, 1945, became known as V-J Day, signaling victory over Japan, but the Empire of Japan did not officially surrender until September 2, 1945.[3] After nearly three hundred thousand Americans had died in the conflict, the end of World War II had finally come for Americans.

For the United States and its veterans, World War II ended amid celebration and patriotism, but for Japanese American citizens the readjustment process lasted for decades. On December 18, 1943, the Emergency Service Committee had issued a formal request to include Japanese Americans in the draft, citing the accomplishments of the 100th Battalion and the Military Intelligence Service as evidence that Japanese Americans could be trusted.[4] During the war, the War Relocation Authority (WRA) issued loyalty tests in the relocation camps and registered eligible men for the draft. It asked the men two questions: (1) "Are you willing to serve in the armed forces of the United States on combat duty, wherever ordered?" and (2) "Will you swear an unqualified allegiance to the United States of America and faithfully defend the United States from any or all attack by foreign or domestic forces, and foreswear any form of allegiance or obedience to the Japanese Emperor, or any other foreign government, power, or organization?" The men in the camps who answered yes to both questions could then be drafted.[5]

Yoshiharu Ogata never had to answer these questions, but his attitudes toward the war serve as a case study for the dilemmas Japanese Americans faced. Since he had not been interned, he was not forced to answer the WRA's loyalty questions regarding willingness to serve in the armed forces or to swear an unqualified allegiance to the United States. As a free citizen, he also refused to fill out the Morale Committee forms recruiting volunteers for the military. He had cultural ties to Japan as a result of his plantation upbringing, family customs, and knowledge of the Japanese language. But his nationality was American; he did not feel any allegiance to the emperor of Japan. His letters, though, do not give a clear indication of what his answer would have been to the WRA's question regarding military service. He obviously did not want to join the military, preferring to serve his community and his family. He was never ordered into military service. Instead, he volunteered locally and worked to ensure his deferment from the draft. There are moments in his letters when he seems to have acquiesced and admitted that if drafted, he would serve, although not happily. Ogata's upbringing, the very factor that made him so determined to stay at home, was also the impetus that would have induced him to serve if drafted. Ogata obtained his much-desired deferments, and after he married, his draft status was no longer I-A. In his later years, Ogata rarely spoke of the war but recognized that he had missed an opportunity to serve his country and thus did not share the same experiences of many of his peers.

World War II had allowed Japanese Americans a unique opportunity to prove their patriotism. Altogether, 33,000 of them served in the armed forces, including more than 16,000 Nisei from the internment camps.[6] The most famous stories of Japanese Americans fighting for the United States during World War II came from the efforts of the 442nd Regimental Combat Team, whose motto was "Go for Broke!" Organized in March 1943, the 2,686 volunteers from Hawaii and 1,500 from the mainland traveled to Camp Shelby, Mississippi, the following April and went into combat on June 26, 1944. The 442nd served primarily in Italy and France and became the most decorated unit of its size and length of service in combat. A lesser-known aspect of the contributions of the 442nd came through the efforts of the men who served in the Military Intelligence Service. These Nisei, with their bilingual skills, trained at military language schools at the Presidio of San Francisco and at Camp Savage and Fort Snelling in Minnesota. They translated enemy documents, interrogated Japanese prisoners of war, intercepted and deciphered communications, and gathered intelligence material that made them "America's secret weapon in the war against Japan."[7] After the war, many of these men returned to Hawaii, having seen more of the world than their peers and family at home. They had experience from serving in combat, interacting with mainland Americans as well as Europeans, and living on the continental United States among a multitude of races.

After the war, both the government and society questioned the loyalty and patriotism of Japanese Americans. On the mainland, men and women returned home from internment camps and military service to find their businesses bankrupted, their property stolen, and some of their neighbors openly hostile and suspicious of them. Japanese Americans returning to their former communities found it hard to obtain housing and discovered that they had been replaced at their jobs by people of other ethnicities.[8] They saw their civil rights denied; public services and access to public places did not extend to them.[9] Still, with the help of a college education, Japanese American residents in both Hawaii and on the mainland found greater socioeconomic success after the war than they previously had. By 1945, Japanese American students took a greater interest in their future and returned to public schools. In fact, Japanese Americans "emerged as one of the better educated groups in American society and took advantage of an expanding white-collar sector."[10] Japanese Americans moved away from agricultural work to professional, technical, clerical, and sales jobs, with 82 percent of the Japanese American population living in urban areas by 1960.[11]

Civilian courts reopened in Hawaii in February 1943, but the territory remained under martial law until October 1944. Even after that, civilian life never returned to prewar conditions.[12] After the war, divorce rates and the number of illegitimate births increased. Young local girls found themselves pregnant or new mothers of babies whose fathers had shipped out with the military when the servicemen received new assignments. One Japanese American student at the University of Hawaii explained that having a baby with a white soldier was "patriotic."[13] In rural communities like those on Kauai, teenagers never completed high school, because the disruption of their schooling and the changes in society discouraged them from doing so. Many identified themselves as members of the "Class of World War II" and even held class reunions into the twenty-first century. But for Japanese American women in urban areas, the war had opened new opportunities, and Naoko's experiences are representative of this. These women had worked in offices, schools, and factories. They dated men of other ethnicities, saw an increase in marriage rates, and hoped to marry for love. These women read advice columns that addressed equality in marriage, and they wanted to be treated like "all modern brides in America." As modern as these women were, however, they still expected to serve husbands, protect children, cook, and meet the needs of the family.[14]

Japanese Americans had expressed a strong desire for education even before the war, and in Hawaii they continued their university education throughout the war years. Sixty-seven of the 127 graduating seniors in 1944 (more than half) were Japanese Americans.[15] Toward the war's end, the 1945 commencement program from the University of Hawaii listed 265 students receiving degrees or certificates, of which 169, or 63 percent, had Japanese last names.[16] Just as the relocation of Hawaii's Japanese population during the war would have been impractical and even economically disastrous, so too would have been the closing of the University of Hawaii to Japanese Americans. At a time when many Japanese Americans on the mainland were denied a college education, and white students on the mainland often chose military service or defense jobs over college, the Nisei in Hawaii attended college in larger numbers than ever before. Those attending summer school were allowed inter-island travel, and that served as a motivation for some to continue their schooling. But the promise of a better education, a future away from the manual labor of the plantations, drew this generation to the university even before returning soldiers attended college with funds from the Servicemen's Readjustment Act, also known as the GI Bill.

After the war, the blackout's curfews and covered windows no longer stifled Japanese Americans, and many took active roles in their communities. Some chose to segregate themselves from other races by playing on the Japanese-only teams of the Americans of Japanese Ancestry Baseball League. Japanese Americans also reopened Buddhist temples and Shinto shrines, as well as teahouses and Japanese-language schools. In the latter half of the twentieth century, Japanese Americans dominated the political and economic arenas in Hawaii. They had begun to expand beyond the plantations' ethnic boundaries with labor strikes in the early twentieth century, and as historian Franklin Odo observes, they learned that they needed a policy of racial tolerance and inclusion if they were going to survive during the war. After the war, Japanese Americans did not want the "privilege" of being white, Odo argues, but they did manage to "negotiate the difficult haole/local boundaries in Hawaii."[17]

The Tsukiyama family, by virtue of being merchants and living in the city, had straddled the boundary between haole and local even prior to the war. Being Christian, going to English Standard Schools, and interacting with haoles established the Tsukiyama children in the larger American society; they were not part of the plantation communities on the islands. The eldest son, James, who had attended New York University and earned a degree in engineering well before most other Nisei in Hawaii ventured beyond the territory, spent the war years in Japan and was conscripted into the Japanese Army. At the war's end, the United States revoked his citizenship because of his experiences in Japan, and he did not regain entry into the United States until a federal court decided that his service in the Japanese military had been under duress. Only then did he regain his American citizenship. He moved to the U.S. mainland, where he gained employment in the aerospace industry, first with North American Aviation and then Hughes Aircraft Company.

The younger Tsukiyama son, Ted, served his country with patriotism and vigor as a member of the 442nd Regimental Combat Team and the Military Intelligence Service. He spent much of his time in service in Burma and India. After returning to Hawaii, he attended college on the GI Bill, went to Yale Law School, and became a lawyer and arbitrator. Kazu, who had graduated from the University of Hawaii just prior to the outbreak of World War II, earned a job as a social worker for the State of Hawaii. She married Ralph Vossbrink. After the war, the youngest Tsukiyama daughter, Martha, attended MacMurray College, a Methodist school in Jacksonville, Illinois. She then worked at the University of Hawaii and later married John Giovanelli. The Tsukiyamas' family business catered to the influx of haoles in Hawaii, and their religious activities gave them further contact with whites. The Nisei generation of this family certainly did not become haole, but it did assimilate by incorporating American customs and ideals, and future generations were indeed part haole.

The Tsukiyama family's leanings toward white society stood in evident contrast to the Ogatas' customs. The Tsukiyamas ate breakfast at dining tables set with cloth napkins and egg cups, whereas the Ogatas' breakfast, which they ate with chopsticks, often included rice and shoyu (soy sauce). But the more notable contrast came as the Nisei grew up. Both of Tsukiyama's brothers married Japanese American women, but her two sisters married white men. The Ogata children all married local Japanese (except Yoshiyuki, who never married). Many of the Ogata children were older than the Tsukiyamas and had married and started life on their own before the war, but even those who had not yet married remained in Hawaii after the war. Once Naoko and Yoshiharu married, they moved to the more rural setting of Kauai. By blood and by tradition, they were Japanese Americans, but through their economic status, they again stood apart from the local plantation community, even on Kauai. After the war, status became based on occupation, and ethnicity, once a primary determinant of one's occupation, was no longer the deciding factor. During and after the war, Naoko and Yoshiharu Ogata lived a quiet life on the rural island of Kauai, but they saw their friends and family members on Oahu climb Hawaii's social and economic ladders. These men and women had proven their Americanism during and after the war by accepting their situation and not making waves within their communities. Many Nisei men expressed their patriotism by serving in the military and later attended college with the help of government funding. They then became successful professionals and reared fully assimilated American children. Nisei soldiers had contemplated their place in U.S. society as Americans of Japanese ancestry. They wanted to become first-class citizens and learned that involving themselves in politics would help level the playing field. The GI Bill provided them a stipend to attend college, and the war gave them pride in their ethnicity—they expected to become part of Hawaii's economic, social, and political scene. After graduating, some went to law schools like Yale and Columbia, and others became university professors and politicians.[18] They were inspired to become doctors, lawyers, educators, labor union leaders, businessmen, and economists with the hope of building a Hawaii with equal rights and opportunities for everyone, regardless of color. Veterans, after seeing the "scum of the white race on the mainland," lost their "instinct of looking up to the *haole*."[19] The combination of their war experiences and ethnic pride led to a "new belief of many Island people that Hawaii's society must be democratized." One element of this democratization was stronger labor unions, which allowed for interethnic cooperation, including the organizing of a strike by all sugar workers in 1946.[20] That same year, six Americans of Japanese ancestry gained seats in the territorial legislature.[21] The Nisei were ready to shape their future, to end the haole regime in the islands.[22] In the "bloodless revolution" of 1954, fifty years of haole Republican dominance in Hawaii came to an end and Japanese Americans took the helm of the prevailing Democratic Party.[23] The Nisei used the lessons they had learned through discrimination, service, perseverance, and patriotism to craft their rise in society. American studies expert Dennis M. Ogawa emphasizes the phrase *okage sama de* ("I am what I am because of you") to express the "interdependency of ethnic members in a common wealth of interest, goal, identity, and mobility" that epitomized the Nisei.[24]

The third generation of Japanese Americans, the Sansei, found their lives shaped by their parents' and grandparents' experiences. Only 9 percent of Nisei married outside their race in 1940, but 22 percent did in 1945. Soldiers' travels had made them ambitious, confident, and experienced and thus more comfortable with dating white women.[25] Some recognized that being Japanese had been a "crime" that had sent their parents to internment camps. Thus, they "purposely distanced themselves and their children from all that was Japanese," and the Sansei grew up "almost oblivious to their Japanese heritage." Ogawa asserts, "No generation of nonwhite people in Hawaii, without the sacrifices of hard work and perseverance, had enjoyed so much of the affluence and abundance of Island living as had the Sansei." They obtained a college education and inherited homes, businesses, and material success from their parents. Their goals, problems, and ideals were those of contemporary American youth, as the mass media played a large role in their lives.[26] They participated in the civil rights movement of the 1960s and even pushed for programs in Asian American studies at their colleges and universities.[27] They still held on to traditional values like aspiration for success, fear of failure, and obligation to their parents. But they also married outside their race more than any other racial minority (60 to 70 percent by the 1990s).[28] Toward the end of the twentieth century, Japanese customs and cultural practices, from Buddhism to festivals and food, became a part island life for Hawaii's locals.[29]

World War II changed the idea and identity of being Japanese American in Hawaii. Being white in Hawaii was never the norm, and the war ended the elite status of haoles. First, the large influx of defense workers, some of whom chose not to leave the islands after the war, introduced new laborers—the working-class haoles. The identity of Japanese

Americans also changed. No longer did the majority work on plantations as manual laborers, and as they rose in class status, they climbed in Hawaii's racial hierarchy. The Nisei's patriotism at home and heroism abroad helped them gain respect in the eyes of the rest of Americans. The Territory of Hawaii, separate from the continental United States, had developed its own sense of race and identity before the war. The influence of mainstream America, the pressures of war, and a multicultural heritage all combined to create a local identity that the Nisei shaped through their efforts as part of "the Greatest Generation."

Epilogue
Until We Meet Again

WITH Japan's surprise bombing of Pearl Harbor, the citizens of the Territory of Hawaii and of the mainland United States faced confusion, anger, and worry. Naoko Tsukiyama experienced those emotions, but she also felt certain of two facts, as was evident in the reflection she wrote on December 7, 1941, and in her actions that followed that fateful day. First, she knew she was a loyal American citizen, and second, she accepted that her Japanese ancestry would require her to make sacrifices during wartime. Over the next four years, she saw how true that was. The war affected her work as a public school teacher, it limited her ability to be with her loved ones, and it emphasized to her that even though she could behave as a patriot, she would still face racism because she shared the physical features and common ancestry of the enemy. Yet, as was characteristic for the myriad Americans in the Hawaiian Islands, she persevered and carried on with her life as normally as she could.

For Naoko Tsukiyama and Yoshiharu Ogata, the drama of being in love in wartime culminated with their marriage in Honolulu on June 19, 1943. They exchanged their vows at the Tsukiyama family's church, the Harris United Methodist Church. Numerous friends and family members celebrated with them. The bridal party included Naoko's two sisters, Kazu and Martha. Baker Taniguchi, Yoshiharu's best friend from Kauai, stood as the best man. The ushers were close friends, along with people they knew from church and the YMCA. Naoko mentioned that because of the ongoing war and with so many men serving in the armed forces, there was simply a shortage of men from whom to choose. "The pickings were slim," she remarked in 2011, but many of the couple's friends in common, including Yozo Shigemura and Doris Fukuda, attended.[1] As mentioned earlier, Yoshiharu's parents could not attend the wedding, because their Issei status prevented them from being able to fly to Oahu.

The couple quickly settled into married life. They spent a few days honeymooning on Oahu, in a cottage at Camp Kokokahi, and then stayed at a beach house in Poipu on Kauai. They lived with Yoshiharu's parents and youngest sister in Wahiawa while Yoshiharu fixed up the family's other house on their property in the neighboring town of Kalaheo. Once that was done, the newlyweds moved there. During their lifetime together, they had two children, a son named Jon, born in 1944, and a daughter named Joy, born in 1946. In early 1953 the family moved to a house in Waimea that Yoshiharu had helped build, just across the street from Waimea High School and across from the Waimea Christian Church. The Ogatas fell into the lifestyle of the schoolteachers on

The couple's wedding picture, June 19, 1943. Photo in author's collection.

Kauai. They were active members of their community, participating in school events, helping to build the community swimming pool, and hosting swim meets as part of the Kauai Interscholastic Federation. They picnicked at the beach with the other Waimea High School teachers and their families. The Ogatas did not live among plantation workers or embrace the same kind of working-class culture that Japanese Americans who lived on the sugar plantations did. Although their children went to public schools alongside those who lived in plantation camps, the experiences of the Ogata children were different from those of the children whose parents were manual laborers. For example, the Ogata children did not eat typical plantation foods like green mango and dried fish, and they did not grow up around the Buddhist church (after the war, locals referred to it as the Buddhist church, not the Buddhist temple). Their family even had domestic help, including a laundress. Jon and Joy expected to go to college after high school and to work in white-collar jobs. The family embraced both Japanese and American traditions, but the Ogatas' positions as teachers meant that they behaved in ways that the locals who grew up on the sugar plantations considered more haole than Japanese. In the postwar era, it had become easier to rise in class and social status, but upbringing more than ethnicity helped form one's identity.

As teachers within the statewide school system, both Yoshiharu Ogata and Naoko Tsukiyama (or Mrs. Ogata, as she became known) were influential in their community. Ogata taught industrial arts classes at Waimea High School, including woodshop, metal shop, and mechanical drawing. He often took charge of *Ka Menehune* (the high school yearbook) and acted as the school photographer for many years. He took his family to the high school football games and captured pictures of the events, developing the photographs in the school's darkroom. He even colorized the yearbook photos by painting on them. Among his other duties were coaching tennis, selling tickets to football games, and chaperoning dances and class outings. Mrs. Ogata taught kindergarten

The Ogata clan on Kauai, January 1947. Naoko Ogata is on the left, kneeling and holding the couple's daughter, Joy. Yoshiharu Ogata is kneeling, on the far right, and carrying their son, Jon. Photo in author's collection.

and later worked as a librarian at Waimea Elementary School. Eventually she served as a part-time librarian at Kaumakani School and Kekaha School, both near Waimea. Naoko retired from the State of Hawaii in 1972, when the couple's first granddaughter was born, and she embraced a new job—that of grandmother and babysitter. She was active in the Waimea United Church of Christ and still participates in the numerous activities that the neighborhood's senior center offers. Yoshiharu's retirement story is not as clear. The family believes that he retired from Waimea High School in 1973. The schoolteachers went on strike that year, but Ogata continued to work. After being labeled a "scab," he was no longer happy working there and chose to retire. Ogata then dedicated his time to working in his woodshop and playing golf.

The family spent most of their time on Kauai and also visited Oahu. They went to Christmas Eve services at the Waimea Christian Church,

The Ogata family at their family home in Waimea, Kauai, ca. 1963. They are sitting on a bench that Yoshiharu Ogata made. *Left to right:* Jon, Joy, Naoko, and Yoshiharu. Photo in author's collection.

whose members were primarily Japanese Americans.[2] They celebrated New Year's Day with their extended family, eating traditional Japanese foods like *mochi* (a rice-based pastry) and drinking sake. When the family visited relatives on Oahu, they saw the Tsukiyamas' Japanese store in Chinatown, but they also attended Harris Church with both haole and Japanese families. Naoko remembers returning to the Big Island only once after the war, to participate in a hula competition in the 1980s.

On June 19, 2007, Yoshiharu and Naoko uneventfully passed their sixty-fourth wedding anniversary. Yoshiharu Ogata died of congestive heart failure nine days later. Naoko lives in her home in Waimea that the couple built. She spends some of her free time planting flowers and vegetables in the garden on the church grounds across the street from her home. At the time when the research phase of this project began, she was ninety-four years old and beginning to slow down. As she reflected on her and Yoshiharu's courtship—what she fondly recollects as "the good old days"—she shared that she had had a number of boyfriends but "the only man [she] really loved," "the only man [she] intensely loved," was her "dear husband." And instead of saying "goodbye," she prefers to say, "a hui hou," or "until we meet again."[3]

NOTES

Book Epigraph

Tom Coffman, *The Island Edge of America: A Political History of Hawaiʻi*, 49.

Preface

1. "Nikkei Legacy Project," University of Hawaii at Manoa Library (hereafter cited as UHM Library), accessed July 26, 2012, http://libweb.hawaii.edu/digicoll /nikkei/RASRL.html.

1. We Should Be Made to Suffer

Epigraph. Naoko Tsukiyama, December 7, 1941. Copy in possession of author.

1. Nordyke, *Peopling of Hawaii*, 63.

2. Takaki, *Pau Hana*, 25–27, 42.

3. Residents of Hawaii refer to the continental United States as "the mainland." Historian Eileen Tamura notes that this has been the pattern since Hawaii became a U.S. territory. Tamura, *Americanization*, xvii.

4. Takaki, *Strangers from a Different Shore*, 44, 45, 147.

5. Japanese people in Hawaii and on the mainland celebrated Japan's accomplishments in the Sino-Japanese War and the Russo-Japanese War. The development of Japan into a world power made some Americans see the Japanese as a threat, and states passed laws promoting segregation and restricting Japanese laborers. Hawaii did not restrict Japanese laborers, but Japan's aggression contributed to racial tension in the islands. Tamura, *Americanization*, 19, 71; Robinson, *Tragedy of Democracy*, 13; Robinson, *By Order of the President*, 4.

6. Adams, preface to *Peoples of Hawaii*, 3.

7. Nordyke, *Peopling of Hawaii*, 66.

8. Ogawa, *Kodomo No Tame Ni*, 52; Fugita and Fernandez, "Religion and Japanese Americans' Views," 115–16.

9. Ninety-eight percent of Japanese children in public schools were also in Japanese-language schools by 1920. Takaki, *Pau Hana*, 117.

10. Daws, *Shoal of Time*, 308.

11. Ibid.; Ogawa, *Kodomo No Tame Ni*, 143, 182; Kinoshita, "Telling Our Roots," 1, 5.

12. This information comes from Yoshiko Tsukiyama's memoir and Seinosuke Tsukiyama's memoir. Copies in possession of author.

13. Odo, *No Sword to Bury*, 57.

14. Tamura, "In Retrospect," 25.

15. According to Ted Tsukiyama, the family was also not part of the upper crust of Japanese society. Odo, *No Sword to Bury*, 55. Seinosuke Tsukiyama had to work and be successful at his business in order to earn money to sustain his family. Yet the work he did was not considered manual labor, as was work on the plantations. The Tsukiyama family was not rich but certainly shared characteristics of the middle class—owning land, sending the children to college, and even hiring domestic help.

16. Odo, *No Sword to Bury*, 27, 55.

17. Fugita and Fernandez, "Religion and Japanese Americans' Views," 115; Ogawa, *Kodomo No Tame Ni*, 49, 188.

18. Odo, *No Sword to Bury*, 84.

19. Ibid., 40, 41.

20. Coffman, *Island Edge of America*, 41.

21. When plantation laborers arrived in Hawaii, they met both Christian and Buddhist missionaries, but of the 100,000 Japanese in Hawaii in 1916, only 1,700 identified as Christian. Daws, *Shoal of Time*, 308.

22. Tamura, *Americanization*, 33.

23. Harris United Methodist Church, *Century of Growth*, 4, 8. At the turn of the century, "Orientals" were refused acceptance at the YMCA, but by 1927 they could join either the Central YMCA or the Nuuanu YMCA in Hawaii. Harada, "Social Status," 7.

24. Harris United Methodist Church, *Century of Growth*, 12.

25. Yoshiharu Ogata, in discussion with Joy Miyamoto, December 6, 2001.

26. The YMCA grew in importance in Hawaii in the 1930s and provided physical space, programs, and leadership training for more than twenty-five thousand boys. Odo, *No Sword to Bury*, 41, 75.

27. Laselle Gilman, "Kauai Morale Group Works Out Solution for 'Jap' Problem: Noboru Miyake Called Example of Trustworthy US Citizen," *Honolulu Advertiser*, June 20, 1943, Box 13, Folder 5, Ka-37, Romanzo Adams Social Research Laboratory (RASRL) Confidential Files, Archives and Manuscripts Collections, UHM Library (hereafter cited as RASRL Confidential Files).

28. Naoko Ogata, in discussion with the author, July 2008.

29. Michael Omi and Howard Winant use this idea in relation to African Americans, but the same pattern existed for Japanese Americans in Hawaii, which did

not have a sizable African American community. Omi and Winant, *Racial Formation*, 27–28.

30. Adams, preface to *Peoples of Hawaii*, 3, 5.

31. Thalia Massie, the wife of a navy officer, reported that five local men kidnapped, beat, and raped her. Although the men were found not guilty (and there was no proof that they were), white vigilantes retaliated against the five with violence, even murdering one of them. When the vigilantes did not receive appropriate penalties for their actions in the ensuing Massie-Kahahawai case, a sharp divide was created between the local community and the haole elite in Hawaii. David Stannard, "The Massie Case: Injustice and Courage," *Honolulu Advertiser*, October 14, 2001, accessed August 15, 2012, http://the.honoluluadvertiser.com/article/2001/Oct/14/op/op03a.html. Historian John Rosa explains that the Massie-Kahahawai case "has often been cited as the first time the term 'local' was used in Hawaii with any salience." Rosa, "Massie-Kahahawai Case," 4; Rosa, "Local Story," 94. And ethnic studies expert Jonathan Y. Okamura argues: "Hawai'i was a highly racialized society with virtually every aspect of institutional and individual life greatly influenced, if not determined, by race. Race . . . constituted the ultimate barrier of exclusion and subordination for local people." Okamura, "Massie-Kahahawai Case," 6.

32. John Rosa, who studies the impact of the Massie case from a twenty-first-century perspective, asserts that post-1965 immigrants do not count as local. Rosa, "Local Story," 94.

33. Coffman, *Island Edge of America*, 10.

34. Foo, "Hawaii," 163.

35. Ogawa, *Kodomo No Tame Ni*, 195.

36. Rosa, "Local Story," 95, 101.

37. Nordyke, *Peopling of Hawaii*, 174–75, 178–79.

38. Beth Bailey and David Farber point out that "white" was not a coherent category either. Bailey and Farber, *First Strange Place*, 26, 22. However, the authors note that Hawaiian locals did not see the variations of whites (categories like Jewish, Catholic, Anglo-American, eastern European, and so on,). Instead, the basic distinction that locals made was between local and haole. Ibid., 139.

39. Daws, *Shoal of Time*, 337.

40. Takaki, *Pau Hana*, 64–67.

41. Daws, *Shoal of Time*, 337–38.

2. These Things I Love

1. Yoshiharu Ogata, interview by Joy Miyamoto, Waimea, Hawaii, December 6, 2001.

2. Conn, Engelman, and Fairchild, *Guarding the United States*, 199.

3. Anthony, *Hawaii under Army Rule*, 1–2; Office of the Coordinator, Major Disaster Council, "Protection of Industrial Plants and Public Buildings,"

October 22, 1941, Box 17, unnumbered folder, Uncataloged Subject Files, Archives and Manuscripts Collections, UHM Library (hereafter cited as USF).

4. Office of the Coordinator, Major Disaster Council, "Defend Your Home Country against Fire," October 22, 1941, Box 17, unnumbered folder, USF.

5. Office of the Coordinator, Major Disaster Council, "Emergency Food Storage List for Private Families," October 22, 1941, Box 17, unnumbered folder, USF.

6. Anthony, *Hawaii under Army Rule*, 4.

7. Department of Public Instruction, Kauai—Kekaha School, "A History of Our War Report, 1941–1944," Original Subject Files, Hawaii War Records Depository, Archives and Manuscripts Collections, UHM Library (hereafter cited as HWRD).

8. Naomi Benyas, "This Realm of Ours," Box 17, Folder Young America Wants to Help, USF.

9. Elizabeth B. Bell to Mrs. Tennent, November 12, 1940, Box 17, Folder Madge Tennet [*sic*] Group, USF.

10. Robinson, *By Order of the President*, 49–70.

11. Tamura, *Americanization*, 5.

12. Fiset, *Imprisoned Apart*, 14–15, 27–28.

13. Coffman, *Island Edge of America*, 52–55.

14. The Nationality Law of Japan allowed all children of subjects of Japan to be Japanese citizens if their parents recorded their births with the Japanese Consul within two weeks. Harada, "Social Status," 12.

15. Ogawa, *Kodomo No Tame Ni*, 256, 272, 299–300.

16. Coffman, *Island Edge of America*, 29.

17. Gary Y. Okihiro, *Storied Lives*, xi.

18. Masuda, *Letters from the 442nd*, 169.

19. Schrum, *Some Wore Bobby Sox*, 98, 102, 129, 154.

20. This song may actually be Jimmy Dorsey's "The Things I Love." The song "Nighty Night" debuted in 1941, by Yvonne King. The Armed Forces Radio Network often played it to sign off at the end of the broadcast day. "'King Sister' Yvonne Dies at 89," CNN Entertainment, December 18, 2009, accessed February 2, 2011, www.cnn.com/2009/SHOWBIZ/Music/12/17/yvonne.king.burch.obit/; "Alvino Rey: Nighty Night," Lyrics Vault, accessed October 18, 2012, www.lyricsvault.net/php/artist.php?s=19427.

21. Naoko Tsukiyama to Yoshiharu Ogata, July 28, 1941; Yoshiharu Ogata to Naoko Tsukiyama, August 1, 1941. Copies of all correspondence between Naoko Tsukiyama and Yoshiharu Ogata are in the author's possession.

22. Kessler, *Stubborn Twig*, 131–32, 169.

23. Michael Okihiro, *AJA Baseball in Hawaii*, 7–8, 11.

24. Even in the twenty-first century, many of the islands have Americans of Japanese Ancestry (AJA) Baseball League teams, in which only those who can trace their bloodline back to Japan are allowed to play. There is no minimum blood quota,

nor does the organization require proof of biological race, but those who are not AJAs are not allowed to join the league. Chinen, "Hawaii's AJAs 'Play Ball!'"; Miyamoto, "Last Samurai."

25. Ogawa, *Kodomo No Tame Ni*, 204.

26. Bailey and Farber, *First Strange Place*, 19.

27. Tamura, *Americanization*, 128.

28. Ibid., 93.

29. Yoo, *Growing Up Nisei*, 22; Odo, *No Sword to Bury*, 245.

30. Bailey and Farber, *First Strange Place*, 204. Michelle Morgan argues that the DPI sought to "limit Japanese entry into the [teaching] corps," while Nisei in Hawaii believed that "education and the teaching profession [were] vehicles to middle-class American life." Morgan, "Americanizing the Teachers," 154–55.

31. Mount Waialeale, whose name means "rippling water," is touted as the wettest spot on earth, but there are a few other contenders, depending on the rainfall average over a particular period. Terrell Johnson, "Where, Exactly, Is the Wettest Spot on Earth?" The Weather Channel, accessed October 30, 2014, http://wap.weather.com/news/science/nature/wettest-place-earth-20130529. Mount Waialeale has an elevation of more than five thousand feet.

32. The "Hawaii" identified here is Hawaii Island, or the Big Island of Hawaii. The distance between Oahu and the Big Island of Hawaii is just over two hundred miles.

33. She is referring to Wahiawa, in the central part of Oahu. This town was known for its rural community and was the home of Dole Food Company. That town should not be confused with the plantation community on Kauai where Yoshiharu's family lived.

34. Ala Moana Beach Park is in Honolulu, near Waikiki.

35. The "breakers" refer to the breakwater.

36. Naoko knew Doris Fukuda, who was from downtown Honolulu and went to McKinley High School. Fukuda went to the University of Hawaii, where she was a member of Wakaba Kai, the Japanese sorority, and then to Columbia University for her master's degree. Afterward, she moved to Kauai and taught at Waimea High School. She married George Crowell, who became the chief of police on Kauai.

37. Stricker, "Cookbooks and Law Books," 480.

38. Welshimer, "'My Husband Says—.'"

39. Mizuno, *Ka Palapala*, 132.

40. Matsumoto, "Japanese American Women," 389.

41. Tamura, *Americanization*, 26.

42. In 1890 the emperor of Japan proclaimed the Imperial Rescript on Education, setting a sixth-grade standard of reading for Japanese citizens. Coffman, *Island Edge of America*, 16.

43. Yoo, *Growing Up Nisei*, 18.

44. Gary Y. Okihiro, *Storied Lives*, 19, 64.

45. Robinson, *Tragedy of Democracy*, 26–27.

46. Gary Y. Okihiro, *Storied Lives*, 9.

47. Sasai, "Two Years," 84.

48. Yamate, "Sugamo Prison," 328; Fugita and Fernandez, "Religion and Japanese Americans' Views," 166.

49. Harada, "Social Status," 6.

50. Sasai, "Two Years," 83.

51. Matsunaga, "Rededication," 396.

52. Ogawa, *Kodomo No Tame Ni*, 196.

53. Sasai, "Two Years," 82–83; Ogawa, *Kodomo No Tame Ni*, 195. Tamura argues that the English Standard Schools encouraged elitism—about one-half of all students at the Standard Schools were white, whereas only 3 to 8.5 percent were Japanese. Tamura, *Americanization*, 110–13.

54. Ogawa, *Kodomo No Tame Ni*, 215–16.

55. Odo, *No Sword to Bury*, 37.

56. Kessler, *Stubborn Twig*, 284.

57. Tamura, *Americanization*, 152.

58. Ogawa, *Kodomo No Tame Ni*, 109.

59. Kessler, *Stubborn Twig*, 133.

60. Ogawa, *Kodomo No Tame Ni*, 218–20.

61. William C. Smith, "Second Generation," 9.

62. Ogawa, *Kodomo No Tame Ni*, 87.

63. Mizuno, *Ka Palapala*, 207–49. The 1940 *Ka Palapala* shows that of 309 graduating seniors in 1940, 128 (or 41.4 percent) had distinctly Japanese last names. Sherman Seki, email message to author, June 29, 2012. Seki is the archivist technician at the University of Hawaii at Manoa Archives and Manuscripts.

64. Ibid., 133–57. In 1940 the university had a number of social fraternities and sororities organized and separated by race. Worthy of note is that the 1944 yearbook, which was almost not published, does not contain any records of the racial fraternities and sororities. The university setting blurred class and geographic lines, but the ethnic sororities and fraternities demonstrated that Americans used race for social structure and for cultural representation. Omi and Winant, *Racial Formation*, 56.

65. Omi and Winant, *Racial Formation*, 55.

66. Tamura, *Americanization*, xv.

67. Naoko Tsukiyama to Yoshiharu Ogata, August 17, 1941.

68. Yoshiharu Ogata to Naoko Tsukiyama, August 20, 1941.

69. Naoko Tsukiyama to Yoshiharu Ogata, August 17, 1941.

70. The Asahi (meaning "Morning Sun" or "Rising Sun") baseball team began in the Japanese communities of the sugar plantation camps and gained fame by participating in the Hawaii Baseball League and making trips to Asia before World War II, and even as late as 1974, to play in the Japan Goodwill Semi-Pro Series. "Fabled Asahi Ball Club Celebrates Centennial," *Honolulu Advertiser*,

September 12, 2005, accessed March 17, 2011, http://the.honoluluadvertiser.com /article/2005/Sep/12/ln/FP509120333.html.

71. "About Us," Central Middle School, accessed August 19, 2011, https://sites .google.com/site/centralmiddleschoolhonolulu/about-us.

72. Naoko Tsukiyama to Yoshiharu Ogata, August 31, 1941.

73. Shizue Katashima is another of Naoko's classmates. Katashima, whose grades were better than Naoko's, got a job in administration while Naoko took a job as faculty. Katashima later married Ernest Watanabe, who was a soldier stationed in Australia during World War II. When Watanabe was in Brisbane, he grew flowers outside of his barracks as a way to pass the time. The flowers made him think of Katashima, his fiancée, and he also thought of the couples separated by war. Upon his return to Hawaii, he started a floral business, selling roses to returning soldiers and their loved ones. Watanabe, along with his new wife and later his children, built what is now known as Watanabe Floral, one of the preeminent floral shops in Hawaii. "About Watanabe Floral," Watanabe Floral, accessed May 7, 2014, www.watanabefloral.com/about/.

74. The town of Kalapana is south of Hilo.

75. The couple's first date included a walk up Wilhelmina Rise, a steep hill off Tenth Avenue in the area of Kaimuki, near the Tsukiyama family's Honolulu home.

3. The Sun Still Shines

1. Details on the bombing of Pearl Harbor are provided in Lyons, *World War II*, 145–47.

2. Inouye, foreword to *Japanese Eyes: Personal Reflections*, ix.

3. Robinson, *Tragedy of Democracy*, 66; Conn, Engelman, and Fairchild, *Guarding the United States*, 200–201; David White and Daniel P. Murphy, "Hawaii under Martial Law," Netplaces.com, accessed July 30, 2013, www.netplaces.com /world-war-ii/the-united-states-enters-the-war/hawaii-under-martial-law.htm.

4. Anthony, *Hawaii under Army Rule*, 103.

5. Acceptable lights included ones of no more than twenty-five watts, with an opaque coating, and only one light was allowed in a space less than one hundred square feet. Office of the Military Governor, Territory of Hawaii, General Orders Nos. 18 and 25, September 28 and October 5, 1943; Anthony, *Hawaii under Army Rule*, 171.

6. Anonymous, "Report of Groups Appointed to Study Problems and Needs of Youth," February 20, 1943, Box 15, Folder 8-RHa–Rural Hawaii, RHa-56a, RASRL Confidential Files.

7. Bailey and Farber, *First Strange Place*, 11–13.

8. Anthony, *Hawaii under Army Rule*, 10; Brown, *Hawaii Goes to War*, 89; Allen, *Hawaii's War Years*, 375. Allen explains that the basic monthly ration was ten gallons a month, and on Kauai, individuals could buy three gallons a week. Brown

notes that liquor permits, once obtained, allowed the bearer one quart of hard liquor, one case of beer, or one gallon of wine each week.

9. Simpson, *Hawai'i Homefront*, 165.

10. Cornelius C. Smith, Jr., as cited in Jones and Jones, *Hawaii Goes to War*, 3, 87–88.

11. Brown, *Hawaii Goes to War*, 110.

12. Coffman, *Island Edge of America*, 106; Anthony, *Hawaii under Army Rule*, 42.

13. Anthony, *Hawaii under Army Rule*, 13, 15, 93.

14. King Kamehameha V Judiciary History Center, Honolulu (hereafter cited as Judiciary History Center), "Martial Law: Hawaii under Martial Law: 1941–1944," accessed July 26, 2012, http://jhchawaii.net/martial-law; Conn, Engelman, and Fairchild, *Guarding the United States*, 203; Anthony, *Hawaii under Army Rule*, 174.

15. Robinson, *Tragedy of Democracy*, 226. Anthony provides an example of one man receiving a punishment of five years hard-labor for assaulting a police officer, when a peace-time punishment for that offense would have been a fine of twenty-five dollars. Anthony, *Hawaii under Army Rule*, 18–19.

16. Akita, "Days of Infamy," 39–42.

17. "Hawaii War Records Depository Photographs: Jan–Jun 1942," HWRD, accessed January 17, 2013, http://libweb.hawaii.edu/digicoll/hwrd/HWRD_html /HWRD42a.html.

18. Brown, *Hawaii Goes to War*, 66, 67, 78; Jones and Jones, *Hawaii Goes to War*, 9; *Honolulu Advertiser*, as reprinted in Simpson, *Hawai'i Homefront*, vi.

19. "Hawaii War Records Depository Photographs."

20. Jones and Jones, *Hawaii Goes to War*, 83–84.

21. Naoko Tsukiyama, "Untitled," December 7, 1941.

22. Dower, "Race, Language, and War," 173–74; Kenneth Ozaki, "The Japanese Hysteria," Box 10, Folder 17-J-Japanese, Jj-10-I, RASRL Confidential Files.

23. Kanaka Kondo, "No Title," Folder SJ 339–55 (Spring '43) (Interracial Dating), UHSj-347-I, RASRL Student Papers; Heather Todd, "Post-War Ethnic Group Controls," Folder Student Journals 191–205 Soc. 151 1943, UhShe-195-I, RASRL Student Papers; Yoshida, "Speak American," 330.

24. Ogawa, *Kodomo No Tame Ni*, 316.

25. Ibid., 191.

26. Gary Y. Okihiro's study examines the efforts and experiences of Japanese American college students during World War II. The author focuses on the "anti-racism" displayed between whites and Japanese Americans at the time, as many of them worked together to further the education of Nisei college students. Gary Y. Okihiro, *Storied Lives*, 32, 82–85.

27. Franklin Odo's work on the Japanese American men who mobilized to participate in the war effort remains one of the seminal studies on war efforts of Japanese Americans in Hawaii. Odo, *No Sword to Bury*, 146.

28. Ted Tsukiyama, as quoted in Odo, *No Sword to Bury*, 161.

29. Martin's "Tonight We Love" is based on Tchaikovsky's Piano Concerto No. 1 in B-Flat Minor. "Tonight We Love," International Lyrics Playground, accessed February 9, 2011, http://lyricsplayground.com/alpha/songs/t/tonightwelove.shtml.

30. *Tom, Dick and Harry* was released in 1941 by RKO Radio Pictures. "Tom Dick and Harry," IMDb, accessed March 18, 2011, www.imdb.com/title/tt0034299/.

31. Brown, *Hawaii Goes to War*, 66, 76.

32. Office of Civilian Registration, "The Enumeration Instruction Bulletin," Original Subject Files, HWRD.

33. Jones and Jones, *Hawaii Goes to War*, 89; Klass, *World War II on Kauai*, 36, 37.

34. Morgan, "Americanizing the Teachers," 153; Odo, *No Sword to Bury*, 245.

35. Mits Fukuda, Doris's cousin, was the husband mentioned in the letters. He became a high-ranking officer in the 100th Battalion of the 442nd. Additional information can be found at 100th Infantry Battalion Veterans Education Center in Honolulu. Michael Markrich, "History: Mitsuyoshi Fukuda, Born to Lead," 100th Infantry Battalion Veterans Education Center, accessed October 30, 2014, www.100thbattalion.org/history/veterans/officers/mitsuyoshi-fukuda/2/. Fukuda married Toshiko Okazaki. Naoko Tsukiyama to Yoshiharu Ogata, February 1, 1942.

36. Naoko Tsukiyama to Yoshiharu Ogata, January 11, 1942.

37. Yoshiharu Ogata to Naoko Tsukiyama, February 3, 1942. He wrote her that message on his twenty-third birthday.

38. Odo, *No Sword to Bury*, 197–198.

39. Kapiolani Elementary School is in Hilo. Mrs. Beers earned the nickname "Ma" Beers, as will be seen in upcoming letters.

40. Honokaa is a coastal city, about one hour away from Hilo, traveling in a counterclockwise, northwestward direction.

41. Naoko remembered Tokuji Ono as a fellow student at the University of Hawaii who lived at the YMCA. He later became part of the 100th Infantry Battalion.

42. Yoshiharu is referring to Yoshiyuki, who joined the military, and to Yoshio, the oldest brother, who had three children and another on the way.

43. Masao Yamada, interview by Andrew W. Lind, Hanapepe, Hawaii, March 2, 1943, Box 12, Folder 23, Kaj-22c, RASRL Confidential Files.

44. Anonymous, "Report of Groups."

45. Kondo, "No Title."

46. Takaki, *Strangers from a Different Shore*, 383.

47. Department of Public Instruction, Misc. Circular No. 669 and Supplement to Misc. Circular No. 669, "A Letter to Teachers," January 10, 1942, Box 20, Folder 20-TS–Teachers Schools, TS-80-I, RASRL Confidential Files.

48. Morris Fox, recorder, "Report of the Keymen's and Laymen's Conference," November 8, 1942, Box 15, Folder 8, RHa-58, RASRL Confidential Files.

49. Anonymous, "Impact on Public Schools," *Honolulu Star-Bulletin*, April 1, 1942.

50. Department of Public Instruction, Kauai, "History of Our War." *Kiawe* is the Hawaiian word for mesquite. Many of the beachfronts had mesquite jungles that needed to be cleared to prevent enemies from sneaking onto the islands.

51. "Hawaii War Records Depository Photographs."

52. Naoko Tsukiyama to Yoshiharu Ogata, January 15, 1942.

53. Naoko Tsukiyama to Yoshiharu Ogata, January 26, 1942.

54. Naoko Tsukiyama to Yoshiharu Ogata, January 26, 1942, and February 1, 1942.

55. Yoshiharu Ogata to Naoko Tsukiyama, January 27, 1942. Columbia Pictures released *Here Comes Mr. Jordan*, a romantic comedy, in 1941. "Here Comes Mr. Jordan," IMDb, accessed February 9, 2011, www.imdb.com/title/tt0033712/.

56. Waipahu was a rural town in central Oahu, about fifteen miles west of Honolulu.

57. Yoshiharu Ogata to Naoko Tsukiyama, January 20, 1942.

58. Yoshiharu Ogata to Naoko Tsukiyama, January 27, 1942.

59. Yoshiharu Ogata to Naoko Tsukiyama, January 20, 1942.

60. Yoshiharu Ogata to Naoko Tsukiyama, January 27, 1942, and February 3, 1942.

61. Naoko Tsukiyama to Yoshiharu Ogata, January 26, 1942.

62. Blank line; nothing written here.

63. Blank line; nothing written here.

64. As the war effort grew and more military men moved into the islands, they began living at the schools. The military took over some schools entirely, also using the grounds, teachers' cottages, and other specified buildings. That forced Naoko and other teachers to move their class sites. Naoko explained that they taught up to eight students at a time in the basements of people's homes. On some days, they taught three hours in the morning and an additional three hours in the afternoon or evening.

65. "Period," according to Naoko, was their secret code for "kiss." This is the first letter in which she uses the code, and both Yoshiharu and Naoko signed many of their letters from this point with "Period" or "Periods," sending their long-distance kisses to each other.

66. The "him" referred to here is probably Mr. Gordon, the principal.

67. It looks like he wrote "P.T.A." here. This might be the Parent Teacher Association.

68. Tondryk, *Nineteen-Forty Tower*, 63.

69. Yoshiharu Ogata to Naoko Tsukiyama, February 13, 1942.

70. Yoshiharu Ogata to Naoko Tsukiyama, April 12, 1942.

71. Yoshiharu Ogata to Naoko Tsukiyama, February 13, 1942.

72. Naoko Tsukiyama to Yoshiharu Ogata, February 18, 1942.

73. Ted Tsukiyama, "Remembering Brother Jimmy," eulogy, December 21, 2009, copy in possession of author.

74. The Nisei increasingly participated in church. Buddhist temples changed to Buddhist churches as an attempt at Americanization, but the new generation also went to Christian churches and Sunday schools because those were in English, the language with which they felt more comfortable. Ogawa, *Kodomo No Tame Ni*, 193; Harada, "Social Status," 9.

75. Anonymous, "Report of Groups."

76. "Oil: Ration Time," *Time Magazine*, March 23, 1942, accessed August 15, 2011, www.time.com/time/magazine/article/0,9171,802299,00.html#ixzz1G7T 304jW.

77. "Stitch in Time," *Time Magazine*, March 30, 1942, accessed August 15, 2011, www.time.com/time/magazine/article/0,9171,773154,00.html#ixzz1G7RDXIib.

78. Robinson, *By Order of the President*, 201.

79. Brown, *Hawaii Goes to War*, 97.

80. Mike Fern, "Kauai Goes to War," and Paradise of the Pacific, "Ke Kauwa Nei O Kauai (Kauai at War)," Folder 37 Kauai, Island of, HWRD.

81. Todd, "Post-War Ethnic Group Controls."

82. Ogawa, *Kodomo No Tame Ni*, 313–15; Coffman, *Island Edge of America*, 67.

83. Robinson, *Tragedy of Democracy*, 114.

84. Kamishita, "Honor Thy Country," 45–46.

85. Harada, "Social Status," 5.

86. Yamate, "Sugamo Prison," 329; Ted Tsukiyama, "An American," 336.

87. Odo, *No Sword to Bury*, 1, 2, 105–27.

88. Ibid., 128.

89. Ibid., 1, 2, 103, 122, 151, 183–94. Schofield Barracks was the biggest army post in the United States. Daws, *Shoal of Time*, 317; Coffman, *Island Edge of America*, 78–79.

90. Odo, *No Sword to Bury*, 194, 206.

91. Sasai, "Two Years," 86.

92. As quoted in Odo, *No Sword to Bury*, 161.

93. Odo, *No Sword to Bury*, 44.

94. "Army & Navy and Civilian Defense—Manpower: More from the Bowl," *Time Magazine*, March 16, 1942, accessed May 1, 2011, www.time.com/time /magazine/article/0,9171,801397,00.html#ixzz1G7W011Au.

95. Naoko mentioned going on a coastal ride with a Mrs. Chang, who lived near the airport, but could not provide further information on her.

96. Davis is a beach area on the windward side of Oahu. It is about thirty minutes from Honolulu.

97. Conn, Engelman and Fairchild, *Guarding the United States*, 217. The population on Oahu rose from two hundred thousand in 1940 to five hundred thousand at the height of the war. Anthony, *Hawaii under Army Rule*, 3; Bailey and Farber, *First Strange Place*, 27, 31.

98. Bailey and Farber, *First Strange Place*, 34–35.

99. Ibid., 43, 38.

100. Anthony, *Hawaii under Army Rule*, 40, 23, 80.

101. Bailey and Farber, *First Strange Place*, 98–107. Bailey and Farber point out that brothels would keep lower-class white men and nonwhite men away from "respectable" white women.

102. Ibid., 140.

103. Kawasaki, "No Title," Folder Student Journals 191–205 Soc. 151 1943, UHSj-204-I, RASRL Student Papers.

104. Anonymous, "No Title," Box 12, Folder 22, KaJ-20-a, RASRL Confidential Files.

105. Kondo, "No Title."

106. Isami Kurasaki to Dr. Lind, April 1, 1943, Box 12, Folder 22, RASRL Confidential Files.

107. Masao Yamada, interview.

108. Lai Sew Choy, "Immediate Effects of This War on the Races in the Territory," Folder Student Journals 191–205 Soc. 151 1943, UHSk-193-I, RASRL Student Papers.

109. Kawasaki, "No Title."

110. Mrs. N. Y. School Teacher, interview by H. Suzuki, Eleele, Hawaii, June 24, 1943, Box 20, Folder 20 TS–Teachers Schools, TSj-78-III, RASRL Confidential Files.

111. Bailey and Farber, *First Strange Place*, 194.

112. William Valentine or Valentin, "Interracial Dating and Marriage," Folder SJ 339–355 (Spring '43) (Interracial Dating), UHShe-342-I, RASRL Student Papers.

113. Bailey and Farber, *First Strange Place*, 198.

114. Ruth Ansai, "The Problems with Americans of Japanese Ancestry in War-Time Hawaii," Folder SJ 206–220 (Summer '43 Race Relations), UHSj-216-IV, RASRL Student Paper; Todd, "Post-War Ethnic Group Controls."

115. Choy, "Immediate Effects."

116. Kondo, "No Title."

117. Bailey and Farber, *First Strange Place*, 197, 201.

118. Mrs. N. Y. School Teacher interview.

119. Jane Hamamura, "Interracial Dating," Folder SJ 295–314 (Summer 1943) (Effect of War on My Community), UHSj-345-I, RASRL Student Papers.

120. Anonymous, "Report of Groups."

121. Bailey and Farber, *First Strange Place*, 173–88.

122. The Waiakea Sugar Mill Company in Hilo was part of the Theo H. Davies and Company enterprise. At this time, Naoko lived with the Shinoda family. The Shinodas ran the Shinoda Dormitory, which housed students attending schools in Hilo, and most of the boarders were Japanese Americans. Naoko remembers that Mrs. Shinoda cooked Japanese food for them, and Mr. Shinoda was a Japanese language teacher. During World War II, he faced being interned. However, the

Shinodas' daughter dated a Portuguese man named Bruno Nunes, who had a civil service job. She believes that his connections at first saved Mr. Shinoda from being interned at Sand Island. Although the Shinoda daughter married Nunes, Mr. Shinoda was later removed from his home and family and interned. Roger Daniels addresses internment further in *Prisoners without Trial*, 47–48.

123. For more details on the Hotel Street vice district, see Bailey and Farber, *First Strange Place*.

124. Tondryk, *Nineteen-Forty Tower*, 5–13, 63.

125. Anonymous, "Education: High-School Students Build Plane Models," *Life Magazine*, March 23, 1942, accessed May 2, 2011, http://books.google.com/books ?id=x1EEAAAAMBAJ&lpg=PP1&pg=PA118.

126. Anonymous, "Schools Asked to Build Model Planes," *Honolulu Star-Bulletin*, February 25, 1942, Box 49, Folder 13, HWRD.

127. Anonymous, "Model Plane Builders Can Help Uncle Sam," *Honolulu Star-Bulletin*, March 18, 1942, Box 49, Folder 2, HWRD.

128. Anonymous, "Youth of Hawaii to Build 2000 Model Planes in National Drive," Box 49, Folder 13, HWRD.

129. Naoko Tsukiyama to Yoshiharu Ogata, March 2, 1942.

130. Naoko Tsukiyama to Yoshiharu Ogata, April 15, 1942.

131. Yoshiharu Ogata to Naoko Tsukiyama, March 18, 1942.

132. Naoko Tsukiyama to Yoshiharu Ogata, March 21, 1942.

133. Naoko Tsukiyama to Yoshiharu Ogata, March 27, 1942.

134. "U.S. at War: War Brides," *Time Magazine*, March 30, 1942, accessed January 18, 2013, www.time.com/time/magazine/article/0,9171,773155,00.html#ixzz 1G7RW1yiW.

135. Naoko Tsukiyama to Yoshiharu Ogata, April 1, 1942.

136. Neither of the two state their feelings, but in this letter and in Naoko's dated March 14, the couple reveal their feelings toward each other and begin their commitment to each other.

137. No additional information about Dr. Hamre has been found.

138. This is probably referencing Tom Imada, another alumnus of the University of Hawaii.

139. Fingerprinting was part of the enumeration and identification process.

140. Tsukiyama identified Toshi as Toshiko Okazaki, and her "Lieut. husband" was Mits Fukuda. She had mentioned the couple earlier in regard to the war's leading to quick marriages.

141. Kau is on the southern side of the Big Island. The drive from Kau to Hilo takes about eighty minutes today.

142. Shigeno Hamada taught with Naoko in Olaa. She later married Sada Iwashita. The two women remained friends even after they married and had their own children.

143. It is probable that this "Mitz" is "Mits" Oka.

144. Tsukiyama could not provide any more information on Jean Okita.

145. Dr. Alsup was the family doctor for the Tsukiyama children when they were growing up. Naoko remembers that he took out their tonsils and gave them their immunizations.

146. Naoko identified Tom Hoon as one of Yoshiharu's friends, but gave no further information. Ted Tsukiyama identified Lefty as Lefty Nakano, whom he remembered as the best Japanese tennis player in Hawaii in the 1920s and 1930s. Nakano also played baseball.

147. The word "tsukemono," Japanese pickled vegetables, is written in Japanese katakana characters in the letter.

148. At that time, only Sueko lived with Yoshiharu's parents.

149. Yoshiharu's brother Yoshitaka worked for the Dole Food Company on Oahu.

150. Itagaki, "Dream for Tomorrow," 353–54.

151. Bailey and Farber, *First Strange Place*, 7–8.

152. Coffman, *Island Edge of America*, 97; Yamate, "Sugamo Prison," 329. And in fact, Tsukiyama and Ogata never use the term "Nisei" in their letters.

153. Masuda, *Letters from the 442nd*, 4.

154. Judiciary History Center, "Martial Law."

155. Robinson, *By Order of the President*, 4; Masuda, *Letters from the 442nd*, 5.

156. Coffman, *Island Edge of America*, 75–76.

157. Bailey and Farber, *First Strange Place*, 5.

158. Territorial Office of Defense, Health and Welfare Services, memo, May 21, 1942, Box 10, Folder 20, RASRL Confidential Files.

159. Fugita and Fernandez, "Religion and Japanese Americans' Views," 115.

160. Coffman, *Island Edge of America*, 76.

161. As quoted in Takaki, *Strangers from a Different Shore*, 380.

162. Coffman, *Island Edge of America*, 79; Daniels, *Decision to Relocate*, 27–28; Robinson, *By Order of the President*, 155–57.

163. Coffman, *Island Edge of America*, 76.

164. Ogawa, *Kodomo No Tame Ni*, 274.

165. Robinson, *Tragedy of Democracy*; 113; White and Murphy, "Hawaii under Martial Law."

166. Coffman, *Island Edge of America*, 95–96; Ogawa, *Kodomo No Tame Ni*, 274–84.

167. Ogawa, *Kodomo No Tame Ni*, 300–301.

168. Naoko Tsukiyama to Yoshiharu Ogata, April 22, 1942.

169. Coffman, *Island Edge of America*, 52–53.

170. Naoko Tsukiyama to Yoshiharu Ogata, April 22, 1942.

171. She is referring here to her brother Jimmy, who spent the duration of the war in Japan.

172. This reference is probably to Mr. Ed Hood, an African American man who was a longtime member of the Harris United Methodist Church.

173. No article on Yoshiharu Ogata can be found in the *Honolulu Star-Bulletin* dated May 4, 1942. However, there is a small blurb on model planes being on display at the Honolulu Academy of Arts in the May 5 issue of the *Star-Bulletin*. The article goes on to say that the Navy Bureau of Aeronautics had requested the models, which would be sent to the mainland. Built to exact specifications, the models would "help civilians to 'spot' friendly and enemy planes." Anonymous, "Model Planes Are Placed on Display," *Honolulu Star-Bulletin*, May 5, 1942.

174. Tsukiyama includes this quotation here, but no quotation appeared in the *Honolulu Star-Bulletin* article on model planes on May 5, 1942. It is not clear if she made up the quotation or found it in a different article.

175. The Academy Award–winning film *Kitty Foyle: The Natural History of a Woman*, released by RKO Radio Pictures in 1940, tells the story of a romance that crosses class lines. "Kitty Foyle," IMDb, accessed February 9, 2011, www.imdb.com /title/tt0032671/.

176. Odo, *No Sword to Bury*, 119.

177. Simpson, *Hawai'i Homefront*, 59.

178. Anonymous, "Report III of the Kauai Morale Committee, December 30, 1942," Box 13, Folder 4, Ka-37, RASRL Confidential Files; Kauai Morale Committee, "No Title," Box 12, Folder 22, Kaj-20-a, RASRL Confidential Files.

179. Anonymous, "Quarterly Report of the Kauai Morale Committee, January–March 1943," Box 12, Folder 23, Ka-21, RASRL Confidential Files.

180. Kauai Morale Committee, "Division of Research—Kauai Morale Committee Bulletin Number One, October 12, 1942, Three Year Plan for Morale Work among Residents of Japanese Ancestry," Box 12, Folder 23, Ka-26, RASRL Confidential Files. In addition to serving religious functions, churches provided youth, athletic, and cultural activities for Japanese Americans. Fugita and Fernandez, "Religion and Japanese Americans' Views," 115.

181. Naoko did not provide further details on Mr. Christensen.

182. *Kapu*, loosely translated, means "forbidden" or "taboo." For example, if there is a sign marking a place as kapu, it means to keep away from it. If an object is marked kapu, it means to leave it alone. Often in Hawaii, one can find signs saying, "Kapu: Keep Out."

183. He has not been identified.

184. Reverend Yamada headed the Morale Committee on Kauai.

185. Niihau, a privately owned island, is reserved for Native Hawaiians, and the DPI did not send teachers there. Honolulu was the most coveted spot for teachers, and thus new teachers needed to put in their time on the outer islands before being assigned to Honolulu schools.

186. Hanalei and Kilauea are on the north shore of Kauai. Because Kauai has only one main road that follows the circumference of the island but does not complete a full circle, Eleele and Kilauea are about forty miles apart and at opposite points on the island's perimeter.

187. Later, Tsukiyama could not recall much about their discussions of marriage. She said that there was no "dramatic proposal" and Yoshiharu did not get down on one knee. Rather, it was more along the lines of the next logical step of their relationship.

4. If You Still Want Me

1. Johnson, *Pacific Campaign*, 100, 114, 135, 281.

2. "Oil: Ration Time."

3. Ogata did not mention Etsuko Hayashi later in his life and Tsukiyama recalled having met her once. She described her as "very frail and fragile, pale and delicate looking." Naoko Ogata, in discussion with author, June 2011. In this letter, Yoshiharu mentions that Hayashi had gotten married, but in later ones, it seems as if she remained single, and the woman he referred to as having gotten married was someone else.

4. "We've a Story to Tell the Nations" is a hymn by H. Ernest Nichol. "We've a Story to Tell the Nations," United Methodist Hymnal Number 569, HymnSite.com, accessed April 8, 2011, www.hymnsite.com/lyrics/umh569.sht.

5. "Education: Schools and the War," *Time Magazine*, March 9, 1942, accessed January 18, 2013, www.time.com/time/magazine/article/0,9171,885937,00 .html#ixzz1G8NvGrSO.

6. Yoshiharu Ogata to Naoko Tsukiyama, October 21, 1942.

7. Tsukiyama did not provide details of the love triangle here. She did say, however, that Ogata was not a romantic and that, in fact, he was "different" and that attracted her to him.

8. Charles Ishii, chairman, Kauai Morale Committee, interview by A. W. Lind, Nuuanu, Hawaii, August 24, 1943, Box 13, Folder 2, Kaj-34, RASRL Confidential Files.

9. Morale Committee, "No Title."

10. Ishii, interview.

11. Captain Fallon, interview by A. W. Lind, Eleele, Kauai, March 2, 1943, Box 12, Folder 20, Ka-13, RASRL Confidential Files.

12. Hatsuko T. Kawahara to Dr. Lind, September 1, 1942, Box 12, Folder 21, Ka-17a, RASRL Confidential Files.

13. Ishii, Kaj-34.

14. Yoshiharu Ogata to Naoko Tsukiyama, November 24, 1942.

15. Anonymous, "Report III."

16. Bailey and Farber, *First Strange Place*, 177, 195–96.

17. Matsumoto, "Redefining Expectations," 45.

18. Ibid., 48, 49.

19. Yoshiharu Ogata to Naoko Tsukiyama, November 27, 1942. *It Happened in Flatbush*, about the Brooklyn Dodgers' pennant win in 1941, was released in 1942 by Twentieth Century Fox and had "Take Me Out to the Ballgame" on its soundtrack. "It Happened at Flatbush," IMDb, accessed April 8, 2011, www.imdb .com/title/tt0034905/.

20. *Lydia*, tagged as a drama romance from Alexander Korda Films, debuted in 1941. "Lydia," IMDb, accessed April 8, 2011, www.imdb.com/title/tt0033858/.

21. "Miss Laurie Will Be Late Tonight" is a story about a mechanic the night before he leaves for the army. He finds the courage to tell the woman he loves about his feelings after being conflicted about the contrast between his being a rough, working-class man and her being fair and a scholar. Upon his confession, he finds out his love is requited and realizes that although he would be away from her, he could carry her memory with him, even to his death. Dennison Smith, "Miss Laurie Will Be Late Tonight."

22. Yoshiharu Ogata to Naoko Tsukiyama, November 29, 1942.

23. Ibid. The original magazine article has not been found.

24. Bailey and Farber, *First Strange Place*, 171.

25. Etsuo Higuchi, interview by A. W. Lind, Kauai, Hawaii, March 2, 1943, Box 13, Folder 9, Ka-12, RASRL Confidential Files.

26. Gerstle, "Interpreting the 'American Way,'" 109.

27. Higuchi, interview.

28. Elaine Tyler May, "Rosie the Riveter," 129.

29. As quoted in ibid., 133–34.

30. Brandt, *No Magic Bullet*, 131.

31. Tone, "Women, Birth Control, and the Marketplace," 368.

32. Lary May, "Making the American Consensus," 90.

33. Elaine Tyler May, "Rosie the Riveter," 134; Erenberg, "Swing Goes to War," 158.

34. Brandt, *No Magic Bullet*, 161–70.

35. Bailey and Farber, *First Strange Place*, 33–39.

36. Jones and Jones, *Hawaii Goes to War*, 85.

37. *Los Angeles Times*, August 22, 1942, as quoted in Jones and Jones, *Hawaii Goes to War*, xxv.

38. "U.S. at War: War Brides."

39. Naoko Ogata, in discussion with author, December 3, 2012.

5. A Dream for Two

1. Nash, *Crucial Era*, 134.

2. Lyons, *World War II*, 210.

3. Axelrod, *Real History*, 368; Lyons, *World War II*, 254.

4. Robinson, *By Order of the President*, 178.

5. Robinson, *Tragedy of Democracy*, 212–13.

6. Coffman, *Island Edge of America*, 90.

7. Ibid., 100.

8. Ted Tsukiyama to Yoshiko Tsukiyama, January 27, 1943, copy in possession of author.

9. *Japanese Eyes: Personal Reflections*, 3–5.

10. Ted Tsukiyama to Folks, April 8, 1943, copy in possession of author; Odo, *No Sword to Bury*, 228–32.

11. Growing up in Hawaii as Japanese Americans, locals learned early in life that there was a distinct difference between a Japanese American in Hawaii and a Japanese American on the mainland. Mainland-born Japanese Americans were "kotonks," a pejorative based on "the sound that their empty heads made when you knocked them together," and those born in Hawaii were "locals." They looked similar but did not speak the same way, and "locals" thought that at times "kotonks" "acted more haole" than Japanese. Many of the differences between the two groups were due to acculturation (or lack of it), but each side perceived the other as different, and as lacking, even though they both shared a Japanese heritage.

12. "Army & Navy and Civilian Defense."

13. Ogawa, *Kodomo No Tame Ni*, 324, 325.

14. Just as there was no singular "American style" wedding, there was no singular "Japanese style" wedding either. Specific traditions depended on the prefecture in Japan. Some commonalities in Japanese culture, though, included a go-between or matchmaker to arrange the marriage, a visit by the groom's family (through a family representative) to the bride's family to propose marriage, a meeting of the families, and an exchange of gifts between the families. Azusa Ono, email to author, January 29, 2013. Ono is a professor at the Osaka University of Economics and is an expert in American history and Japanese culture. Also see Ogawa, *Kodomo No Tame Ni*, 416–17.

15. Momoe Inouye, interview with Jon Ogata, Honolulu, Hawaii, July 21, 2000. She could not explain the discrepancy between the dates and recognized that the Ogatas had had several children by 1911.

16. Yoshiko Tsukiyama, memoir.

17. Odo, *No Sword to Bury*, 31. Odo notes the Gift Box as the name of the Isoshimas' store, but Naoko Tsukiyama recalled it as "the Japanese Bazaar." By the turn of the century, it was not uncommon to find Japanese-owned businesses in Hawaii, including stores, theaters, and restaurants, and the Japanese Merchants Union formed in 1895. Coffman, *Island Edge of America*, 22.

18. While living in Tokyo, Seinosuke had been baptized as a Christian and had attended night school to learn English. This exposure to Christianity introduced

him to Western culture and increased his interest in the English language. Odo, *No Sword to Bury*, 55. Louis Fiset, in his study *Imprisoned Apart*, 5, addresses the impact of the Christian church on the Issei.

19. Coffman, *Island Edge of America*, 23.

20. Yoshiko Tsukiyama, memoir.

21. Harris United Methodist Church, *Century of Growth*, 8–13, 41; Seinosuke Tsukiyama, memoir.

22. Yoshiharu had sped through the town of Kalaheo at 33 miles per hour—the speed limit there was (and still is) 25 mph.

23. Mr. Griswold was Yoshiharu's principal at Waimea High School.

24. This notion of "haole style" came up for the couple throughout the planning of their wedding, referring to the traditions of a Westernized, or Americanized, ceremony rather than a Japanese one. The couple intended to have a Christian wedding and to follow the etiquette promoted by women's magazines in the 1940s.

25. This refers to his brother-in-law Yoshio Inouye (Momoe's husband), who was a first-generation immigrant from Japan.

26. Port Allen is located in Eleele.

27. He is referring to Walter Miyake, who attended the University of Hawaii. Miyake, like Ted Tsukiyama, joined the ROTC, then the VVV and the 442nd, and eventually worked for the Military Intelligence Service.

28. Packard, *American Nightmare*, 194–95.

29. Bailey and Farber, *First Strange Place*, 133, 157, 163.

30. Ibid., 205.

31. Naoko Ogata, in discussion with author, July 2010.

32. At this point, the Varsity Victory Volunteers had been disbanded. Ted then volunteered for the 442nd and was preparing to head to the mainland for training.

33. This is in reference to the Reverend Harry Komuro. He was the Japanese-language pastor at Harris United Methodist Church, taught Sunday school, and, with the help of Naoko's father, translated his sermons into Japanese in order to minister to the Issei. Harris United Methodist Church, *Century of Growth*, 18.

34. Kats Tomita was a good friend of Ted Tsukiyama's and a fellow member of the VVV.

35. Mooheau Park is in Hilo, near the coast.

36. Bailey and Farber, *First Strange Place*, 204.

37. "Education: Schools and the War."

38. He is referring to his brother-in-law Tomoiichi Yamamoto, Tomoe's husband.

39. Ah Chew Goo played basketball for the Hawaii Senior League and coached and refereed. The "Mandarin Magician," as he was known, was 5'4" and described as "better than the top-rated ballhandling and playmaking professionals in the NBA." "Ah Chew Goo," *Honolulu-Star Advertiser*, accessed April 6, 2015,

http://obits.staradvertiser.com/2015/02/05/ah-chew-goo/. Joe Kaulukukui was a Roosevelt High School graduate and the first player from Hawaii to sign with the University of Hawaii football team. Dan Cisco, *Hawai'i Sports: History, Facts and Statistics* (Honolulu: University of Hawaii Press, 1999), 176–77.

40. Jones and Jones, *Hawaii Goes to War*, 85.

41. Naoko Tsukiyama to Yoshiharu Ogata, March 3, 1943

42. Naoko Tsukiyama to Yoshiharu Ogata, February 28, 1943.

43. Ibid.

44. Yoshiharu Ogata to Naoko Tsukiyama, March 4, 1943.

45. See page 178 for more information on the Revenue Act of 1942.

46. Tsukiyama identified "Brat" as Brat Urabe, a friend of a friend of Yoshiharu's. *Wahine* is the Hawaiian word for "woman."

47. The *Honolulu Advertiser* began as the *Pacific Commercial Advertiser* in July 1856. During World War II, when martial law ruled the territory, the *Advertiser* served as the military government's public affairs advertiser. "Honolulu Star-Advertiser—About Us," *Honolulu Star-Advertiser*, accessed April 28, 2011, www.staradvertiser.com/about/; "The Honolulu Advertiser 'News Building,'" *Historic Hawaii Foundation*, accessed October 24, 2014, http://historichawaii.org/?wpdmact =process&did=NDkuaG90bGGluaw==.

48. Artie Shaw gained fame in the 1930s and 1940s as a clarinet player and band leader performing swing music of the era. After the bombing of Pearl Harbor, Shaw joined the U.S. Navy. Instead of doing combat work, he formed a service band and performed throughout the Pacific. "Swing Music Net Biography: Artie Shaw," Swingmusic.net, accessed April 22, 2011, www.swingmusic.net/Shaw_Artie .html. The Civic Auditorium was located in Honolulu and hosted musical and sporting events.

49. "There Are Such Things," recorded by Frank Sinatra, became a hit in 1940. During the war, Sinatra's songs "expressed the hopes of a generation of pure love in a mad world, but his strong sex appeal for women of all ages underscored the fragility of those dreams of home." Erenberg, "Swing Goes to War," 158.

50. The song "You'd Be So Nice to Come Home To," written by Cole Porter, was featured in the movie musical *Something to Shout About*, released in 1943 by Columbia Pictures. "Something to Shout About," IMDb, accessed April 28, 2011, www .imdb.com/title/tt0036375/.

51. Hannun, "The Favorite Suit."

52. Tsukiyama thinks that Komatsu, referred to in the letter, was Komatsu "Dorothy" Kohatsu, the daughter of a Dr. Kohatsu.

53. *Puka* is the Hawaiian word for "hole."

54. McEvoy, "Our 110,000 New Boarders."

55. In this letter, Naoko and her fellow teachers complained to Mrs. Koga about Mrs. Duncan "in a humorous way." Mrs. Duncan claimed that the teachers

described her as "militantly obnoxious" and lacking in "finer feelings." Naoko explained to Yoshiharu that they had not said exactly that, but maintained that Mrs. Duncan should not have read the personal letter. She declared, "So I'm not saying I'm sorry." Naoko Tsukiyama to Yoshiharu Ogata, March 10, 1943.

56. Ogata often spelled morale as "moral." It is not clear if he did so intentionally as a sarcastic way to show his disenchantment with the committee, or if it is simply a misspelling.

57. Bailey and Farber, *First Strange Place*, 174.

58. War Production Board, "No. 287 Memorandum," January 12, 1943, Box 17, Folder 5, USF.

59. Buchanan, *United States in World War II*, 2:316; Revenue Act of 1942, www .constitution.org/tax/us-ic/hist/RevAct1942.pdf.

60. "Stitch in Time."

61. Bailey and Farber, *First Strange Place*, 173.

62. Odo, *No Sword to Bury*, 10–11, 16.

63. Ogawa, *Kodomo No Tame Ni*, 82–84.

64. Ibid., 84.

65. Shields, "Love Is a Man Trap."

66. "Desperate Journey," IMDb, accessed March 11, 2013, www.imdb.com/title /tt0034646/; Naoko Tsukiyama to Yoshiharu Ogata, March 17 and 24, 1943.

67. Naoko Tsukiyama to Yoshiharu Ogata, March 24, 1943.

68. Yoshiharu Ogata to Naoko Tsukiyama, March 20, 1943; Naoko Tsukiyama to Yoshiharu Ogata, March 24, 1943.

69. Yoshiharu Ogata to Naoko Tsukiyama, March 20 and 24, 1943.

70. The reference here is to Robert and Kuulei Taira. Robert was a University of Hawaii classmate who became an officer in the 100th Battalion of the 442nd during World War II.

71. Naoko retired in 1972 and Ogata in 1973. Although the couple never gained riches, they retired comfortably.

72. This Spencer Tracy movie from MGM debuted in 1942. "Tortilla Flat," IMDb, accessed March 7, 2011, www.imdb.com/title/tt0035460/.

73. Bailey and Farber, *First Strange Place*, 50, 54, 95,176, 178, 194, 204, 205.

74. Kimie Hironaka, "No Title," Folder SJ 295–314 (Summer 1943) (Effect of War on My Community), UHSj-299-I, RASRL Student Papers.

75. Bailey and Farber, *First Strange Place*, 179, 51, 53–54, 58, 83, 36, 85.

76. Waichi Takemoto was another University of Hawaii colleague. "Uke" is short for "ukulele."

77. Two days earlier, Ted Tsukiyama had been inducted into the 442nd, and then headed out for training with 522nd Field Artillery Battalion at Camp Shelby in Mississippi. Ralph Yempuku worked as the University of Hawaii sports director in the 1930s and became the supervisor of the VVV.

78. Naoko later remembered Inouye as a member of the Harris Church Choir and commented that she did not remember him as a professor. He is not listed in the University of Hawaii yearbooks. Naoko Ogata, in discussion with Joy Miyamoto, March 14, 2013.

79. Yoshiharu Ogata to Naoko Tsukiyama, April 4, 1943, and April 12, 1943; Naoko Tsukiyama to Yoshiharu Ogata, April 7, 1943.

80. Naoko Tsukiyama to Yoshiharu Ogata, April 7, 10, and 14, 1943.

81. Naoko later identified Mrs. Chang as Nora Chang, a teacher at Waimea Elementary School. Naoko Ogata, in discussion with Joy Miyamoto, April 29, 2013.

82. The Haraguchis mentioned here are Yoshiharu's sister Hiruyo and her family.

83. This is in reference to Yoshio Inouye's desire to hold on to many traditional Japanese practices.

84. The Hiroses were Naoko's neighbors at Olaa. She could not recall their first names but noted that the Hiroses gave them food and had two sons at the time of the war. Naoko Ogata, in discussion with Joy Miyamoto, April 29, 2013.

85. Naoko Tsukiyama to Yoshiharu Ogata, April 27, 1943.

86. Ibid.; Yoshiharu Ogata to Naoko Tsukiyama, April 29, 1943. Baker Taniguchi was Yoshiharu's best friend from Waimea Elementary and High School. He was the businessman behind Waimea Bakery and hired local people to do the baking. He legally changed his name from Takeshi to "Baker" and has since been identified by his career. In 2012, Taniguchi attended Naoko's ninety-fifth birthday party. Of those in attendance, he was the person who had known Naoko the longest.

87. Edith Nomi was Ted Tsukiyama's college girlfriend.

88. Gene Hirai was a family friend whom the Tsukiyamas knew from the Makiki Castle Church. Gene married Hirobumi Uno, a man from Hanapepe, Kauai.

89. Litheia Wong had been a friend of Naoko's and Kazu's since grade school.

90. Tsukiyama could not identify Fred Hiura further except to say that he was a member of the Harris Church Choir. Naoko Ogata in discussion with Joy Miyamoto, April 29, 2013.

91. Church of the Crossroads was active with students at the University of Hawaii, and it owned a cottage at Kokokahi on the windward side of Oahu. Chris Holmes, an heir to the Fleischmann's Yeast fortune, owned Mokuoloe Island, or Coconut Island, off the coast of Kaneohe on the windward side of Oahu. "Mokuoloe Island," Hawaii for Visitors, accessed March 7, 2011, www.hawaiiforvisitors.com /oahu/attractions/mokuoloe-island.htm.

92. Shigeko Akimoto was Naoko's good friend from Oahu. They both grew up in the same neighborhood and went to Japanese-language school together. She married Tatsuki Yoshida, whom Naoko identified as a member of the University of Hawaii ROTC. Naoko Ogata, in discussion with Joy Miyamoto, April 29, 2013.

Tsukiyama recalled a Cooper Ranch on the Big Island, but the one to which she referred is on the windward coast of Oahu.

93. Naoko Tsukiyama to Yoshiharu Ogata, April 29 and May 8, 1943.

94. Yoshiharu Ogata to Naoko Tsukiyama, May 3 and 9, 1943.

95. Yoshiharu Ogata to Naoko Tsukiyama, May 12 and 16, 1943; Naoko Tsukiyama to Yoshiharu Ogata, May 14, 1943.

96. This is in reference to her not being able to gain passage back to the Big Island from Oahu and thus missing almost a week of teaching.

97. Yoshiharu was marrying Naoko, a city girl from Honolulu, instead of one of the girls from Kauai. His fellow Kauaians could tease him, as they recognized the town-versus-country rivalry.

98. Mrs. Weatherbee has not been identified further.

99. There are two blank lines—nothing written there.

100. "O.P.A." is most likely the Office of Price Administration.

101. Kenneth Kawamoto was a member of the Harris Church Choir.

102. Sukiyaki is a traditional Japanese meal, cooked in one pot. If one were to follow true Japanese tradition, each step of the process, from choosing the meat and vegetables to making the broth and cooking the dish, contains significance.

103. In his February 26, 1942, letter to Naoko, Yoshiharu explained that he had received a deferment until May 26, 1942. He must have obtained another one through May of 1943, though, because the contents of his letters do not dwell on being drafted until 1943.

104. Miss Hundley was the supervising principal on Kauai.

105. Naoko identified Mr. Gavin Bush as "chairman of the labor board or some influential position." Naoko Tsukiyama to Yoshiharu Ogata, June 5, 1943.

6. I Am What I Am

1. Axelrod, *Real History*, 202, 292–95, 299, 301, 307, 328, 368–70; Lyons, *World War II*, 266–67, 300.

2. Lyons, *World War II*, 303, 306, 312–14.

3. Axelrod, *Real History*, 368–70.

4. Odo, *No Sword to Bury*, 248.

5. James, *Exile Within*, 82–84.

6. Takaki, *Strangers from a Different Shore*, 399; James, *Exile Within*, 127.

7. *Japanese Eyes: Personal Reflections*, 5–8.

8. Fiset, *Imprisoned Apart*, 83, 88.

9. Takahashi, *Nisei/Sansei*, 114–15.

10. James, *Exile Within*, 159, 8.

11. In comparison, 70 percent of the nation's general population at that time lived in urban areas. Takahashi, *Nisei/Sansei*, 117.

12. Judiciary History Center, "Martial Law"; Odo, *No Sword to Bury*, 103–104.

13. Brown, *Hawaii Goes to War*, 137.

14. Ogawa, *Kodomo No Tame Ni*, 414–21.

15. Associated Students of the University of Hawaii, *The 1944 Ka Palapala*, 36–49.

16. Sherman Seki, email to author, September 24, 2012.

17. Odo, *No Sword to Bury*, 267, 43.

18. Ibid., 255–63.

19. As quoted in Ogawa, *Kodomo No Tame Ni*, 350.

20. Ogawa, *Kodomo No Tame Ni*, 356.

21. Coffman, *Island Edge of America*, 104, 111; Ara, "Light from One Corner," 350; Kometani, "Nisei and the Future," 365.

22. Ogawa, *Kodomo No Tame Ni*, 355,

23. Odo, *No Sword to Bury*, 257.

24. Ogawa, *Kodomo No Tame Ni*, 362. A more current translation of *okage sama de* is "thanks to you." Azusa Ono, email to author, April 1, 2015.

25. Ibid., 320, 349.

26. Ibid., 441, 442.

27. Takahashi, *Nisei/Sansei*, 164–65.

28. Kessler, *Stubborn Twig*, 284–86, 289.

29. Ogawa, *Kodomo No Tame Ni*, 536.

Epilogue

1. Naoko Ogata, in discussion with author, December 2011.

2. At that time, three Christian churches, divided by ethnicity into the 1960s, served the residents of Waimea. Tsukiyama went to the "Japanese Church," and the other two churches were the "Haole Church" and the "Hawaiian Church." The economic hardships of supporting three pastors and three parsonages, and perhaps the lessening of the racial divide due to the civil rights movement, led to the combining of the three. Today, the Waimea United Church of Christ, housed in what was once called the Haole Church, serves the town. Joy Miyamoto, in discussion with author, October 2011.

3. Naoko Ogata, in discussion with author, December 2011.

BIBLIOGRAPHY

Archival Sources

Hawaii War Records Depository. Archives and Manuscripts Collections. University of Hawaii at Manoa Library.

Romanzo Adams Social Research Laboratory. Confidential Files; Student Papers. Archives and Manuscripts Collections. University of Hawaii at Manoa Library.

Uncataloged Subject Files. Archives and Manuscripts Collections. University of Hawaii at Manoa Library.

Books, Articles, Papers, and Yearbooks

Adams, Romanzo. Preface to *The Peoples of Hawaii: A Statistical Study*. Edited by Romanzo Adams, T. M. Livesay, and E. H. Van Winkle. Honolulu: Institute of Pacific Relations, 1925.

Adams, Romanzo, T. M. Livesay, and E. H. Van Winkle, eds. *The Peoples of Hawaii: A Statistical Study*. Honolulu: Institute of Pacific Relations, 1925.

Akita, George. "Days of Infamy: The Journal of George Akita." In Hawaii Nikkei History Editorial Board, *Japanese Eyes: Personal Reflections*, 36–44.

Allen, Gwenfread. *Hawaii's War Years, 1941–1945*. Kailua, Hawaii: Pacific Monograph, 1999.

Anonymous. "Model Planes Are Placed on Display." *Honolulu Star-Bulletin*. May 5, 1942.

Anthony, J. Garner. *Hawaii under Army Rule*. Stanford, Calif.: Stanford University Press, 1955.

Ara, Ryokan. "The Light from One Corner." In *Japanese Eyes: Personal Reflections*, 409–12.

Associated Students of the University of Hawaii. *The 1944 Ka Palapala*. Honolulu: Associated Students of the University of Hawaii, 1944.

Axelrod, Alan. *The Real History of World War II: A New Look at the Past*. New York: Sterling, 2008.

Bailey, Beth, and David Farber. *The First Strange Place: Race and Sex in World War II Hawaii*. Baltimore: Johns Hopkins University Press, 1992.

Banner, Lois W. *Women in Modern America: A Brief History*. Belmont, Calif.: Thompson Wadsworth, 2005.

Bauer, Lt. Col. E. *The History of World War II: The Full Story of the World's Greatest Conflict*. New York: Military Press, 1966.

Bottoms, D. Michael. *An Aristocracy of Color: Race and Reconstruction in California and the West, 1850–1890*. Norman: University of Oklahoma Press, 2013.

Brandt, Allan M. *No Magic Bullet: A Social History of Venereal Disease in the United States since 1880, with a New Chapter on AIDS*. Oxford: Oxford University Press, 1987.

Brown, DeSoto. *Hawaii Goes to War: Life in Hawaii from Pearl Harbor to Peace*. Honolulu: Editions Limited, 1989.

Buchanan, A. Russell. *The United States and World War II*. Vols. 1 and 2. New York: Harper and Row, 1962.

Calvocoressi, Peter, and Guy Wint. *Total War: Causes and Courses of the Second World War*. New York: Penguin Books, 1979.

Chafe, William H. *The American Woman: Her Changing Social, Economic, and Political Roles, 1920–1970*. New York: Oxford University Press, 1972.

Chinen, Karleen. "Hawaii's AJAs 'Play Ball!'" *Hawaii Herald*, June 7, 1996.

Cisco, Dan. *Hawai'i Sports: History, Facts and Statistics*. Honolulu: University of Hawaii Press, 1999.

Coffman, Tom. *The Island Edge of America: A Political History of Hawai'i*. Honolulu: University of Hawaii Press, 2003.

Conn, Stetson, Rose C. Engelman, and Byron Fairchild. *Guarding the United States and Its Outposts*. Washington, D.C.: Center of Military History, United States Army, 2000.

Conzen, Kathleen Neils, David A. Gerber, Ewa Morawska, George E. Pozzetta, and Rudolph J. Vecoli. "The Invention of Ethnicity: A Perspective from the USA." In *American Immigration and Ethnicity: A Reader*, edited by David A. Gerber and Alan M. Kraut, 85–98. New York: Palgrave Macmillan, 2005.

Cott, Nancy F., and Elizabeth H. Pleck. *A Heritage of Her Own: Toward a New Social History of American Women*. New York: Simon and Schuster, 1979.

Daniels, Roger. *The Decision to Relocate the Japanese Americans*. Malabar, Fla: Robert E. Krieger, 1986.

———. *Prisoners without Trial: Japanese Americans in World War II*. Rev. ed. New York: Hill and Wang, 2004.

Daws, Gavan. *Shoal of Time: A History of the Hawaiian Islands*. New York: Macmillan, 1968.

Dower, John W. "Race, Language, and War in Two Cultures: World War II in Asia." In Erenberg and Hirsch, *The War in American Culture*, 169–201.

DuBois, Ellen Carol, and Lynn Dumenil. *Through Women's Eyes: An American History with Documents*. Boston: Bedford/St. Martin's Press, 2004.

Erenberg, Lewis A. "Swing Goes to War: Glenn Miller and the Popular Music of World War II." In Erenberg and Hirsch, *The War in American Culture*, 144–65.

Erenberg, Lewis A., and Susan E. Hirsch, eds. *The War in American Culture: Society and Consciousness during World War II*. Chicago: University of Chicago Press, 1996.

Fiset, Louis. *Imprisoned Apart: The World War II Correspondence of an Issei Couple*. Seattle: University of Washington Press, 1997.

Foo, Lora Jo. "Hawaii: The Asian State." In *Asian American Women: Issues, Concerns, and Responsive Human and Civil Rights Advocacy*, 163–73. New York: Ford Foundation, 2002.

Fuchs, Lawrence H. *Hawaii Pono: A Social History*. San Diego, Calif.: Harcourt Brace Jovanovich, 1961.

Fugita, Stephen S., and Marilyn Fernandez. "Religion and Japanese Americans' Views of Their World War II Incarceration." *Journal of Asian American Studies* 5, no. 2 (June 2002): 113–37.

Geiger, Andrea. *Subverting Exclusion: Transpacific Encounters with Race, Caste, and Borders, 1885–1928*. New Haven, Conn.: Yale University Press, 2011.

Gerber, David A., and Alan M. Kraut. *American Immigration and Ethnicity: A Reader*. New York: Palgrave Macmillan, 2005.

Gerstle, Gary. "Interpreting the 'American Way': The Working Class Goes to War." In Erenberg and Hirsch, *The War in American Culture*, 105–27.

Hannun, Alberta Pierson. "The Favorite Suit." *Good Housekeeping*, February 1943, 32, 33, 118, 120–125.

Harada, Tasuku. "The Social Status of the Japanese in Hawaii: Some of the Problems Confronting the Second Generation." In *Institute of Pacific Relations Preliminary Paper[s] Prepared for Second General Session, July 15–29, 1927*, 1–13. Honolulu: Institute of Pacific Relations, 1927.

Harris United Methodist Church. *Harris United Methodist Church: A Century of Growth*. Honolulu: Harris United Methodist Church, 1988.

Hawaii Nikkei History Editorial Board, ed. *Japanese Eyes . . . American Heart: Personal Reflections of Hawaii's World War II Nisei Soldiers*. Honolulu: Tendai Educational Foundation, 1998.

———. *Japanese Eyes . . . American Heart*. Vol. 2, *Voices from the Home Front in World War II Hawaii*. Honolulu: Watermark Publishing, 2012.

Inouye, Daniel K. Foreword to Hawaii Nikkei History Editorial Board, *Japanese Eyes: Personal Reflections*, ix–xi.

Itagaki, Joseph. "The Dream for Tomorrow—Letters between Joseph R. Itagaki and Charles R. Hemenway." In Hawaii Nikkei History Editorial Board, *Japanese Eyes: Personal Reflections*, 351–58.

James, Thomas. *Exile Within: The Schooling of Japanese Americans 1942–1945.* Cambridge, Mass.: Harvard University Press, 1987.

Jameson, Elizabeth. *All That Glitters: Class, Conflict and Community in Cripple Creek.* Urbana: University of Illinois Press, 1998.

Johnson, William Bruce. *The Pacific Campaign in World War II: From Pearl Harbor to Guadalcanal.* New York: Routledge, 2006.

Jones, Wilbur D., Jr., and Carroll Robbins Jones. *Hawaii Goes to War: The Aftermath of Pearl Harbor.* Shippensburg, Pa.: White Mane Books, 2001.

Kamishita, Seiso. "Honor Thy Country." In Hawaii Nikkei History Editorial Board, *Japanese Eyes: Personal Reflections,* 45–48.

Kelley, Judith. *Marriage Is a Private Affair.* New York: Harper and Brothers, 1941.

Kessler, Lauren. *Stubborn Twig: Three Generations in the Life of a Japanese American Family.* New York: Penguin Group, 1993.

Kessler-Harris, Alice. *Out of Work: A History of Wage-Earning Women in the United States.* New York: Oxford University Press, 2003.

Kinoshita, Gaku. "Telling Our Roots in the Sugar Plantation: Collective Identities of Japanese American Elderly in Puna, Hawaii." In Okamura, *The Japanese American Contemporary Experience,* 1–20.

Klass, Tim. *World War II on Kauai.* Portland, Oreg.: Westland Foundation, 1970.

Kometani, Katsumi. "The Nisei and the Future." In Ogawa, *Kodomo No Tame Ni,* 364–65.

Lyons, Michael J. *World War II: A Short History.* 3rd ed. Upper Saddle River, N.J.: Prentice Hall, 1989.

Masuda, Minoru. *Letters from the 442nd: The World War II Correspondence of a Japanese American Medic.* Edited by Hana Masuda and Dianne Bridgman. Seattle: University of Washington Press, 2008.

Matsumoto, Valerie. "Japanese American Women during World War II." In Norton and Alexander, *Major Problems in American Women's History,* 385–97.

———. "Redefining Expectations: Nisei Women in the 1930s." In "Japanese Americans in California," special issue, *California History* 73, no. 1 (Spring 1994): 44–53.

Matsunaga, Spark. "Rededication." In Hawaii Nikkei History Editorial Board, *Japanese Eyes: Personal Reflections,* 395–400.

May, Elaine Tyler. "Rosie the Riveter Gets Married." In Erenberg and Hirsch, *The War in American Culture,* 128–43.

May, Lary. "Making the American Consensus: The Narrative of Conversion and Subversion in World War II Films." In Erenberg and Hirsch, *The War in American Culture,* 71–102.

McEvoy, J. P. "Our 110,000 New Boarders." *Reader's Digest,* March 1943, 65–68.

Miyamoto, Melody M. "The Last Samurai: The Culture of American Japanese Association Baseball." Paper presented at the Western History Association Conference, Tempe, Ariz., 2005.

Mizuno, Larry Y., ed. *Ka Palapala: University of Hawaii—1940*. Vol. 25. Honolulu: Associated Students of the University of Hawaii, 1940.

Morgan, Michelle. "Americanizing the Teachers: Identity, Citizenship, and the Teaching Corps in Hawai'i, 1900–1941." *Western Historical Quarterly* 45, no. 2 (Summer 2014): 147–67.

Murin, John M., Paul E. Johnson, James M. McPherson, Gary Gerstle, Emily S. Rosenberg, and Norman L. Rosenberg. *Liberty, Equality and Power: A History of the American People*. Vol. 2, *Since 1863*. Belmont, Calif.: Thompson Wadsworth, 2006.

Nash, Gerald D. *The Crucial Era: The Great Depression and World War II, 1929–1945*. 2nd ed. New York: St. Martin's Press, 1992.

Nordyke, Eleanor C. *The Peopling of Hawaii*. 2nd ed. Honolulu: University of Hawaii Press, 1989.

Norton, Mary Beth, and Ruth M. Alexander, eds. *Major Problems in American Women's History*. 4th ed. Boston: Houghton Mifflin, 2007.

O'Brien, David J., and Stephen S. Fugita. *The Japanese American Experience*. Bloomington: Indiana University Press, 1991.

Odo, Franklin. *No Sword to Bury: Japanese Americans in Hawaii during World War II*. Philadelphia: Temple University Press, 2004.

Ogawa, Dennis M., ed. *Kodomo No Tame Ni/For the Sake of the Children: The Japanese American Experience in Hawaii*. Honolulu: University of Hawaii Press, 1978.

Okamura, Jonathan Y., ed. *The Japanese American Contemporary Experience in Hawaii*. Social Process in Hawaii, no. 41. Honolulu: Department of Sociology, University of Hawaii at Manoa, 2002.

———. "The Massie-Kahahawai Case and Race Relations in Hawai'i in the 1930s." In *Original Plays and Classic Humanities: A Special Series from Kumu Kahua Theatre, for Its 2003–2004 Season*, 6. Honolulu: Kumu Kahua Theatre, 2003.

Okihiro, Gary Y. *Storied Lives: Japanese American Students and World War II*. Seattle: University of Washington Press, 1999.

Okihiro, Michael. *AJA Baseball in Hawaii: Ethnic Pride and Tradition*. Honolulu: Hawaii Hochi, 1999.

Omi, Michael, and Howard Winant. *Racial Formation in the United States: From the 1960s to the 1990s*. 2nd ed. New York: Routledge, 1994.

Packard, Jerrold M. *American Nightmare: The History of Jim Crow*. New York: St. Martin's Press, 2002.

Robinson, Greg. *By Order of the President: FDR and the Internment of Japanese Americans*. Cambridge, Mass.: Harvard University Press, 2001.

———. *A Tragedy of Democracy: Japanese Confinement in North America*. New York: Columbia University Press, 2009.

Roosevelt, Franklin. Exec. Order No. 9066. 3 CFR 1092–93 (1938–43). February 19, 1942.

Rosa, John P. "Local Story: The Massie Case Narrative and the Cultural Production of Local Identity in Hawaii." In "Whose Vision? Asian Settler Colonialism in Hawai'i," edited by Russell C. Leong, special issue, *Amerasia Journal* 26, no. 3 (2000): 93–115.

———. "The Massie-Kahahawai Case: A Local Story of Enduring Importance." In *Original Plays and Classic Humanities: A Special Series from Kumu Kahua Theatre, for Its 2003–2004 Season*, 4–5. Honolulu: Kumu Kahua Theatre, 2003.

Sasai, Samuel. "Two Years, Eight Months, and Nineteen Days That Changed My Life Forever." In Hawaii Nikkei History Editorial Board, *Japanese Eyes: Personal Reflections*, 81–93.

Schrum, Kelly. *Some Wore Bobby Sox: The Emergence of Girls' Culture, 1920–1945*. New York: Palgrave Macmillan, 2004.

Shields, Frances. "Love Is a Man Trap." *Woman's Home Companion*, March 1943, 13, 14, 109–10, 114.

Simpson, MacKinnon. *Hawai'i Homefront: Life in the Islands during World War II*. Honolulu: Bess Press, 2008.

Smith, Dennison. "Miss Laurie Will Be Late Tonight." *Good Housekeeping*, November 1942, 40, 41, 206–16.

Smith, William C. "The Second Generation Oriental in America." In *Preliminary Paper[s] Prepared for Second General Session, July 15–29, 1927*, Institute of Pacific Relations, 1–36. Honolulu: University of Hawaii, 1927.

Stannard, David. "The Massie Case: Injustice and Courage." *Honolulu Advertiser*, October 14, 2001. Accessed August 15, 2012, http://the.honoluluadvertiser.com/article/2001/Oct/14/op/op03a.html.

Stricker, Frank. "Cookbooks and Law Books: The Hidden History of Career Women in Twentieth-Century America." In *A Heritage of Her Own: Toward a New Social History of American Women*, edited by Nancy F. Cott and Elizabeth H. Beck, 476–98. New York: Simon and Schuster, 1979.

Takahashi, Jere. *Nisei/Sansei: Shifting Japanese American Identities and Politics*. Philadelphia: Temple University Press, 1997.

Takaki, Ronald. *Pau Hana: Plantation Life and Labor in Hawaii, 1835–1920*. Honolulu: University of Hawaii Press, 1983.

———. *Strangers from a Different Shore: A History of Asian Americans*. New York: Little, Brown, 1998.

Tamura, Eileen H. *Americanization, Acculturation, and Ethnic Identity: The Nisei Generation in Hawaii*. Urbana: University of Illinois Press, 1994.

———. "In Retrospect: Second-Generation Japanese Americans in Hawai'i." In Okamura, *The Japanese American Contemporary Experience*, 21–36.

Tondryk, Joseph, ed. *The Nineteen-Forty Tower.* Menomonie, Wisc.: Stout Institute, 1940.

Tone, Andrea. "Women, Birth Control, and the Marketplace in the 1930s." In Norton and Alexander, *Major Problems in American Women's History*, 360–69.

Tsukiyama, Ted. "An American—Not a Japanese Living in America." In Hawaii Nikkei History Editorial Board, *Japanese Eyes: Personal Reflections*, 335–39.

Ueda, Reed. "The Changing Path to Citizenship: Ethnicity and Naturalization during World War II." In Erenberg and Hirsch, *The War in American Culture*, 202–16.

Walker, Nancy A., ed. *Women's Magazines 1940–1960: Gender Roles and the Popular Press.* Boston: Bedford/St. Martin's, 1998.

Walz, Eric. *Nikkei in the Interior West: Japanese Immigration and Community Building 1882–1945.* Tucson: University of Arizona Press, 2012.

Welshimer, Helen. "'My Husband Says—,' *Good Housekeeping*, February 1940." In *Women's Magazines 1940–1960: Gender Roles and the Popular Press*, edited by Nancy A. Walker, 100–102. Boston: Bedford/St. Martin's, 1998.

Yamate, Sohei. "On the Way to Sugamo Prison." In Hawaii Nikkei History Editorial Board, *Japanese Eyes: Personal Reflections*, 328–34.

Yoo, David K. *Growing Up Nisei: Race, Generation, and Culture among Japanese Americans of California, 1924–49.* Urbana: University of Illinois Press, 2000.

Yoshida, Shigeo. "Speak American." In Ogawa, *Kodomo No Tame Ni*, 329–31.

INDEX

difficulties to and from, 102–103, 108*ltr*, 112; YO's comments on, 26*ltr*, 115
Kauai High School (Lihue, Hawaii), 13
Kauai Interscholastic Federation, 230
Kauai Morale Committee: establishment of, 67; Kiawe Corps, 145; mission of, 103–104; Reverend Yamada's role, 122, 189, 249n184; Women's Auxiliary, 125; YO's relationship with, 112, 123, 154*ltr*, 155*ltr*, 181*ltr*, 219, 255n56. *See also* Kiawe (Keawe) Corps (volunteer labor battalions)
Kauai Soto Zen Temple Zenshuji, 13
Kaulukukui, Joe, 164, 165*ltr*, 254n39
Kaumakani School (Kauai), 231
Kawamoto, Kenneth, 206, 211*ltr*, 257n101
Keawe Corp. *See* Kiawe (Keawe) Corps (volunteer labor battalions)
Kekaha, Kauai, Hawaii, 204
Kekaha School, 231
Kiawe (Keawe) Corps (volunteer labor battalions), 103, 112, 145, 151*ltr*, 165*ltr*, 189, 190*ltr*, 214*ltr*; *Kiawe* defined, 54, 244n50
Kilauea, Kauai, Hawaii, 108*ltr*, 113*ltr*, 250n186
Kilauea Military Camp (internment location), 91
Kim (family), 39*ltr*, 50*ltr*
Kim, Richard, 56*ltr*, 58*ltr*
Kimura, Sue (née Hokada), 167*ltr*
King, Yvonne (King Sisters), 238n20
Knox, Frank (Secretary of State), 81, 91
Koga, Mrs. (teacher), 175*ltr*, 254n55
Kohatsu, Dr. (father of Komatsu), 254n52
Kohatsu, Komatsu ("Dorothy"), 172*ltr*, 254n52
Komuro, Rev. Harry, 157*ltr*, 184, 253n33
Kumamoto, Japan, 6

Ladies' Home Journal, 8
letters: and "period" code, 244n65
Lihue, Kauai, 13, 148*ltr*, 149*ltr*, 204*ltr*
Los Angeles Times, 133

MacMurray College (Jacksonville, Ill.), 224
"mainland," 235n3
Major Disaster Council (Honolulu), 19–20

Makaweli, Kauai, Hawaii, 113*ltr*, 161*ltr*
Makiki Castle Church, 256n88
Manpower office, 204*ltr*
marriage/dating (during wartime): 6, 247n140; customs, 252n14, 253n24; extramarital sex, 129; gender role expectations, 28, 222; interethnic, 6, 74–77, 125–26; rates of, 49, 133–34; and soldiers, 75, 126, 186
martial law, 4, 42–45, 221; air raids, 43, 45, 54, 71*ltr*, 72*ltr*, 79*ltr*, 84*ltr*; blackouts, 3, 19, 42–45, 50–51*ltr*, 54, 71–72*ltrs*, 79*ltr*, 84*ltr*, 241n5; and children/schools, 51*ltr*, 52–53, 244n64; curfews, 43, 52, 223; effect on general population, 44–45, 52–54, 65, 163–64; effect on NT and YO, 43–44, 45, 47, 93, 97, 122, 200; government use of the *Advertiser*, 254n47; and the Issei, 42, 92, 229; and the judiciary system, 44–45, 221; and rationing of cloth, 178–79; and rationing of consumer goods, 44, 164, 208; and rationing of gasoline and tires, 45, 52, 66, 112, 241n8; and rationing of liquor, 43, 49, 70*ltr*, 78*ltr*, 139*ltr*, 164, 167*ltr*, 169*ltr*, 241n8; and shortages of food, 67; and shortages of men (eligible locals), 229; and shortages of teachers, 121, 161; and shortages of women, 73, 76, 187; and shortages of workers, 171, 121; and travel, 44, 49–50, 97, 148*ltr*, 196, 208, 212*ltr*; victory (home) gardens, 54, 64, 66, 103; violation penalties, 45, 242n15
Martin, Freddy, "Tonight We Love," 243n29. *See also* popular music: "Tonight We Love"
Massie, Thalia, 237n31. *See also* Massie-Kahahawai case
Massie-Kahahawai case, 16–17, 237nn31–32
May Act (1941), 132
McBryde Sugar Plantation, 179
McEvoy, J. P., 174–75
McKinley High School, 12
mesquite jungles (*kiawe*), 244n50; clearing beachfronts of, 54, 103
Mid-Pacific Institute, 30
Military Intelligence Service, 219, 220, 224, 253n27

Mits. *See* Fukuda, Mitsuyoshi ("Mits"); Oka, "Mitz" ("Mits")

Miyake, Walter, 153*ltr*, 253n27

Miyama, Rev. Kenichi, 14

Mokuoloe Island (Coconut Island), 256n91

Mooheau Park (Hilo), 159, 253n35

morale committees, 67, 123; power of, 107, 122, 155*ltr*; and recruiting, 181, 219; and responsibilities of teachers, 122; and the responsibilities of women, 125–26; and sexual morality, 126; survey questions, 103–104; Territorial Office of Civilian Defense, Public Morale Division, 103; YO's comments on, 123*ltr*, 124–25*ltr*, 180–81*ltr*

Morgan, Michelle, 239n30

Mount Waialeale, 25*ltr*, 239n31

MPs (Military Police), 204

Mussolini, Benito, 218

Nagasaki, Japan, 219

Nagata, Akiko (wife of Yoshitaka Ogata), 13

Nakano, Lefty, 89*ltr*, 248n146

Napier, Donald, *11*

National Home-workshop Guild, 62

Nationality Law of Japan, 238n14

Navy Bluejackets (basketball team), 165*ltr*

New York University, 29, 31, 223

Nichol, H. Ernest, "We've a Story to Tell the Nations," 114*ltr*, 250n4

Niihau (Island), 107*ltr*, 249n185

Nisei (second-generation immigrants), 4, 13, 15, 17, 42, 90, 103, 179, 226, 248n152; abandoning Japanese culture, 46, 103; Americanization, 21–23, 223–24; education and the teaching profession, 29–31, 179, 222, 223–24, 239n30, 242n26; as "enemy alien," 42, 44, 68, 130; language skills, 31, 220; *okage sama de*, 226; participation in military service, 63, 67, 142, 220, 225; participation in politics and governance, 225–26; and religion (church), 245n74; volunteer work, 46, 48, 69

Nishimura, Kimiko (wife of Yoshio Ogata), 13

Nomi, Edith, 196*ltr*, 256n87

North American Aviation, 223

Nunes, Bruno, 247n122

Oahu (island), Hawaii, 5, 16, 18; population increase, 245n97

Odo, Franklin, 24, 69, 223, 242n27, 252n17

Office of Civil Defense Hospital, 182

Office of Price Administration ("O.P.A." *in letters*), 178, 204*ltr*, 257n100

Ogata, Hiruyo (sister of YO), 12. *See also* Haraguchi, Sueji (husband of Hiruyo Ogata)

Ogata, Jon (son of NT and YO), 229, 230, *231*, *232*

Ogata, Joy (daughter of NT and YO), 229, 230, *231*, *232*

Ogata, Jyo (née Ojo Ohashi; mother of YO), 12, 146–47

Ogata, Momoe (aka Mrs. Inouye; sister of YO), 12, 147, 252n15

Ogata, Sakae (sister of YO), 12

Ogata, Sueko (sister of YO), 12, 13, 248n148

Ogata, Tomoe (sister of YO), 12. *See also* Yamamoto, Tomoiichi (husband of Tomoe Ogata)

Ogata, Yoshiharu (YO), 4, *14*, *231*, *232*; advice to NT, 36*ltr*, 52*ltr*, 118*ltr*; Americanization of, 129; career (teacher), 14–15, 48, 80, 104, 155*ltr*; and civic duty, 81, 104, 130; craft and-building skills, 88*ltr*, 114, 163, 182; death, 232; draft/deferment; early years, 4–5, 12–14; education, 19, 33, 144; family obligations, 13, 49, 81–82, 123, 127*ltr*, 144, 179; and gender roles, 115, 117*ltr*, 171, 182–83; grammar/language skills, 27*ltr*, 33, 55, 136*ltr*; love triangle with Etsuko Hayashi, 250n7; model plane building project, 80–81, 84*ltr*, 85*ltr*, 87*ltr*, 96*ltr*, 98*ltr*, 117*ltr*, 129–30, 249nn173–74; as a Nisei, 13, 17, 224–25, 248n152; on NT's proper behavior, 34, 115, 146, 200–201; plantation life of, 55, 69, 112, 144, 219. *See also under* Department of Public Instruction (DPI; D.P.I. *in letters*); draft (military); Hayashi, Etsuko; moral committees; Nisei (second-generation immigrants); plantation life; Stout Institute (Menomonie, Wisc.)